HACKED!

HACKED!

High Tech Election Theft in America

11 Experts Expose the Truth

Edited by
ABBE WALDMAN DELOZIER
and
VICKIE KARP

TRUTH ENTERPRISES PUBLISHING

Hacked!
High Tech Election Theft in America
11 Experts Expose the Truth

TRUTH ENTERPRISES PUBLISHING
7010 Hwy. 71 West
Suite 340, PMB 162
Austin, TX 78735
www.hackedelections.com

First Edition
August 2006

ISBN 0-615-13255-3

Printed in the United States of America

Dedication

WE WOULD LIKE TO DEDICATE this book to Bev Harris.

Bev has worked tirelessly since the year 2000 to enlighten the public regarding the facts on compromised elections in America. She deserves a well-earned place in history as an American heroine. With her dogged commitment to revealing the truth, Bev is a beacon of light in a dark chapter of American history. This is a time when our election process has been corrupted beyond belief in a country formerly considered to be a worldwide example of democracy at its finest.

Ignorance amongst our citizens is widespread on the topic of elections today. Few people know and understand the truth and complexities of this issue. Bev Harris does. She has an encyclopedic knowledge of the details surrounding every vendor of voting machines; how any voting machine works; its failures, vulnerabilities, performance ratings; election officials' names in counties across America; election anomalies, issues, problems; federal and state statutes; testing labs; computer scientists' opinions and research; and anything else you could think of related to this topic. She has led the charge to gather the finest scientific and engineering minds in America today to quantify, qualify and prove her research. Bev and her team have produced the most solid evidence available (which is quite considerable), that electronic voting is unsafe for use by voters. She has shown repeatedly that it can be errantly programmed and corrupted and easily hacked. These breeches remain undetected by testing under current federal and state guidelines.

She has been legally threatened, bugged, followed, stolen from, wrongfully accused, libeled, and still she quietly goes on working. It has been proven that at least some of her critics are the vendors of these machines who financially benefit to the tune of millions of dollars in state contracts. That kind of money has certainly created a vested interest in trying to deter this woman from her mission.

Still, against all opposition, she visits county election offices, voting system testing labs, secretaries of state, citizens' groups; she files open records requests, probes, questions, and investigates day in, day out looking for answers, clues and evidence. She seeks solutions and offers citizens actions they can take to reclaim their elections.

At night she blogs, writes, sends out press releases with a determination and spirit that is unflagging and amazing. We would not know what we know on this issue today if it were not for Bev Harris. She is our mentor and heroine. She will go to the ends of the earth to solidly document her allegations and conclusions.

What began as research for her book, *Black Box Voting: Ballot Tampering in the 21st Century*, has led to her creation of the nonprofit organization "Black Box Voting," the first consumer protection organization for elections, and to her lifetime commitment to research and to expose the truth about privatized elections until we citizens stand up and reclaim them for ourselves. Bev's book is the absolute must-read for anyone wanting to understand the full picture on electronic voting. She was kind enough to allow us to use chapters from her book to help complete our overview in this book. Her Web site, *www.blackboxvoting.org*, is a key source for critical information and solutions.

Bev Harris is telling the truth. All Americans need to listen to what this woman is telling us. Wake up, America! Your democracy has been stolen right out from under you!

We would also like to thank and acknowledge the thousands of voting activists across America who are working so hard on this issue. They consist of election workers, journalists, media spokespeople, bloggers, mathematicians, statistical analysts, computer programmers and security engineers; but mainly the heroes and heroines of this movement are simply **citizens.** Citizens who fear for our democratic process and have devoted endless hours on this issue because they all care so deeply about our country. We have a list of election reform organizations across the country at the conclusion of this book. We hope you, our readers, will find one in your state and choose to take action toward restoring safe, hand-counted paper ballots with nonpartisan citizen oversight as the standard for voting in America.

Special thanks to Laura Webb, Melinda Esco, Jayme Huff, and Cyndi Hughes for all the great edits and extra help; to Cindy Goldman and to Scot Hill, our cover photographer; to Terry Sherrell, Blake Mitchell and Stephen Bright; to Karen Renick and VoteRescue, Sharona Merel, Nancy White, Nancy Tobi, Sheila Parks, Ellen Theisen, Pokey Anderson, James Garland, Brian Buffini, Kirsten Parent, and Ed Spencer, for inspiration; to Kat L'Estrange, Liz Carpenter, Helen Thomas, Greg Palast, and Leni Von Eckhardt for believing in this book; to Radio Free Austin for telling the truth; and to Robert DeLozier and Milton Jones for their tremendous support and enduring patience.

Table of Contents

Why using voting machines is disenfranchising Americans. Landes is one of the nation's leading journalists on voting technology and democracy issues.

Well-documented examples of problems with machines in various elections. Bev Harris is founder of the nonprofit "Black Box Voting." Includes an Appendix of serious voting machine problems.

Background on the misunderstood federal mandate, "Help America Vote Act," and how election officials have been pressured and baited with tax dollars to use it as an excuse to purchase millions of dollars of unsafe voting machines.

Preface
Vote Fraud "Hounds of Hell"

Vickie Karp

*AS LONG AS THE WARREN Report stays on
the books as the officially recognized "truth" about
the JFK case, there will be an open wound in the body politic that defies
healing. Assassination researchers are so virulent in scavenging the field
in search of any shred of evidence; they have come to be known as the
"Hounds of Hell."*

*But there's another public cause that has captured the imagination
of the Hound mentality. Vote fraud. Consider the strong emotional val-
ues that we Americans attach to the sanctity of the U.S. ballot. The
ballot is America's number one export. It is the hallowed ground and shed
blood of ten generations of "those who made the supreme sacrifice."*

*As with the JFK breed of Hound, vote fraud trackers have the gut
feeling that some fundamental outrage has occurred and is being covered up in the highest levels of government.*

*One never knows the exact moment of transition from common citi-
zen to Hound.*

—James and Ken Collier from
Votescam: The Stealing of America, 1992

I actually remember the day, even the moment, when I began
my shift from common citizen to one of the vote fraud "Hounds
of Hell."

It was a sweltering day in July of 2003, in Austin, Texas, when I
learned that our elections could be stolen. Before then, I was just a
Realtor selling homes, hanging out with friends, and taking dive

vacations to the Caribbean. Then suddenly, everything changed, just by turning on the radio.

En route to look at a home in North Austin, I found myself listening to a fascinating interview. The guest, clearly intelligent and extremely articulate, was discussing voting machines. She turned out to be Bev Harris, a dedicated, determined investigator who is uncovering the inner workings of computerized vote fraud—something I had no idea even existed.

Harris was explaining how she discovered massive security holes within the secret software manufactured by the second largest electronic voting machine vendor in America: Diebold. Diebold maintains that its software, used to count multi-millions of votes in every election, is absolutely secure. But amazingly, Bev Harris downloaded it off the Internet! The software read like a "handbook on how to tamper with an election." Harris described how she set up a mock election on her laptop, and using instructions found within the software, discovered a hidden "back door" in the code. She was able to hack into the central tabulator where the final vote totals of an election reside. Harris "flipped" the election in minutes, effectively rigging the vote count, and exited out of the system *with no trace.*

I was so stunned as I listened to her story that I pulled into the Whole Foods parking lot, grabbed a yellow legal pad and began taking notes. As a Toastmaster for over 15 years, I'm always looking for more speech material, and if this was true, well . . . WOW! What a speech topic this would make!

Harris described how the new Diebold touchscreen voting machines, being certified for use in precincts throughout America, not only lack a paper ballot or receipt—making any meaningful recount impossible—they are also equipped with modems. This allows data to be uploaded and downloaded from remote locations, and should *never* be present on any secure voting system. When she first made this discovery, she called the Diebold company. Their representative actually denied that there were any modems on their voting machines—all the while, Harris was staring at a photo of a Diebold machine on the Internet with the modem clearly evident!

"It reminds me of the old Richard Pryor joke," Harris recalled, "where the woman comes home and finds her husband in bed with her best friend, and the husband says, 'Who're you going to believe? Me or your lying eyes?'"

I felt like I'd been punched right between *my* eyes. Could electronic voting machines actually be rigged from a remote location, without detection? Could it be that, as so many people have claimed, Al Gore really *did* win the 2000 election—not George W. Bush? If Bush, or any other candidate, rigged himself in with the help of computer-savvy insiders, how would we ever know? And what would that mean for the upcoming 2004 election, where millions of votes would be counted by these riggable computers?

Please understand. I considered this frightening question from the point of view of a political Independent, *not* as a "sour grapes" Democrat. Most important, I considered it from the perspective of an American citizen. Regardless of partisan politics, if elections were being stolen, I wanted to know the whole truth about it—and I wanted to make sure that everyone I came into contact with knew it too. As citizens, we could not let it continue!

At that moment, I ceased being just a Realtor. I became a vote fraud Hound.

I was soon to discover that Bev Harris was not alone. There were others who had awakened to the sickening reality of vote fraud in America, and they were doing something about it. Researchers, investigators, activists, academics scattered throughout the country— all of them patriots in the truest, highest meaning of the word. Journalists James and Kenneth Collier, authors of *Votescam: The Stealing of America,* had even risked their lives to uncover their evidence. Their self-sacrifice and passion for democracy inspired me, and their information helped me to understand exactly how the foundations of our country are being undermined—and what I could do about it.

Since that time, I have become a speaker on the subject of vote fraud and have delivered talks to Republicans, Democrats, Independents, Greens, Libertarians, the League of Women Voters, and many concerned citizens' groups. I now proudly serve on the board of Bev Harris's non-profit 501(c)(3), Black Box Voting. I am the National Chair of the Coalition for Visible Ballots, and I assist Karen Renick with Austin-based VoteRescue.

I recruited one of my closest friends, Abbe Waldman DeLozier, to work on this issue with me. Her dedication to various activist projects, her media savvy, her creative energy and persistence, and her intuitive ability to "smell a rat" in political situations made her a natural partner to help me get the truth out about vote fraud.

In this book, we have gathered together some of the best minds behind what we believe is the most important movement in America today—the movement to take back our democracy by taking back our vote. We are honored to offer you their hardwon evidence, their clear thinking, and their vital solutions. Each contributor has approached the topic from his or her unique perspective. Together, these essays and testimonials make a compelling argument for the shocking premise that *elections are being regularly stolen in our country.*

In this book you will learn of the fundamental dangers inherent in the electronic voting process that our mainstream media has neglected to investigate or report:

- The software that runs all the computerized voting systems is "secret and proprietary." No citizens or government agencies can review it for honesty and integrity.

- Many of the systems have modems, allowing for manipulation of elections from remote locations.

- Touchscreen systems have no paper ballot or receipt that can be recounted in case of question or audit.

- Ownership ties to the major e-voting system vendors link back to top political operatives.

- Felons have been employed as programmers.

- Thousands of problems have arisen with the machines in real election conditions: "flipped" votes where you vote for one candidate and the name of the opponent appears; "overvotes" (more votes than registered voters); "undervotes" (fewer votes than registered voters); machines breaking down and needing recalibration; machine vendors running elections because election officials do not understand how to operate the software; and many, many more.

- The programming that allows for undetectable fraud is present in two of the top four electronic vendors' software. It may also be in the other two; their software has not been revealed to the public or any election officials for review.

- The proposed solutions that involve adding printers to touchscreens but only auditing 2% of all the paper "ballots" or "receipts" are dangerously ineffective.

- Fraud in the Ohio recounts in 2004 prove both audits and re-counts to be ineffective solutions.

- An election can be hacked using optical scan counters that count paper ballots.

We hope that the growing body of vote fraud evidence—much of it discussed in this book—will help break the silence on the part of the mainstream press and help reporters ask the right questions of elections officials.

Just two months before the 2004 presidential race, over 100 members of the media attended press conferences in Washington, D.C., where Bev Harris and a team of computer experts demonstrated six ways to hack an election. It was more than dismaying when *every* story that reported on that event ended with the same lame quote from the vendors of electronic voting machines: *The event was a "circus act" that could not be duplicated in real election conditions.*

The only problem with that conclusion is that *it isn't true*. The evidence is in: **These machines can be hacked; our elections rigged without detection**. There is simply no reason to trust software created by Diebold or any other electronic voting machine vendor when their software is secret, or when there is no paper ballot to validate the final electronic vote total. Even the optical scan counters that count paper ballots are computers that have proven to be highly hackable.

It's very simple: Voting systems must be transparent. Citizens should *not* need a degree in computer science to know whether their vote was accurately counted. Voting should be no more complex than marking choices on a paper ballot, inserting it into a transparent ballot box, and being able to return at 7 P.M. to watch the vote count. The hand count of the paper ballots should be done first at the precinct, in public, and videotaped. The totals should be posted at the precinct.

As Bev Harris has always said, "An election is basically like accounting. Every vote should be accounted for."

Everything Abbe and I have learned about electronic vote fraud in the last three years has made us more afraid for the future of our country and for the freedom of American citizens. Our freedoms are dependent upon honest elections, and as you will learn from this book, we just don't have those anymore.

Any democratic country is in deep trouble when its elections are privatized and controlled by unaccountable corporations, not citizens. That is where we find ourselves today. And it will be We the People, the citizens of America, who ultimately *have to take our elections back*. Citizens who have become the vote fraud Hounds of Hell! Read this book, learn the truth, and then join us! We cannot save our elections—we cannot save our country—without your help.

Vickie Karp
August 2006

Preface
Who Stole our Votes?

Abbe Waldman DeLozier

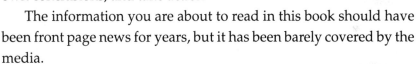

AMERICA, WAKE UP!

Your elections have been stolen!

If you love America, we ask you to read this book, consider the implications of it, draw your own conclusions, and take action.

The information you are about to read in this book should have been front page news for years, but it has been barely covered by the media.

Yes, the truth is this: America has abdicated to private corporations the responsibility of handling elections and counting the votes; corporations that are manufacturing very expensive, highly vulnerable, computerized voting equipment run with secret, proprietary software. **These machines can be easily manipulated and errantly programmed!** The vote you cast may not have been recorded as you intended, and as long as you are voting using these machines for either casting or counting, you will never know if your vote was counted the way you cast it.

That is why we produced this book. Our goal is to help educate people on the subject of vote fraud. I think you deserve to know that your democracy is in grave danger.

Second, we believe that it's been years since we've had fair elections in America. *Some of the people currently "representing" you in federal and state governments were not truly elected by We the People!* When you read this book, you will come to understand how and why we believe this to be true.

When first presented with this information, I thought, "This is impossible! " How could this come to pass in America? Isn't the government monitoring elections? We monitor elections in third world countries around the world, don't we? These were my initial reactions when I was first told in 2003 by my friend, Vickie Karp, that electronic voting machines were corrupting elections in America. The first questions I asked myself were:

1. Why have our government and/or election officials not been noticing that there were election discrepancies and problems and doing something about this?

2. Why are our election officials not filing lawsuits? Why aren't there federal, state, and county investigations being launched to determine if vote fraud is occurring?

It has taken more than six years of problems with electronic voting machines for the Government Accountability Office (GAO) to finally conduct a study of electronic voting machine problems. In summary, on page two of this 107-page report critical of electronic voting equipment, it states that ". . . **cast ballots**, ballot definition files, **and audit logs could be modified. . . .**" Do you need to read more? Their report can be found at: *www.gao.gov/new.items/ d05956.pdf.*

Upon learning that our elections have been compromised, recent events started making sense to me. I knew something was wrong with our election process starting with the presidential "election" of 2000. I prefer not to call it an "election" because I went into shock when I saw judges in federal and state courts deciding *to not allow citizens' votes in America* to be recounted in numerous states where ballot counting results were questionable or unfinished. My heart was *broken* when the Supreme Court ordered vote counts stopped before a final, complete analysis was in. Is this not what democracy in America is about—one person, one vote? How could this be happening in our country?

Everything I knew and loved about America and the democracy I assumed we live in went down in flames in the months following the 2000 "election." I got angry. Then, thanks to a piece I saw on a television show called *NOW*, I finally took action. Bill Moyers, the wonderful long-time author and journalist then affiliated with PBS, had a program featuring what people across America were doing in their own way to change the world around them.

One citizen was taking every congressman to lunch, one at a time on his own dime, to discuss his concerns about our country. Mr. Moyers concluded his program by saying that until you actually take action and do something to change your world, you, too, are part of the problem. His words spoke to me that day and still do.

The next day, I took action and started producing a variety of political actions and projects and have not looked back with regret since.

I consider it my patriotic duty to help educate and inform the public about election fraud in America. I am still in a constant state of disbelief and anger over what is going on under our noses with elections and voting in America today. We can never have proper representation in our government until we are legally guaranteed that our votes are being properly hand counted for the people we choose.

I have hope and faith in America's future. The most important thing I can impart to you, the reader, is to ask you to get involved in your community. The America we all know and love is in a sad state of affairs. We are supposed to have a government of, by, and for the people. This is no longer the case.

You are going to read information in this book that may shock you. You will probably react as I did. You will probably question why our state and federal governments are not carefully regulating voting systems in America. After reading our book and examining this issue carefully, you may come to see, as I and others have, that they are not regulating voting systems if we are not even allowed to review what the vendors refer to as their "proprietary" source code that programs the computer!

You will find that in the vast majority of cases, election and government officials will adamantly insist that our elections are closely monitored and meet state and federal guidelines and certification standards. Many probably honestly feel that they are right.

However, consider just one example of how naive (or deceptive) this attitude is (clearly indicating that at best our officials do not grasp the underlying severity of the issue). Dr. Aviel Rubin, a computer security expert with Johns Hopkins University, wrote the following on December 16, 2005, regarding a voting system testing lab summit hosted by the California Secretary of State, Bruce McPherson. Regarding the matter of Independent Testing Authorities (ITAs), mandated by law to test voting machines for security, Dr. Rubin states that he heard the following remarks from a Systest Labs representative (one of three labs in the country approved to test electronic voting equipment): ". . . A representative replied that they were only required to test against the standard (current U.S. regulations). **When pressed about whether the ITAs would fail a system if a serious flaw was found, the reply was that a memo would be written, but that the system would still pass**. I couldn't believe it. The company that was tasked with certifying machines for elections in the United States would still pass them, even if a serious flaw was found, as long as the machine did not violate any aspects of the standard. Unbelievable. . . ."

Dr. Rubin went on to clarify another point about the three certified testing labs in America that test the machines citizens use to vote when he stated ". . . **The ITAs are hired by and paid by—the vendors. When a vendor has a voting machine that they want certified, they find an ITA who is willing to certify it. Any memos about flaws that are discovered remain confidential.**

There is no requirement to disclose any problems that are found with the machines. In fact, the entire ITA report is considered proprietary information of the voting machine vendor. *After all, they paid for it*. This provides an incentive for ITAs to certify machines to satisfy their clients. . . ." "Unbelievable" is right! Want something else that is unbelievable? A former California Secretary of State has been a paid consultant for Sequoia Voting Systems, one of the largest voting machine DRE vendors. Unbelievable. Yet, sadly true.

Additionally, many election and government officials simply have little, or not enough, technical background. Many are earnest and probably honest, but not sophisticated enough with technical matters to properly review and oversee computerized machines. You will hear election officials say that they had "no problems" with their elections, or that they had "a fine election and things went smoothly." *They have no way of knowing the accuracy! Did they have an accurate election? Do they know whether they might have been misled or hacked?*

Our answer is NO! Voting systems and equipment today are regulated by archaic laws mostly written before the advent of the newer Direct Recording Electronic (DRE) voting machines. The fox (voting machine companies) is guarding the henhouse and telling everyone that there is no problem, to simply take their word and trust them. They know that there is not enough legal policy to oversee them. We also have documented proof, beyond what Dr. Rubin stated in the previous quotes, that some of the testing labs used to test electronic voting equipment have their fees paid by the vendors of these machines and furthermore ". . . are not required to disclose any problems that are found with the machines! . . ." See "The Dirty Little Secrets of Voting System Testing Labs" by Dr. Aviel Rubin, December 16, 2005, available at: *http://www.huffingtonpost.com/avi-rubin/the-dirty-little-secrets-_b_12354.html.*

Let the Spin Begin

The reactions to this book will be swift and predictable. We will be called conspiracy theorists and worse. We, however, discuss the hard facts, not theories, regarding the voting problems covered in our book. I am sure there will be comments that every election has human error; that the problems we are experiencing are normal election worker errors that should be expected. I ask you to particularly pay attention to author May Schmidt's article. She has been an election worker for 35 years and she explains that with hand-counted paper ballots every ballot was accounted for! Seems like a reasonable approach to me. We need a return to more oversight and protection as with hand-counted paper ballots. Let's get to work on it to ensure honest elections.

You will probably also hear vendors state that tests by independent computer security experts proving voting machine vulnerabilities are simply "unproven dog-and-pony shows" using computers or software that are not state or federally certified or tested. **That is simply not true! Beware of the spin!** Go to *www.blackboxvoting.org* and read the reports of computer security tests performed by the Black Box Voting team (reference "Hursti reports" linked on the home page.)

Another favorite claim made by vendors and election officials is that the government closely monitors election equipment and that your vote is "...safer, easier, faster..." (quote taken from the Texas Secretary of State's Web site). Yet, I read some of the transcripts of the Texas Secretary of State's *closed door certification hearings* of the Texas Voting Systems Examiners' Board, the body which evaluates voting systems and makes recommendation to the Secretary of State regarding which voting systems to certify for use. Those transcripts from 2004 stated that the certifications were *based solely on vendor input* and no outside independent experts were consulted, other than the state-appointed certification examiners. To my knowledge, for example, the state of Texas has not ordered outside independent testing on voting systems used by taxpayers other than the standard testing under lax regulations described previously. This is unacceptable. All anyone seems to be saying, be they governmental or corporate officials, is, **Trust us**. This is an unacceptable review process.

Time and again, I have seen comments in the transcripts of these Texas voting examiners indicating that in spite of various security and operating concerns, examiners recommend recertification of these voting machines. Is this representing the citizens of our country? To allow unknowing citizens to pick up the tab for expensive, secretly programmed and faulty voting equipment with their hard-earned tax dollars, and then to certify for public use computers that are shown in certification hearings to be unworthy of a public trust as important as voting is totally irresponsible.

Computerized voting machines are vulnerable to attack by virtue of just being machines. These computerized machines have a history of wildly inaccurate and suspect performance, election after election, evidenced by breakdowns, miscounts, and loss of thousands of votes. **What is so wrong with having publically accountable elections? There is no accountability or transparency with voting machines!**

We ask you to read this book, inform yourself, but don't take our word for it: Do your own research.

We will provide you resources and Web sites for further documented information on this subject. After you have read the evidence, ask yourself these questions: What makes sense to you? For whom are the proponents of electronic voting machines working? How many millions of dollars are the vendors of these machines profiting from YOUR tax dollars? *Who stands to gain, economically or politically?* Follow the money, as Woodward and Bernstein have stated.

Are the election officials who support the use of these machines, the very officials who rushed to authorize their purchase with your tax dollars, now unwilling to retract their decisions for fear of tarnished reputations now that these machines are proving unreliable? To some of these officials' credit, the Help America Vote Act (HAVA) dangled millions of dollars for their use if they would upgrade their voting equipment by their primary election of 2006. However, it has been widely presumed that HAVA was a mandate to purchase electronic equipment. Not so! Because of that, county election officials in most states across the country had their secretaries of state demanding they purchase equipment immediately or lose millions of federal dollars.

Can We Prove That Elections Have Been Hacked?

This is the question everyone asks us. We can prove that the machines can be hacked. We can prove that elections have been manipulated. What we cannot prove in most cases is the extent to which the manipulations affected the results.

Can we prove widespread fraud across the country has taken place? No. Our government has allowed our elections to be privatized to companies who are allowed to use secret proprietary source code to control how these machines record votes. Even the election officials who buy the machines are not allowed to look under the hood.

Like a criminal trial where the motive, weapon and body must be demonstrated, we will show you the evidence step by step in the following pages to prove our case that we believe elections are being hacked and compromised. Criminals have been convicted of murder with far less evidence then what you are about to read in this book. As you read, keep in mind the following question:

Why is our government allowing its citizens to vote on privately owned machines, without citizen oversight, using secret programming, without proper testing or certification, and looking the other way every time a machine miscounts an election?

We do not consent.

The information that follows documents *specific election tampering* that has occurred. I find it unacceptable that this is going on in America, and that we have no way of knowing how widespread this problem is.

[*Editors Note:* The following information was provided to us by Bev Harris, Executive Director of Black Box Voting. Keep in mind the implications of what you are reading.]

Have Computerized Voting Systems Been Hacked During Real Elections?

When 18 ½ minutes went missing from a critical Watergate audiotape, we didn't shrug and call it "a glitch." In King County, Washington on Sept. 14, 2004, three hours was deleted from a central tabulator audit log during the middle of the count in a primary election. The log contained the record of what was going on in the main King County tabulator. All of the automatically generated entries from around 9 P.M. to midnight (the most active results-generating period of the evening) simply vanished. During a time period when hundreds of precincts were tabulated and no less than five interim results reports were calculated by the machine, then-King County elections chief Logan claimed that the audit records are missing because the machine was inactive. As with the missing 18 minutes in the Nixon tapes, no one will ever know what the logs contained.[1]

In Palm Beach County, Florida during the 2004 presidential election, four dozen voting machine logs contained votes cast with time and date-stamps weeks before the election, sometimes in the middle of the night—and in one case, votes are date-stamped seven years after the election. Battery failure and re-setting the clock have been ruled out. The simplest explanation, given all the surrounding details, is that the out-of-whack dates are a side effect of tampering with program code. Palm Beach County has been unwilling to let citizens examine the machines with the crazy dates to try and replicate the "error." The machines are paperless touch-screens and no one will ever know what the votes really were or who may have benefited from the tampering.[2]

[*Editors note*: Ms Harris had to file a lawsuit in order to obtain this information from Palm Beach County.]

In Volusia County, Florida during the 2000 presidential election, a memory card (the ballot box, for computerized voting machines) produced correct results. Strangely, the correct electronic ballot box (memory card #0) was later replaced with another ballot box (memory card #3), which produced different results: *Minus 16,022 votes for Al Gore. In a remarkable coincidence, this happened to be just the margin that was needed to call the election for George W. Bush.* Nine minutes after the Volusia County electronic ballot box was replaced, all major networks erroneously called the election for Bush, based on according to an internal CBS report—the 16,000 vote spread that suddenly occurred in Volusia County. Pressure was put on Gore to concede, and he finally did, privately, to Bush. He was on his way to concede to the nation—only two blocks away—when he learned of the bogus results and withdrew his concession. Had he conceded to the nation as planned, the 2000 presidential election would have ended on Election Night.[3]

Motive. Means. Opportunity.

I think you will understand, after reading our book, why a change in our election systems must take place immediately. We believe hand counted paper ballots are the only acceptable method for holding elections now and in the future.

We produced this book to demonstrate the reasons why we believe this is the only *safe* solution for citizens' votes to be properly counted.

We, along with all our authors, want to sincerely thank you in advance for reading our book. We urge you to take action to restore safe elections in America.

Our future and the future of our democracy depend on the actions you will take. We hope you join us in hope and participation.

Thank you.
Abbe Waldman DeLozier
August 2006

Endnotes

1. Source: Public records from King County Washington.
http://www.bbvdocs.org/kingcounty.pdf

2. Source: Public records from Palm Beach County, Florida
http://www.bbvforums.org/forums/messages/1954/19421.html

3. Source: Black Box Voting: Ballot-Tampering in the 21st Century pp. 170-178.

http://www.blackboxvoting.org/bbv_chapter-13.pdf ; CBS report:
http://www.bbvforums.org/forums/messages/2197/23140.html

Faking Democracy
Americans Don't Vote, Machines Do, & Ballot Printers Can't Fix That

Lynn Landes

MACHINES WILL PROCESS 95% of all the election results for the upcoming elections. With all the hoopla over voting machine "glitches," porous software, leaked memos, and the creepy corporations that sell and service these contraptions, and with all the controversy that surrounds campaign financing, voter registration, redistricting issues, and the general privatization of the election process, we are missing the boat on the biggest crisis facing our democracy.

Americans aren't really voting. Machines are. Call it faking democracy.

And no one seems to be challenging it. As far as I can tell from my own investigations and from discussions with law professors, attorneys, and others, there has never been a lawsuit that challenges the right of machines to be used in the voting process. Recent lawsuits that have been filed by Susan Marie Webber of California and Congressman Robert Wexler (D-FL) are based on verification. The plaintiffs want voting machines to produce paper ballots so that voters can verify that the machine's output matched their input. They also want paper ballots for manual audits and recounts.

But these lawsuits, as well as proposed legislation in Congress from Congressman Rush Holt and Senator Bob Graham, leave voting machines in control of election results. The public is being offered a set of false choices: paperless touchscreen voting machines or touchscreen machines with ballot printers. Machine-free elections are not on the menu.

Part of the reason may be that people believe the Help America Vote Act (HAVA) requires states to use voting machines. **It does no such thing, not even for the disabled**. Another reason the machine-free option is not widely discussed is the popular misconception that people will not "go back" to paper ballots. But they already have. Absentee voting continues to grow in popularity despite real security problems with the chain of custody of the ballots.

It is particularly confounding to this writer that our foremost legal scholars and political scientists have yet to address this issue. Instead, a bold band of tech heads is leading a charge against paperless voting machines. But, they are not looking at the broader Constitutional issues. Being technical, they're calling for a technical fix—ballot printers.

The only fix that will give Americans back their Constitutional right to vote is to ditch the machines.

In *Bush v Gore*, the Supreme Court stated that a "legal vote" is one in which there is a "clear indication of the intent of the voter." Voting machines (lever, optical scan, touchscreen, the Internet, etc.) produce circumstantial evidence of the voter's intent, at best. Think of voting as a three-step process: marking, casting, and counting ballots. Once a machine is involved in any one of those steps, the result is hard evidence of the machine's output and circumstantial evidence of the voter's input.

Many activists are calling for ballot printers, hand counts, and strict audits to ensure honest election results. That will not fix the problem of using voting machines. Voting rights are for people, not machines. The voting process must be transparent in order for voting rights to be enforced. Machines are not transparent.

When voting machines are used, critical parts of the Voting Rights Act can't be enforced. Under Section 8 of the Voting Rights Act, 42 U.S. Code §1973f, Federal Observers are authorized to observe

". . . whether persons who are entitled to vote are being permitted to vote. . . (and) whether votes cast by persons entitled to vote are being properly tabulated. . . ."

Under "Prohibited acts" in §1973i, the "Failure or refusal to permit casting or tabulation of vote. . ." can result in civil and criminal penalties. " No person acting under color of law shall fail or refuse to permit any person to vote who is entitled to vote. . . (and) Whoever. . . knowingly and willfully falsifies or conceals a material fact. . . shall be fined not more than $10,000 or imprisoned not more than five years, or both." Voting machines violate those provisions. Vote casting and tabulation take place inside of a box. Federal Observers can't observe ". . . whether persons who are entitled to vote are being permitted to vote. . . (and) whether votes cast. . . are being properly tabulated." Voting machines by their very design "conceal a material fact."

Although Susan Marie Webber and Congressman Wexler are suing to force states to require manufacturers to attach ballot printers to voting machines, the resulting ballot would still be only circumstantial evidence of the voter's intent. It's been predicted by election officials (and it makes common sense, to boot) that many voters won't bother to verify their ballots. In which case, who is to say if the vote cast matched the voter's intent? Some will say that it's the voter's responsibility to verify his or her ballot, but that view misses the point. Why should people verify the work of a machine? That puts the voter playing second fiddle to technology. Whose right to vote is it?

The contention that voters too often don't fill out ballots properly or the elections officials too often don't count correctly is not borne out by the facts, but is moot, regardless. Again, the right to vote and to observe your vote counted properly belongs to people, not machines.

Consideration of time and convenience is another red herring in this debate. Those issues have simple no-tech solutions, anyway. If officials want a fast ballot count then they can limit the size of the voting precincts or increase the number of elections officials. If more elections officials are needed they can be drafted into public service as is done all year around for jury duty. Likewise, voters who don't understand English could order ballots in their own language in advance of an election.

Voting machines have been marketed as "assisting voters" (i.e., President Bush's Elections Assistance Committee), rather than what they really do, which is to interfere with a citizen's right to vote. It's particularly galling to see the needs of the disabled voters used to force voting machines down the throats of the electorate. The simple ballot template, which is used in Rhode Island, Canada, and around the world, allows the blind to vote privately and independently, or as independently as possible. Actually, when the disabled use voting machines they certainly are not voting independently. They are relying on the machine to vote for them, just like able-bodied voters.

It's insane when you think about it. Using machines in elections. Yet, we've been doing it since 1888. How can Americans be so naive? How can we surrender our precious right to vote to some hunk of junk and so few people seem to notice or to care? How can we call ourselves a democracy?

It is painful to think that as African Americans intensified their struggle for the vote in the 1960s, voting machines were already in widespread use and perfectly positioned to control election results, and according to some accounts, were already doing so. Just imagine how the Iraqi people would react if the U.S. government told them that their elections will be electronic and that Halliburton, the Carlyle Group, and Microsoft will provide the machines and the software they run on? Exactly. The Iraqis would burn the place down, some more.

Yet, here we Americans go again. Not connecting the dots. Shooting at the wrong target. Attaching printer machines to the voting machines that don't belong there in the first place. Asking voters to verify a machine's output, leaving the voter's input indirect and in doubt.

I wonder what the United Nations think about a country that fakes democracy? They probably already know.

❖ ❖ ❖

Article reprinted with minor edits, with permission of author. Originally published in April of 2004.

Lynn Landes is one of the nation's leading journalists on voting technology and democracy issues. Readers can find her articles at EcoTalk.org. Lynn is a former news reporter for DUTV and commentator for the British Broadcasting Corporation (BBC). In 2004, Lynn filed a lawsuit in U.S. District Court in Philadelphia challenging the use of electronic voting machines and absentee voting as unconstitutional. The U.S. District Court ruled against her and she appealed the case to the U.S. Third Circuit Court of Appeals, and eventually to the U.S. Supreme Court which let stand the lower court's decision that Landes had no standing to challenge the constitutionality of election laws. Contact info: lynnlandes@earthlink.net / (215) 629-3553.

Can We Trust These Machines?

Bev Harris

IN THE ALABAMA 2002 GENERAL election, machines made by Election Systems and Software (ES&S) flipped the governor's race. Six thousand three hundred Baldwin County electronic votes mysteriously disappeared after the polls had closed and everyone had gone home. Democrat Don Siegelman's victory was handed to Republican Bob Riley; the recount Siegelman requested was denied. Six months after the election, the vendor shrugged. "Something happened. I don't have enough intelligence to say exactly what," said Mark Kelley of ES&S.[1]

When I began researching this story in October 2002, the media was reporting that electronic voting machines are fun and speedy, but I looked in vain for articles reporting that they are accurate. I discovered four magic words, "voting machines and glitch," which, when entered into the *DJInteractive.com*[2] search engine, yielded a shocking result: A staggering pile of miscounts was accumulating. These were reported locally but had never been compiled in a single place, so reporters were missing a disturbing pattern.

I published a compendium of 56 documented cases in which voting machines got it wrong.

How do voting-machine makers respond to these reports? With shrugs. They indicate that their miscounts are nothing to be concerned about. One of their favorite phrases is: "It didn't change the result."

Except, of course, when it did:

In the 2002 general election, a computer miscount overturned the House District 11 result in Wayne County, North Carolina. Incorrect programming caused machines to skip several thousand party line votes, both Republican and Democratic. Fixing the error turned up 5,500 more votes and reversed the election for state representative.[3]

This crushing defeat never happened. Voting machines failed to tally "yes" votes on the 2002 school bond issue in Gretna, Nebraska. This error gave the false impression that the measure had failed miserably, but it actually passed by a 2 to 1 margin. Responsibility for the errors was attributed to ES&S, the Omaha company that had provided the ballots and the machines.[4]

According to the *Chicago Tribune*, "It was like being queen for a day—but only for 12 hours," said Richard Mitotic, a losing Republican candidate for alderman who was told that he had won a Lake County, Illinois, primary election. He was among 15 people in four races affected by an ES&S vote-counting foul-up.[5]

An Orange County, California, election computer made a 100 percent error during the April 1998 school bond referendum. The Registrar of Voters Office initially announced that the bond issue had lost by a wide margin; in fact, it was supported by a majority of the ballots cast. The error was attributed to a programmer's reversing the "yes" and "no" answers in the software used to count the votes.[6]

A computer program that was specially enhanced to speed the November 1993 Kane County, Illinois, election results to a waiting public did just that—unfortunately, it sped the wrong data. Voting totals for a dozen Illinois races were incomplete, and in one case they suggested that a local referendum proposal had lost when it actually had been approved. For some reason, software that had worked earlier without a hitch had waited until election night to omit eight precincts in the tally.[7]

A squeaker—no, a landslide—oops, we reversed the totals—and about those absentee votes, make that 72–19, not 44–47. Software programming errors, sorry. Oh, and reverse that election, we announced the wrong winner. In the 2002 Clay County, Kansas, commissioner primary, voting machines said Jerry Mayo ran a close race but lost, garnering 48 percent of the vote, but a hand recount revealed Mayo had won by a landslide, receiving 76 percent of the vote.[8]

Apparently voting machine miscounts have been taking place for some time. In a 1971 race in Las Vegas, Nevada, machines declared Democrat Arthur Espinoza to be the winner of a seat on the city assembly, but Republican Hal Smith challenged the election when he determined that some votes had not been counted because of a faulty voting machine. After unrecorded votes were tallied, Smith was declared the winner.[9]

The excuses given for these miscounts are just as flawed as the election results themselves. Vendors have learned that reporters and election workers will believe pretty much anything, as long as it sounds high-tech. They blame incorrect vote counts on "a bad chip" or "a faulty memory card," but defective chips and bad memory cards have very different symptoms. They don't function at all, or they spit out nonsensical data.

In the November 2002 general election in Scurry County, Texas, poll workers got suspicious about a landslide victory for two Republican commissioner candidates. Told that a "bad chip" was to blame, they had a new computer chip flown in and also counted the votes by hand—and found out that Democrats actually had won by wide margins, overturning the election.[10]

We usually don't get an explanation for these miscounts. In 1986 the wrong candidate was declared the winner in Georgia. Incumbent Democrat Donn Peevy was running for state senator in District 48. The machines said he lost the election. After an investigation revealed that a Republican elections official had kept uncounted ballots in the trunk of his car, officials also admitted that a computerized voting program had miscounted. Peevy insisted on a recount. According to the *Atlanta Journal-Constitution*: "When the count finished around

1 A.M., they [the elections board] walked into a room and shut the door," recalls Peevy. "When they came out, they said, 'Mr. Peevy, you won.' That was it. They never apologized. They never explained." [11]

In a Seminole Nation election held in Oklahoma in August 1997, electronic voting machines gave the election to the wrong candidates twice. The private company hired to handle the election announced results for tribal chief and assistant chief, then decided that its computer had counted the absentee ballots twice. So the company posted a second set of results. Tribal officials then counted the votes by hand, producing yet a third, and this time official, set of results. A different set of candidates moved on to the runoff election each time. [12]

If you insist on the right to vote for whom you want (and no one's gonna stop you), does it make a difference if misprogramming, rather than a human being, forces you to vote for someone you *don't* want?

News reports often explain miscounts as "software programming errors," with no follow up and certainly no outrage. Yet incorrect programming is more insidious than Mad Myrtle secretly stuffing the ballot box. At least when we vote on paper ballots, hand counted, we can hold someone accountable. We don't even know the names of our voting machine programmers.

A software programming error gave the election to the wrong candidate in November 1999 in Onondaga County, New York. Bob Faulkner, a political newcomer, went to bed on election night confident he had helped complete a Republican sweep of three open council seats. But after Onondaga County Board of Elections staffers rechecked the totals, Faulkner had lost to Democratic incumbent Elaine Lytel. Just a few hours later, election officials discovered that a software programming error had given too many absentee ballot votes to Lytel. Faulkner took the lead. [13]

Akron, Ohio, discovered its votes got scrambled in its December 1997 election. It was announced that Ed Repp had won the election— no, cancel that, a programming error was discovered—Repp actually lost. (Look! Twins!) Another error in the same election resulted in incorrect totals for the Portage County Board election. (Make that triplets.) Turns out the bond referendum results were wrong, too.[14]

In a 1998 Salt Lake City election, 1,413 votes never showed up in the total. A programming error caused a batch of ballots not to count, though they had been run through the machine like all the others. When the 1,413 missing votes were counted, they reversed the election.[15]

❖ ❖ ❖

Voting machine vendors claim these things are amazingly accurate. Bob Urosevich, who has headed three different voting machine companies under five different corporate names, said in 1990 that his company's optical-scan machines had an error rate of only "one thousandth of 1 percent."[16]

At that time, Urosevich was with ES&S (then called American Information Systems). Recently, the same Urosevich (now president of Diebold Election Systems, formerly called Global Election Systems) gave an even more glowing endorsement of his company's touchscreen accuracy.

"Considering the magnitude of these elections, which includes more than 870,000 registered voters within the four Maryland counties, we are very pleased with the results as every single vote was accurately counted," he said.[17]

When Chuck Hagel accepted his position as chairman of American Information Systems, he offered a rousing endorsement: "The AIS system is 99.99 percent accurate," he assured us.[18]

But do these claims hold up?

According to *The Wall Street Journal*, in the 2000 general election an optical-scan machine in Allamakee County, Iowa, was fed 300 ballots and reported 4 million votes. The county auditor tried the machine again but got the same result. Eventually, the machine's manufacturer, ES&S, agreed to have replacement equipment sent. Republicans had hoped that the tiny but heavily Republican county would tip the scales in George W. Bush's favor, but tipping it by almost four million votes attracted national attention.

"We don't have four million voters in the state of Iowa," said Bill Roe Jr., county auditor.

Todd Urosevich of ES&S said, "You are going to have some failures."[19]

November, 2003: Officials from Boone County, Indiana, wanted to know why their MicroVote machines counted 144,000 votes cast when only 5,352 existed.

"I about had a heart attack," said County Clerk Lisa Garofolo, according to the *Indianapolis Star*. "Believe me, there was nobody more shook up than I was."[20]

If you are an elections official, I hope this litany gives you pause. Do you really need this kind of stress?

With computerized voting, the certified and sworn officials step aside and let technicians, and sometimes the county computer guy, tell us the election results. The Boone County information technology director and a few MicroVote techs "fixed the problem." (For voting, I prefer the term "corrected.")

Better than a pregnant chad—these machines can actually give birth.

In the 1996 McLennan County, Texas, Republican primary run-off, one precinct tallied about 800 votes, although only 500 ballots had been ordered. "It's a mystery," declared Elections Administrator Linda Lewis. Like detectives on the Orient Express, officials pointed fingers at one suspected explanation after another. One particular machine may have been the problem, Lewis said. That is, the miscounted votes were scattered throughout the precincts with no one area being miscounted more than another, Lewis also explained. Wait—some ballots may have been counted more than once, almost doubling the number of votes actually cast. Aha! That could explain it. (Er...excuse me, exactly *which* ballots were counted twice?)

"We don't think it's serious enough to throw out the election," said county Republican Party Chairman M.A. Taylor. Error size: 60%.[21]

Here's a scorching little 66% error rate: Eight hundred and twenty-six votes in one Tucson, Arizona-area precinct simply evaporated, remaining unaccounted for a month after the 1994 general election. No recount appears to have been done, even though two-thirds of voters did not get their votes counted. Election officials said the vanishing votes were the result of a faulty computer program. Apparently, the software programming error and the person who caused it are still at large.[22]

Some voters aren't so sure that *every single vote* was accurately counted during the 2002 general election in Maryland.

According to the *Washington Times*, Kevin West of Upper Marlboro, who voted at the St. Thomas Church in Croom, said, "I pushed a Republican ticket for governor and his name disappeared. Then the Democrat's name got an 'X' put in it." [23]

No one will ever know whether the Maryland machines counted correctly because the new Diebold touchscreen system is unauditable.

Tom Eschberger became a vice president of ES&S not long after he accepted an immunity deal for cooperating with prosecutors in a case against Arkansas Secretary of State Bill McCuen, who pleaded guilty to taking kickbacks and bribes in a scheme related to computerized voting systems.[24]

Eschberger reported that a test conducted on a malfunctioning machine and its software in the 1998 general election in Honolulu, Hawaii, showed the machine worked normally. He said the company did not know that the machine wasn't functioning properly until the Supreme Court ordered a recount, when a second test on the same machine detected that it wasn't counting properly. "But again, in all fairness, there were 7,000 machines in Venezuela and 500 machines in Dallas that did not have problems," he said.[25]

Really?

Dallas, Texas: A software programming error caused Dallas County, Texas's new, $3.8 million high-tech ballot system to miss 41,015 votes during the November 1998 election. The system refused to count votes from 98 precincts, telling itself they had already been counted. Operators and election officials didn't realize they had a problem until after they'd released "final" totals that omitted one in eight votes.

In one of the nonsensical answers that we see so often from vendors, ES&S assured us that votes were never lost, just uncounted.

The company took responsibility and was trying to find two apparently unrelated software bugs, one that mistakenly indicated precinct votes were in when they weren't, and another that forgot to include 8,400 mail-in ballots in the final tally. Democrats were livid and suspicious, but Tom Eschberger said, "What we had was a speed bump along the way."[26]

Caracas, Venezuela: In May 2000, Venezuela's highest court suspended elections because of problems with the tabulation for the national election. Venezuela sent an air force jet to Omaha to fetch experts from ES&S in a last-ditch effort to fix the problem.

Dozens of protesters chanted, "Gringos get out!" at ES&S technicians. Venezuelan President Hugo Chavez accused ES&S of trying to destabilize the country's electoral process. Chavez asked for help from the U.S. government because, he said, the U.S. had recommended ES&S.[27]

❖ ❖ ❖

Some people, when you give them the short but horrifying version of the electronic voting issue, insist on minimizing the problem. You tell them about an election that lost 25 percent of its votes, and they say, "That's just an isolated incident." When you add that another election had a 100 percent error, they call it a "glitch." When you tell them a voting machine was videotaped recording votes for the opposite candidate than the one selected, they say, "There are problems in every election."

No. We are not talking about a few minor glitches. These are real miscounts by voting machines, which took place in real elections. Almost all of them were caused by incorrect programming, whether by accident or by design. And if you run into anyone who thinks we are hallucinating all of these problems, hand them the footnote section, so they can examine sources and look them up themselves.

For the third time in as many elections, Pima County, Arizona, found errors in its tallies. The computers recorded no votes for 24 precincts in the 1998 general election, but voter rolls showed thousands had voted at those polling places. Pima used Global Election Systems machines, which now are sold under the Diebold company name.[28]

Officials in Broward County, Florida, had said that all the precincts were included in the November 5, 2002, election and that the new, unauditable ES&S touchscreen machines had counted the vote without a major hitch. The next day, the County Elections Office discovered 103,222 votes had not been counted.

Allow me to shed some perspective on this. Do you remember when we got excited about a missing ballot box found in a Dade County, Florida, church daycare center in the 2000 presidential election?[29] One hundred and three thousand uncounted votes represents about1,000 ballot boxes. Broward Deputy Elections Supervisor Joe Cotter called the mistake "a minor software thing."[30]

If you are a candidate, you know that participating even in a small election means raising or borrowing money, passing out flyers, going door to door and standing in the rain at various events. How do you feel if your vote is not counted accurately?

"I knew something was wrong when I looked up the results in my own precinct and it showed zero votes," said Illinois Democrat Rafael Rivera, according to the *Chicago Tribune*. "I said, 'Wait a minute. I know I voted for myself.'"

The problem cropped up during the Lake County, Illinois, election held April 1, 2003. Clerk Willard Helander blamed the problem on ES&S, the Omaha company in charge of operating Waukegan's optical-scan voting machines. Rivera said he felt as if he were living an episode of *The Twilight Zone*. No votes showed up for him, not even his own.

"It felt like a nightmare," he said.[31]

Is this not alarming? These voting systems have miscounted our votes, flipping elections even when they are not particularly close. Even more alarming: We have no idea how many miscounts go unnoticed.

No legal authority permits privately employed technicians—often temporary workers—who are not sworn and don't work for the elections office, who sometimes are not even residents of the U.S., to determine the results of the election when there are discrepancies.

Yet they do.

Ten days after the November 2002 election, Richard Romero, a Bernalillo County, New Mexico, Democrat, noticed that 48,000 people had voted early on unauditable Sequoia touchscreen computers, but only 36,000 votes had been tallied—a 25 percent error. Sequoia vice president Howard Cramer apologized for not mentioning that the same problem had happened before in Clark County, Nevada. A "software patch" was installed (more on that risky procedure later) and Sequoia technicians in Denver *e-mailed* the "correct" results.[32]

Not only did Cramer fail to mention to Bernalillo County that the problem had happened before in Nevada—just four months later, Sequoia salespersons also failed to mention it while making a sales presentation to Santa Clara County, California. A Santa Clara official tried to jog their memory. According to the minutes of this meeting,[33] " Supervisor McHugh asked one of the vendors about a statistic saying there was a 25 percent error rate. . . . No one knew where this number came from and Sequoia said it was incorrect."

That meeting was held February 11, 2003. Just 20 days before, in Snohomish County, Washington, at a meeting called because Sequoia optical-scan machines had failed to record 21 percent of the absentee votes,[34] I asked about the 25 percent error in Bernalillo County. The Sequoia representative was well aware of the problem, replying quickly that *that* 25 percent error was caused by something quite different from *this* 21 percent problem. OK. *Nothing to see here—move along.*

❖ ❖ ❖

Sequoia's failure to disclose a miscount when asked about it during a sales meeting really got me wondering: How often do voting companies lie about known errors when they are making sales presentations? Not often, it turns out. They don't have to lie—because our election officials *don't ask*! That's right. When deciding to buy voting machines, our representatives don't ask whether the machines count accurately. And only occasionally does anyone bother to ask whether the machines can be tampered with. Here's what I mean:

Marion County, Indiana Voting Technology Task Force, Meeting Minutes July 30, 1999 ES&S, Global Election Systems, MicroVote. Mr. Cockrum asked a series of questions to each vendor.

> How do you recommend instruction of voters to become
>   familiar with your system?
> How many machines per voter/precinct?
> Could your system handle split precincts?
> Could your systems handle school board elections?
> Does your system allow for party crossover voting?
> What is the recount capability?
> Is your system tamper proof?
> Can your system be leased or does it need to be purchased?
> What is the percentage of availability of spare machines?
> What are the advantages?
> There being no further business before the Voting Technology
> Task Force, Chairwoman Grant adjourned the meeting.

We know the machines have miscounted elections, but could this happen without being discovered?

In Seattle, a malfunction caused voting-machine computers to lose more than 14,000 votes during the November 1990 election. Individual ballots were counted but not the votes contained on them. The computer program didn't catch the problem, nor did any of the election officials. A Democratic candidate happened to notice the discrepancy after the election was over, and he demanded an investigation.

"It was mechanical or electric malfunction with the card reader," said Bob Bruce, then superintendent of elections for King County. "We'd lost the 14,000 votes. We've got them back now. Hallelujah! The prodigal votes have come back. Now we have to make sure we don't have too many votes." [35]

At least two voting machine miscounts resulted in grand jury investigations. In Polk County, Florida, County Commissioner Marlene Duffy Young lost the election to Bruce Parker in November 1996 but regained the seat after a court-ordered hand recount. After the recount, county commissioners unanimously voted to ask for a grand jury probe. Testifying were Todd Urosevich, a vice president with American Information Systems Inc. (now ES&S), the company that had sold the county its ballot-counting equipment.

The machines had given the election to Parker, a Republican, but a hand recount revealed that Young, a Democrat, had won. Todd Urosevich said his machines were not responsible for the miscount. [36]

A grand jury was convened in Stanislaus County, California, to determine what caused computerized voting machines to misreport election results in the November 1998 election. The grand jury concluded that an ES&S computerized counting system miscounted the votes for three propositions. A hand recount of the ballots resulted in Measure A, a state proposition, being reversed: ES&S machines had reported that it had lost badly, but it had won. According to Karen Matthews, county clerk recorder and registrar of voters, the problem occurred because of a programming error. [37]

Who, exactly, must pay lawyers and court costs if errors made by a voting machine result in litigation? Is it the taxpayer?

If an elections official ruins an election—loses votes forever, or mishandles the voting so badly that no one can repair the error —we can fire that person. If an elections *machine* ruins an election, shouldn't we fire that voting system?

In Knoxville, Tennessee, a software programming error caused more than 40,000 votes cast during 15 days of early voting for the 1996 general election to be lumped together, instead of separating the vote tally into city and non-city ballots. Voters considered this programming error to be an outrage because it caused one of the ballot items to fail when it was voted on county-wide.[38]

In the October 16, 2001, Rock Hill, South Carolina city election, voting machines were programmed incorrectly, skipping hundreds of votes cast. In a number of precincts, the software ignored votes for council members when they should have been included, causing omission of 11 percent of the votes cast for these races. In all, voting irregularities were found in seven of the city's 25 precincts.[39]

At its heart, our body of law is on the side of the voter. Our entire governing system is based on the sanctity of the vote. It is not excusable for votes to be counted improperly because of "programming errors." Almost all states have statutes that say something like this:

"If voting machines are to be used, they must count the vote *properly*."

If a system is so complicated that programming errors become "inevitable" or "to be expected," the system must not be used. And yet the problems continue.

In Union County, Florida, a programming error caused machines to read 2,642 Democratic and Republican votes as entirely Republican in the September 2002 election. The vendor, ES&S, accepted responsibility for the programming error and paid for a hand recount. Unlike the new touchscreen systems, which eliminate voter-verified paper ballots, Union County retained a paper ballot. Thus, a recount was possible and Democratic votes could be identified.[40]

In Atlanta, Georgia, a software programming error caused some votes for Sharon Cooper, considered a "liberal Republican candidate," not to register in the July 1998 election. Cooper was running against conservative Republican Richard Daniel. According to news reports, the problem required "on-the-spot reprogramming."[41]

How can computerized vote-counting possibly be considered secure from tampering when "on-the-spot reprogramming" can be used to alter vote totals?

In November 2002, a voting machine was caught double-counting votes in South Dakota. The error was blamed on a "flawed chip." ES&S sent a replacement chip; voters demanded that the original chip be impounded and examined. Who was allowed to examine it? Citizens? (No.) Experts that we choose? (No.) ES&S? (That's it.)[42]

But they are tested and tested and tested again.

This is the official rebuttal when you ask whether machines can miscount. More on this testing later, but for now, suffice it to say that the ultimate invalidation of the testing a voting machine endures would be *a machine that can't count!*

Election officials and voting machine companies can argue 'til they are blue in the face about the excellence of the certification process, but if the testing works, how did this happen: In Volusia County, Florida, during the 2000 presidential election, the Socialist Workers Party candidate received almost 10,000 votes—about half the number he received nationwide. Four thousand erroneous votes appeared for George W. Bush while at the same time, presidential candidate Al Gore received *negative* 16,022 votes.[43]

I think we should pause for a moment to digest this last example. In fact, if an electronic voting system, in this case a Diebold optical-scan system, can register *minus* votes in sufficient quantity to cause a candidate for president of the United States to erroneously concede to his opponent, we should examine the situation in more detail, don't you agree?

❖ ❖ ❖

Sometimes, machines are given a passing grade even when they fail their testing. Dan Spillane, a senior test engineer for the VoteHere touchscreen voting system, says he flagged more than 250 system-integrity errors, some of which were critical and could affect the way votes were counted—yet this system passed every level of certification without a hitch. Spillane claims he brought his concerns up to all levels of VoteHere management but was ignored. Just before the system went through certification testing, Spillane contends, the company fired him to prevent him from flagging the problems during certification. He filed a lawsuit for wrongful termination,[44] which was settled by VoteHere, with details kept confidential.[45]

According to the *Las Vegas Review-Journal*, a member of the Nevada Policy Research Institute's Advisory Council reports the following:

> In July 1996, a public test to certify Clark County's Sequoia Pacific machine for early voting was conducted. During the test, a cartridge malfunctioned; also, the examiner had difficulty casting his vote. He had to vote 51 times rather than the designated 50, an option not afforded the voter should the machine malfunction in an actual election. In spite of these malfunctions, the machine was given certification—the equivalent of declaring it accurate, reliable and secure. (Clark County then trotted right out and bought the machines.)[46]

The testing didn't work here either: In Conroe, Texas, congressional candidate Van Brookshire wasn't worried when he looked at the vote tabulation and saw a zero next to his name for the 2002 primary. After all, he was unopposed in the District 2 primary and he assumed that the Montgomery County Elections Administrator's Office hadn't found it necessary to display his vote. He was surprised to learn the next day that a computer glitch had given all of his votes to U.S. Representative Kevin Brady, who was unopposed for the nomination for another term in District 8. A retabulation was paid for by ES&S, the company that made the programming mistake. The mistake was undetected despite mandatory testing before and after early voting.[47]

What is supposed to happen in theory doesn't always happen in practice. In Tennessee, a computer snafu in the August 1998 Shelby County election temporarily stopped the vote count after generating wildly inaccurate results and forcing a second count that continued into the morning. State Senator Roscoe Dixon huddled with other politicos around a single copy of the latest corrected election returns, which quickly became dog-eared and riddled with circles and "X"s.

"This system should have been checked, and it should have been known that the scanner couldn't read the cartridges," Dixon said.[48]

Here's another system they tested right before the election, but it miscounted anyway, flipping the election: Pamela Justice celebrated her re-election to the school board in Dysart, Arizona, in the March 1998 election. But the computer had failed to count 1,019 votes from one precinct. When those votes were added in, Justice lost the election to her opponent, Nancy Harrower.

"We did an accuracy test before election day and the computers worked fine," said Karen Osborne, county elections director.[49]

And if you're not yet convinced that our certification system doesn't work: A computer defect at the Oklahoma County State Election Board left more than a dozen state and county races in limbo during the 1996 general election. A final count was delayed until sometime the next morning while technicians installed new computer hardware.

Despite several trial runs with computers the week prior to the election, the problem didn't surface until 7:05 P.M.—five minutes after the election board attempted to begin its count. "That's what's puzzling about it," County Election Board Secretary Doug Sanderson said. "It's one of those deals where you can test it one minute and it's working fine, and you can test it the next and it's not."

Two hundred and sixty-seven precincts (and two close races) were involved.

"We could count it by hand, but I'm not going to do that," Sanderson said, as reported by the *Daily Oklahoman*. "We're just going to wait here until we can do it electronically, so there will be no question that the election's integrity was upheld."[50] Really.

Sometimes they omit testing key systems: The manufacturer of Baltimore's $6.5 million voting system took responsibility for the computer failures that delayed the November 1999 city election results and vowed to repay the city for overtime and related costs. Phil Foster, regional manager for Sequoia Pacific Voting Equipment Inc., said his company had neglected to update software in a computer that reads the election results. Although it tested some programs, the company did not test that part of the system before the election. Before Sequoia agreed to reimburse the city for the problems—a cost that election officials said could reach $10,000—Mayor Kurt L. Schmoke had threatened a lawsuit against the company.[51]

After every election, you will hear this happy refrain: "The election went smoothly." More recently, as we have brought concerns to light, this has become: "Though some people expressed concerns about the voting machines, the election went without a hitch."

Here's the hitch: You won't discover miscounts until you do the audit, which does not take place on election night, and errors sometimes aren't identified until several days later, if at all.

Most errors are detected only when voter sign-in sheets are compared with vote tallies. Many of the errors listed in this chapter were found *only* because the number of votes cast did not match the number of voters who had signed in. But suppose 100 votes are cast, 55 for Mary and 45 for John, but the computer says you have 100 votes, 48 for Mary and 52 for John. John wins. How will we know the election was given to the wrong person if no one checks the paper ballots?

The California Institute of Technology and the Massachusetts Institute of Technology mobilized a team of computer scientists, human-factors engineers, mechanical engineers and social scientists to examine voting technology. Touchscreens did not get high marks. Here are voting system error rates, as estimated by the Caltech/MIT Voting Technology Project report, issued in July 2001:[52]

Most lost votes—Congressional and gubernatorial races

1. Lever machines **7.6%**—1.5% for presidential races
2. Touchscreen machines **5.9%**—2.3% for presidential races
3. Punch card **4.7%**—2.5% for presidential races
4. Optical scan **3.5%**—1.5% for presidential races
5. Hand-counting **3.3%**—1.8% for presidential races

The Caltech/MIT study omits three critical issues: programming errors, tampering and dirty politicking.

If we are going to use computerized systems, we need computer scientists to help us create safe voting systems. Dr. Rebecca Mercuri, now with Harvard University, and Dr. Peter Neumann from SRI International Computer Science Laboratory, are among the best known computer scientists in the elections field and were the first to really investigate electronic voting systems. They were joined by Dr. Doug Jones, a computer scientist from the University of Iowa, who became a member of the Iowa Board of Examiners for Voting Machines in 1994. For many years, these were the voices of reason in the mad dash to electronic voting. New faces have entered the fray within the last two years, but for more than a decade, much of the heavy lifting has been done by these three computer scientists.

They've done a stellar job, but computer scientists usually see this as a programming challenge, rather than an auditing problem or a decision about election procedures, and they tend to concentrate their attentions on touchscreen voting, though some of the most disturbing problems take place on optical-scan systems.

Because we have become over-reliant on input from this one type of expert, we have not adequately evaluated simpler, cheaper solutions, like going back to hand-counted paper ballots (perhaps using a computer as a printer, for legibility and accessibility).

Linda Franz, a voting integrity activist, puts it more tactfully.

"Democracy builds from many pieces. We have an absolute need for accounting expertise, and part of the puzzle is the input of experts on good accounting practices. Computer scientists know the theory of plotting out the need before the design, and in current electronic voting systems, it doesn't look like the vendors have done much of that. How do we convince them that the system needs to be thought out with the input of experts in many fields?"

Current voting systems suffer from a very poor understanding of accounting, and make no mistake about it, counting the vote is a form of accounting. We also need better input from candidates and campaign managers, from historians, from legal and civil rights people, and from the officials who run the elections.

"I often see overgeneralization [believing that expertise in one area translates into wisdom in other domains] with top performers in advanced technical fields," says leadership psychologist Dr. Susan Battley, who troubleshoots for organizations such as JP Morgan Chase and Brookhaven National Laboratory. "In reality, when high achievers overlook fundamental differences in skill requirements, it courts not just failure, but disaster."[53]

We may have such a disaster with current auditing systems. We've been using inappropriate statistical models for auditing, and this model (random spot-checks of a tiny percentage of the ballots) has now become the law in many jurisdictions. This can help catch random error, but a more robust procedure is needed to detect fraud.

November 2002, Comal County, Texas: A Texas-sized anomaly on ES&S machines was discovered when the uncanny coincidence came to light that three winning Republican candidates in a row tallied exactly 18,181 votes. It was called weird, but apparently no one thought it was weird enough to audit.[54] Comal County's experience shows why a simple, random, spot-check audit is insufficient.

Suppose you are an auditor but you must follow election audit rules. You are only allowed to spot check, and you can only look at 1 percent of the receipts. You see this:

> $18,181—Utilities
> $18,181—Advertising
> $18,181—Payroll

But you can't do anything about it, because according to the law, you can't audit any more. You have already looked at 1 percent of the receipts. If you try to pull the records on the $18,181 anomaly, party hacks object that you want to "audit and re-audit and then audit some more." A real audit allows you to look at any darn thing you want, even on a hunch, and when you spot an anomaly of any kind, you get to pull all the records.

1950s, Louisiana: Ivory tower, meet raw politics. When automated voting machines were brought into the state as a way to reduce election fraud, then-Gov. Earl Long said, "Gimme five (electoral) commissioners, and I'll make them voting machines sing 'Home Sweet Home.'"[55]

Actually, accountants for Las Vegas casinos have better expertise on fraud-prevention techniques than computer professors. Accountants are never invited onto voting system task forces, nor were they called upon to testify when the Help America Vote Act, which prescribed new voting requirements, was being written. Hint hint. Nudge.

July 1996, Clark County, Nevada: According to a *Las Vegas Review-Journal* article, a technician removed thousands of files from the tabulation sector of the program during the vote count "to speed up the reading of the count." Reconfiguring a computer program that affects the tabulation of votes is prohibited without prior state verification, but they did it anyway.[56] In a real audit, people don't get to remove part of the bookkeeping system; in the real world, people don't always follow instructions.

November 2002, Miami, Florida: Fuzzy math in Miami? On November 10, the *Miami Herald* listed the following figures for the total votes cast at the Democrat-friendly Broward County Century Village precinct in the general election:

> 1994: 7,515
> 1998: 10,947
> 2002: 4,179

Yet an accountant called Century Village and was told that its occupancy had remained stable (around 13,000 residents) since the complex had hit capacity in 1998.[57]

A spot-check audit, in this case, will achieve nothing. Because there is usually no provision in the law to allow an audit based on anomalies, all a fraudster had to do was figure out a way to delete a block of votes and cook the sign-in books. Impossible, you say? Here's a five-letter method: b-r-i-b-e.

❖   ❖   ❖

When a human being handles a voting system, you'll see mistakes, but when a computer handles the voting, you'll see some complete boondoggles.

November 1998, Clearwater, Florida: The voting computer crashed on election night. Republicans who lost complained that the crash could have corrupted files, skewed data or lost votes. Tom McKeon, a county commissioner candidate, said "There's no guarantee the votes went to the right candidate." Elections Supervisor Dot Ruggles said it was not the first time such a crash had occurred.[58]

March 2000, Shelby County, Tennessee: Computer problems halted the voting at all 19 of Shelby County's early-voting sites during the 2000 Republican presidential primary, forcing officials to use paper ballots (which were supposed to be provided by the voting machine company as a backup but were unavailable when needed). Election officials had to make voters wait in line or tell them to come back later. Because early voting turnout in this election was six times normal, this snafu affected about 13,000 voters.[59]

November 2000, Glenwood Springs, Colorado: At a special city council meeting held just after the election, Mayor Skramstad announced that the Garfield County Clerk and Recorder asked that he read a press release. It stated, "The Garfield County Clerk and Recorder wishes to inform the public that she is continuing to experience difficulty with the ES&S Inc. software utilized for tabulating election results. I will receive a corrected computer chip this evening. On Friday, November 10th. . . my office will utilize a new chip to count the ballots for Precinct 20 and re-tabulate the results. . . I anticipate this process will take most of the day. Thank you for your patience during this process. Signed, Mildred Alsdorf."[60]

Question: Did this new chip go through certification? Nope. The only one who knew what was on this chip was some guy in Omaha. What Mildred didn't realize when she accepted that chip was that she had just opened the door for lawsuits, ultimately paid for by you, the taxpayer, and guaranteed to produce a great deal of stress for Mildred, the County Clerk and Recorder.

November 2000, Allegheny County, Pennsylvania: City Councilwoman Valerie McDonald reported that machines in Pittsburgh's 12th and 13th wards and other predominantly black neighborhoods malfunctioned on election day. They began smoking and spitting out jammed and crumpled paper. Poll workers felt the machines had been intentionally programmed incorrectly and had been sabotaged. Whether or not there was sabotage, the spit-and-polish image so carefully crafted in election company press releases didn't seem to apply to the African American precincts that day. Poll workers in the 12th and 13th wards waited hours for repairs, and voters who couldn't spend the day at the polling place were rendered politically voiceless.[61]

February 2000, Passaic, New Jersey: About 75 percent of the voting machines in the city of Passaic failed to work when the polls opened on election day, forcing an undetermined number of voters to use paper ballots during the morning. Independent consultant V. Thomas Mattia, a Philadelphia voting machine supervisor who later examined the machines, concluded the problem was due to sabotage, which led a Democratic candidate to refer the matter to the FBI.

For no discernable reason, Mattia later reversed himself.

"I believe that it was an oversight, and there was no fraud involved," Mattia stated in a letter.

Freeholder James Gallagher, who had referred the matter to the FBI based on Mattia's previous suspicions, said that he was surprised by the reversal and needed more information about why the expert had changed his mind.[62]

November 2002, Tangipahoa Parish, Louisiana: "I can't say every precinct had a problem, but the vast majority did," Tangipahoa Parish Clerk of Court John Dahmer said.

He reported that at least 20 percent of the machines in his parish malfunctioned. "One percent might be acceptable, but we're not even close to that," Dahmer said. He said 15 employees worked to combat the malfunctions.[63]

November 2002, Maryland: Vote Republican (read "Democrat")— In Maryland, a programming error on Diebold touchscreen machines upset a lot of voters when they saw a banner announcing " Democrat" at the top of their screen, no matter whom they voted for.[64]

November 2002, New Jersey: Forty-four of forty-six machines malfunctioned in Cherry Hill, New Jersey: Election workers had to turn away up to 100 early voters when it was discovered that 96 percent of the voting machines couldn't register votes for mayor, despite the machines' having been pretested and certified for use.[65]

November 2002, New Jersey: "What the hell do I do with this?" A bag full of something that looked like rolls of cash register tapes was handed to the Mays Landing County Clerk. A computer irregularity in the vote-counting system caused three of five relay stations to fail, leaving a single county clerk holding the bag for a hand count.[66]

November 2002, Ascension Parish, Louisiana: An elections official gnashed his teeth as more than 200 machine malfunctions were called in. The Parish Clerk said his staff was on the road repairing machines from 5 A.M. to 9 P.M. In one case, a machine wasn't repaired until 12:30 A.M. Wednesday.[67]

November 2002, Ohio: A voting machine malfunctioned with 12 of Crawford County's 67 precincts left to count. A backup machine was found, but it also could not read the vote. Election workers piled into a car and headed to another county to tally their votes.[68]

November 2002, Pickens County, South Carolina: Pickens County couldn't get totals from two precincts due to computer problems.[69]

November 2002, Georgia: Fulton County election officials said that memory cards from 67 electronic voting machines had been misplaced, so ballots cast on those machines were left out of previously announced vote totals. Fifty-six cards, containing 2,180 ballots, were located, but 11 memory cards still were missing two days after the election.

Bibb County and Glynn County each had one card missing after the initial vote count.

When DeKalb County election officials went home, they were missing 10 cards.[70]

What is a memory card? It's a ballot box. Electronic ballot boxes for the Diebold machines used in Georgia are about the size of a credit card. With the new electronic voting systems, you can pocket a dozen ballot boxes at once, slip one up your sleeve or tote 67 ballot boxes around in your purse.

An interesting (and suspicious) anomaly appeared with these missing electronic ballot boxes. I interviewed a Georgia computer programmer named Roxanne Jekot for this book. When Jekot quizzed Dr. Brit Williams, official voting machine certifier for the state of Georgia, during an August 22, 2003, public meeting, Williams explained that the memory cards were not lost, but had inadvertently been left in the machines.

Really?

Something appears to be missing in this explanation. The procedure in Georgia for transmitting electronic votes from Diebold touchscreens is as follows: If you have seven voting machines at a polling place, each one has a memory card which stores its votes. You take all seven cards and, one by one, put them into a single machine, which accumulates them and runs a report. When votes from all seven machines are accumulated, they are transmitted to the county tabulator. A printout of the accumulated results is run, and this is placed in an envelope with the memory cards. The envelope is then sealed, signed and delivered to the county.

Jekot raised this excellent question: If the votes are accumulated from all cards before transmitting to the county, this means all the votes would be transmitted as one batch. So why did 2,180 more votes show up when individual cards were "found" inside the machines?

I also have this question: If the procedure is to accumulate, print the report, place it into an envelope with cards, seal the envelope, sign it and then take it to the county, how is it that different people, at different polling places, forgot to do this 67 times in the same county?

Perhaps we should look into the Georgia election a little more.

❖ ❖ ❖

November 2002, Nebraska—This example shows, I think, just how far we've deviated from the concept of fair and open election procedures. Paul Rosberg, the Nebraska Party candidate for governor, eagerly took advantage of a Nebraska law that lets candidates watch their votes being counted. He first was invited to watch an optical-scan machine, which had no counter on it, and then was taken into the private room, where he was allowed to watch a computer with a blank screen. So much for public counting of votes.[71]

❖ ❖ ❖

"Take the rest of the examples out or put them in an appendix—this is just completely overwhelming," said an editor. So I did. All in all, I documented 100 of these examples, and could have continued for another 100 had space allowed, and our ability to tolerate this outrage permitted. See Appendix A for a continuing compendium.

Reprinted with author's permission from Black Box Voting: Ballot Tampering in the 21st Century, *Copyright 2004.*

———————————————

Bev Harris has been referred to as "the godmother" of the election reform movement by the Boston Globe. *She is the author of the book Black Box Voting. "Harris stumbled onto a national story ignored by every big-city newspaper in the land, and worked it deeper and deeper with scoops that would have made her career at the New York Times or the Washington Post."*—Vanity Fair

In 2003, just weeks after a stunning electoral upset in Georgia that tipped control of the U.S. Senate, Harris discovered 40,000 secret voting machine files on the Web—including a folder called "rob-georgia," containing instructions to replace Georgia's computerized voting files before the election. She downloaded the files and ultimately arranged to set them free into the wild, and the files were then studied by several security experts, revealing deep flaws in voting system security.

Harris's articles revealed that modern-day voting systems are run by private, for-profit corporations, relying on a few cronies for oversight, using a certification system so fundamentally flawed that it allows machines to miscount and lose votes, with hidden back doors that enable "end runs" around the voting system. Harris filed a false claims action against Diebold Election Systems; in 2005, the firm paid $2.6 million in restitution to the state of California. Her investigations have led some to call her the 'Erin Brockovich of elections.'

Her facts check out. Harris's original investigative work has now been covered in The New York Times, *the* Washington Post, Time, *The*

Associated Press, Reuters, Investor's Business Daily, and on CBS, NBC, ABC, CNBC, MSNBC, CNN and Fox News, and in many European media outlets.

End Notes

1. *Mobile Register,* 28 January 2003; *"Voting* Snafu Answers Elusive."

2. Factiva.com is a search engine frequently used by reporters for background. In 2002, it was known as *DJInteractive.com.*

3. *The News & Observer,* 9 November 2002; "'Winners' may be losers."

4. *Omaha World-Herald,* 6 November 2002; "A late night in Sarpy; glitches delay results."

5. *Chicago Tribune,* 4 April 2003; "Returns are in: Software goofed Lake County tally misled. . ."

6. *Newsbytes News Network,* 24 April 1998; "Feature—Glitches of the Week."

7. *Chicago Tribune,* 4 April 2003; "Returns are in: Software goofed. . ."

8. Associated Press reported in the *Wichita Eagle,* 22 August 2002; "Mayo won by a landslide. . . Election reversed. . ."

9. *The Las Vegas Review-Journal,* 30 November 1994; "Voter fraud allegations continue."

10. *Houston Chronicle,* 8 November 2002; "Ballot glitches reverse two election results."

11. *The Atlanta Journal - The Atlanta Constitution,* 3 September 1998; "Elections Board Case: Candidate's lawyer knows the feeling."

12. *Newsbytes News Network,* 5 August 1997; "Glitches of the Week."

13. *Newsbytes News Network,* 22 April 1999; "Glitches of the Week."

14. *Newsbytes News Network,* 9 December 1997; "Glitches of the Week."

15 *The Salt Lake Tribune,* 25 June 1998; "Commission Primary Recount. . ."

16. *The Omaha World-Herald,* 15 June 1990; "Vote Confusion Blamed on Human Error."

17. Company press release: PR Newswire, 12 September 2002; "Diebold Touchscreen Voting Terminals Perform Well in Primary Elections."

18. *The Omaha World-Herald,* 21 April 1992; *"Omaha* Firm Taps North Platte Native."

19. *The Wall Street Journal,* 17 November 2000; "Fuzzy Numbers: Election Snafus Went Far Beyond. . ."

20. *Indianapolis Star,* 9 November 2003; *"Vote* count marred by computer woes."

21. Associated Press, in the *Dallas Morning News,* 13 April 1996; *"Vote* tally miscounted in runoff. . ."

22. *The Arizona Daily Star,* 8 December 1994; "826 votes vanish in Oro Valley. . ."

23. *All Africa*, 11 November 2002; "US Polls Plagued with Glitches. . ." Also *The Washington Times*, 6 November 2002; "Glitches cited at some polls . . ."

24. *The Baton Rouge Advocate*, 5 February 2002; Bill McCuen, guilty plea to felony charges of bribery, tax evasion and accepting kickbacks.

25. *Honolulu Star Bulletin*, 3 February 1999; "Voting checks failed to detect fault twice; A flawed ballot counter passed a manual check and a mechanical test."

26. *The Dallas Morning News*, 11 November 1998; "Election system company apologizes, offers partial refund Fixes proposed for problems that led to undercounts" (related articles November 5th and 28th).

27. *Honolulu Star Bulletin*, June 7, 2000; "Firm admits errors in counting votes for Hawaii, Venezuela."

28. *The Arizona Daily Star*, 11 November 1998; "Computer fails to record 9,675 Pima County votes."

29. CNN: Breaking News, 8 November 2000; "Election 2000: Strange Events Plague Florida Polls."

30. *The Post-Standard*, 5 December 2002; "More Florida Blunders; Precious Votes Should Be Counted."

31. *Chicago Tribune*, 6 November 1993; "Kane Election Results Just Didn't Compute."

32. *Albuquerque Journal*, 19 November 2002; "County Certifies Vote Tally."

33. Notes on "Workshop" on Voting Machine Security for Santa Clara County Supervisors, 11 February 2003;
See *http://verify.stanford.edu/dill/EVOTE/sc-2-11-2003.html*.

34. *The Everett Herald*, 20 January 2003; "*County* to Discuss Ballot-Counting Foul-up."

35. *The Seattle Times*, 22 November 1990; "Thousand of Lost Votes Turn Up. . ."

36. *The Tampa Tribune*, 2 May 1997; "Grand jury probes contested election."

37. *Newsbytes News Network*, 4 June 1999; "Glitches of the Week."

38. *The Knoxville News-Sentinel*, 8 November 1996; "A betrayal of voters; Disaster over early votes on unification demands action."

39. *The Herald*, Rock Hill, SC, 25 October 2001; "The city election foul-up."

40. *The Bradenton Herald*, 17 September 2002; "Sometimes the old ways are best."

41. *The Atlanta Journal; The Atlanta Constitution*, 23 July 1998; "Election '98: Cobb glitch delayed tabulations statewide."

42. NPR: *Morning Edition*, 6 November 2002; "Analysis: Senate races in Minnesota and South Dakota."

43. *Orlando Sentinel*, 7 October 2001; "Election Goal: Low Profile, Changes Aim to Keep Day Fiasco-Free."

44. *Daniel B. Spillane v VoteHere Inc.*, filed in King County, Washington; case no. 03-2-18799-8SFA.

45. *Seattle Times*, 19 November 2003; "Fired engineer reaches deal with election software company."

46. *The Las Vegas Review-Journal*, 19 July 1998; "The Clark County vote: How secure is it?"

47. *Houston Chronicle*, 16 March 2002; "Candidate zeroes in on computer glitch."

48. *The Commercial Appeal*, 7 August 1998; "Vote Totals. . ."

49. *Newsbytes News Network*, 20 March 1998; "Feature—Glitches of the Week."

50. *The Daily Oklahoman*, 6 November 1996; "Big Computer Glitch Causes Election Hitch."

51. *The Baltimore Sun*, 4 November 1999, "Manufacturer of voting system assumes blame for Baltimore's Election Day glitch; Failure to test software resulted in breakdown, delays in vote."

52. Caltech/MIT Voting Technology Project, July 2001; *www.vote.caltech.edu/*.

53. The voter-verified ballot is, in effect, a contract between the voter and his government. An original signed contract trumps a facsimile, and paper trumps machine, unless it can be shown that the original was tampered with.

54. *Deseret News*, 9 November 2002; "Texans tally triple match in exceptional election."

55. *The Virginian-Pilot and The Ledger-Star*, 25 August 1997; "Warner Doggedly Pursues Divisive Election Inquiry."

56. *The Las Vegas Review-Journal*, 19 July 1998; "The Clark County vote: How secure is it?"

57. *Miami Herald*, 10 November 2002; and call-in report from a Miami accountant.

58. *The Tampa Tribune*, 6 November 1998; "Computer crash leads to countywide recount of votes."

59. *The Commercial Appeal*, 5 March 2000; "Computer Glitch Hampers Voting. . ."

60. Minutes of City of Glenwood Springs Special City Council Meeting, 9 November 2000.

61. *Pittsburgh Post-Gazette*, 4 May 2001, "Hearing Gets Landslide of Voting Problems."

62. *The Record*, 23 February 2000; "Expert Finds No Sabotage in Election, Reverses Stance. . ."

63. *The Baton Rouge Advocate*, 7 November 2002; "Voting machine glitches worrisome. . ."

64. *The Washington Times*, 6 November 2002; "Glitches cited at some polls. . ."

65. *Newsday*, 6 November 2003; *"Voting* glitches."

66. *Newsday*, 6 November 2003; *"Voting* glitches."

67. *The Baton Rouge Advocate*, 7 November 2002; Voting machine glitches worrisome. . ."

68. *Telegraph-Forum*, 6 November 2002; "Glitch sends vote count to Richland."

69. Associated Press, 6 November 2002; *"Equipment* causes voting problems in several counties."

70. *Atlanta Journal-Constitution*, 8 November 2002; "2002 Election: 2,180 Fulton ballots located after tally 67 memory cards misplaced . . ."

71. 7 November 2002; Interview with Paul Rosberg, candidate for Nebraska governor.

HAVA and the Rush to Poor Judgment

Vickie Karp

IF YOU LIKED THE ORWELLIAN-named "Clear Skies Initiative" or the "No Child Left Behind" Act, you should really love the "Help America Vote Act," (HAVA), another farce brought to you by our esteemed leaders in the White House and Congress.

How was HAVA created and what is its purpose? Here's some history:

> If someone took a poll today among average Americans on the street and asked them what was the most memorable snafu regarding the 2000 Presidential election, my bet is that overwhelmingly the response would be: the "hanging chad" debacle in Florida.

The media's coverage of hanging chads created one of the most widespread and effective smokescreens ever devised to fool the American people into believing that chads were the reason for all the hubbub in Florida, which ultimately led to the Supreme Court selecting our president—rather than allowing the states and counties to continue to count ballots and determine the real winner of that election.

But hanging chads and the problems that they caused pale in comparison to the REAL reason for the election screw up: intentional (mis)matching of over 50,000 minority voters' names with a list of convicted felons in such a way as to effectively (and illegally) disenfranchise them by not allowing them to vote—50,000 voters who were expected to vote Democratic. This story was broken by investigative journalist Greg Palast, who finally took it to the UK where it was run on their BBC network, because no American mainstream media would run it.

Instead, it was the hanging chad "debacle" that was given all the airplay. In my opinion, it was planned specifically to lead to the later passing by Congress of the "Help America Vote Act"(which does anything but. . .) in October 29, 2002. HAVA dangles the carrot of $3.86 billion in federal funds to the states, county by county, in exchange for upgrading old punch-card and lever voting machine systems for newer, improved voting systems. What is mandatory about HAVA is **NOT** that electronic voting systems must be purchased (widely misinterpreted by election officials); but that the disabled must be provided with a way to vote without assistance.

How clever to use the politically correct and truly important issue of providing an unassisted vote for the disabled as an impetus to create a mad rush of county officials all across the U.S. to purchase paperless electronic voting machines or optical scan counters—whose vendors were standing by with their products waiting to provide the supposed solution to the HAVA requirements. Time is running out for the counties, many of whose officials have been misinformed on the real requirements of HAVA. But one thing is certain: the HAVA deadline, set for primary election day of 2006 in each state, has sent the message to the states: upgrade your voting systems, or no federal funds. The race is on! And the race for HAVA funds is also a race to poor judgment on the part of many well-meaning, but often ill-informed, election officials.

Electronic voting is not new—it started creeping into our country during the '90s. In fact, there was enough evidence of election anomalies produced by these proposed technologically superior machines that Bev Harris, an investigative journalist from Washington state, began researching them in 2003 for her book, *Black Box Voting: Ballot Tampering in the 21st Century*, (available online at *www.blackboxvoting.org*).

Harris got a lucky break when she was surfing the Net and Googled "Diebold," the second largest e-voting machine/software vendor in the United States. Then, by sheer luck, found their secret, "proprietary" software on their Web site.

At first Harris wasn't sure exactly what she had, but she downloaded it and shared it with computer scientists and programmers. The ultimate conclusion they came to? This election software amounted to a "virtual handbook on how to tamper with an election." In July of 2003, Harris set up a "mock election" on a laptop using the same Diebold election software certified for use in many cities across America. She was able to execute a "back-door hack" that allowed her to flip election results in less than ten minutes, then exit out of the system totally undetected.

A Johns Hopkins–Rice University study also done in July of 2003 concluded that electronic voting, with its modems, secret software and no paper trail, poses "a threat to democracy."

Harris and her nonprofit consumer organization, Black Box Voting (.org) has continued to research Diebold as well as the other three top vendors of electronic voting systems: ES&S (Electronic Systems and Software); Sequoia; and Hart InterCivic.

She now has the Diebold hack down to less than 60 seconds with the help of her world-class computer expert team, who states that the election software is "elegantly designed for multiple, sophisticated hacks." **Harris's "hacking" team has discovered the ability to manipulate results at the central tabulator (where the final vote totals for entire counties are stored)** through a "live" computer program they found in the election software's "memory cards." These memory cards are used with optical scan counters that count paper ballots! Each memory card contains the vote totals for an entire precinct, which is why Bev Harris refers to them as "electronic ballot boxes"—and the illicit program that the memory card contains then directs the central tabulator to record the vote in whatever manner designated by IT, and NOT as the votes were actually cast!

What this means to you and me is, the program has the ability to change votes from how they were originally cast, unbeknownst to the voters!

Think about this: Whoever programs the memory card has the ability to manipulate the outcome of the election any way they want! **An anonymous computer programmer can determine the outcome of an election!**

The voting systems' "audit logs," which print all the activity that happens during an election on the central tabulator—and records all the computerized downloads of vote totals for a county—printed *incorrect* vote totals. This was only known because the Black Box Voting hackers set up a simple mock election and everyone in the room knew how many YES and NO votes were fed into the machine. The official audit log printed a completely different set of numbers, "flipping"the result. This event was videotaped and is included in an upcoming major production film to be released this fall.

The software vendors will tell you that the audit log is the "accurate"record of EVERY vote that was cast and of all the vote totals. The problem is, without an expert hacking team testing them out on election day, we cannot ever be sure if that is true or not. Certainly in Leon County, Florida, in 2005, this assertion was NOT TRUE!

This should serve as a somber alert to all Americans, as well as election reform activists: **Legislative efforts toward creating "paper trails" on electronic voting systems are a waste of time. If the hackers of these voting software systems can make the paper audit log reflect differently from the actual votes being cast inside the machine, how can we trust that, just because a printer is attached to an electronic voting machine and the paper "receipt" reads the way we voted, that the computerized voting system actually recorded our votes the same way the paper says it did? WE CAN'T!** (*www.blackboxvoting.org*, report from July 4, 2005 and May 11, 2006, The "Hursti Reports")

Harri Hursti, computer programmer and security engineer, said that hacking into the machines "is an exceptionally flexible, one-man exploit requiring only a few hundred dollars, mediocre technical ability and modest persuasive skills (or, in lieu of persuasive skills, *inside access*)."

Speaking of *inside access*, keep in mind that vendors send out "technicians" regularly *during elections to* "service" electronic voting machines because they are so prone to chronic breakdowns and malfunctions. We are highly suspicious that these "fixes" and "patches" are where tampering and vote fraud commonly occur. Here you have a vendor's representative, without citizen or election official oversight, allowed unfettered access to the machines *on election day*, thus increasing the odds that election manipulation is occurring.

Here are some relevant paragraphs on the subject of "inside access" from Black Box Voting (*www.blackboxvoting.org*):

> One thousand two hundred locations in the U.S. and Canada use Diebold voting machines. In each of these locations, typically three people have a high level of inside access. Temporary employees also often have brief access to loose memory cards as machines are being prepared for elections. Poll workers sometimes have a very high level of inside access. National elections utilize up to two million poll workers, with hundreds or thousands in a single jurisdiction.
>
> Many locations in the U.S. ask poll workers to take voting machines home with them **with the memory cards inside**. San Diego County (Calif) sent 713 voting machines/memory cards home with poll workers for its July 26 election, and King County (Wash.) sent over 500 voting machines home with poll workers before its Nov. 8 election.
>
> Memory cards are held in a compartment protected by a small plastic seal. However, these simple seals can be defeated, and **Hursti has found evidence that the memory card can be reprogrammed without disturbing the seal by using a telephone modem port on the back of the machine.**

When people understand how many temporary poll workers, working without any background checks, have access to these memory cards, it really shows that procedures aren't sufficient as long as there is no citizen oversight in every step of the "chain of custody" of these cards and the machines.

These voting machines and optical scan counters have NO PLACE in what is supposed to be a transparent election process.

Another computer expert, Jeremiah Akin of Riverside, California, gained access to the Sequoia software, downloaded and researched it, and found other easily manipulated features about that vendor's software. To name just one "feature" he found with the Spanish ballot software, used in heavily Hispanic areas of the country: The person who programs the language feature of the election software can decide if a vote will be counted for the person it was cast for—*or the opposite candidate!* His chapter detailing some of his findings is included in this book

The unmistakable conclusion of this research is that *these election systems cannot be trusted with our votes. It appears that they were designed to be hacked.* AND THESE ARE THE VERY SYSTEMS THAT COUNTY ELECTION OFFICIALS ARE RUSHING TO PURCHASE BEFORE their 2006 primary elections—to ensure they get the HAVA federal funds!

In September 2004, at two Washington, D.C. press conferences, Harris, Akin, and other computer experts demonstrated on software then currently certified for use in cities across America six simple hacks that could flip an election in less than 60 seconds. All the media were there, but their later reports made the event sound like some kind of circus sideshow. I was there helping to produce these events along with Abbe DeLozier. Congresswoman Cynthia McKinney even volunteered as a "guest hacker" and was successfully taught how to hack into these voting systems in a "mock election" in less than a minute.

True to form, the controlled media either will not report the issue, or will heavily distort the truth. We wouldn't want the American people to find out that 80% of the voting systems they used in 2004 were highly suspect and in some cases, proven fraudulent systems— would we?

The examples of questionable election results and suspicious, unexplained problems with electronic voting (**all** the major vendors' machines: Diebold, ES&S, Sequoia and Hart InterCivic) in the 2000, 2002 and 2004 elections would likely circle the earth several times if all the reports were put together end-to-end. You can read about these anomalies in chapter two and in our bibliography.

Many would say that mandatory audits where paper ballots are still being used, but counted by these optical scan counters, will serve as an accuracy check against election manipulation. The problem is, where audits are mandated by the states or even by proposed legislation, only 2% of the ballots are designated to be recounted. Nothing less than a 100% recount will really do, BUT the likelihood of that ever happening, even if the states mandated it, is miniscule. Most states place the financial burden of a recount on the candidate who disputes the election. This can cost hundreds of thousands of dollars, money that post-election candidates rarely can pull together.

The solution many experts are promoting is this: Paper ballots, hand counted in public view. This simple voting method, though not perfect, has been identified by Lynn Landes, Harris, other journalists and researchers and the leaders of many other election reform groups as the best solution to fraudulent voting systems. As Harris says, a paper ballot, hand counted election has about five or six "attack vectors"; with electronic voting, there are 50 or 60. Electronic voting simply offers NO transparency. The voter will never know if their vote has been accurately recorded or not. And the means already exist to print paper ballots for elections that can be methodically hand-counted, in many cases, taking less time than electronic counts, which frequently have "snafus" that can extend the counting process for days!

Ironically, many of the e-voting systems themselves do not meet HAVA requirements for the disabled! There are other ways to provide a private vote to the disabled without purchasing electronic voting equipment—the very reason of given by their secretaries of state for making this purchase. One of these simple and inexpensive alternative voting systems for the disabled, the "Vote-PAD," created by election reform activist Ellen Theisen and others (company based in Port Ludlow, WA). The Vote-PAD will allow the physically impaired (in addition to the blind or the deaf) to vote unassisted on **non-electronic** equipment, assisting a larger group of the disabled than even the HAVA mandated rules provide for.

Other voting reform activists, Sherry and David Healey of Mill Valley, California, have created another such non-computerized voting system for the disabled called "Equalivote." Obviously, non-electronic options for fulfilling the HAVA mandate exist!

My message to all decision makers who are about to purchase these machines: Your electorate is counting on you to provide them with the safest, most honest voting system possible—the one you may be using right now! **DON'T LET "HAVA" CREATE A RUSH TO POOR JUDGMENT!**

Elections and Voting
Will the Major Media Finally Cover
the Electronic Election Fraud Issue?

Bob Fitrakis and Harvey Wasserman

THAT THE PRESIDENTIAL ELECTIONS of 2000 and 2004 were stolen has become an article of faith for millions of mainstream Americans. But there has been barely a whiff of coverage in the major media about any problems with the electronic voting machines that made those thefts possible—until now.

A recent OpEdNews/Zogby People's poll of Pennsylvania residents found that "39 percent said that the 2004 election was stolen. 54 percent said it was legitimate. But let's look at the demographics on this question. Of the people who watch Fox news as their primary source of TV news, one half of one percent believes it was stolen and 99 percent believe it was legitimate. Among people who watched ANY other news source but FOX, more felt the election was stolen than legitimate. The numbers varied dramatically."Here, from that poll, are the stations listed as first choice by respondents and the percentage of respondents who thought the election was stolen: CNN, 70 percent; MSNBC, 65 percent; CBS, 64 percent; ABC, 56 percent; Other, 56 percent; NBC, 49 percent; FOX 0.5 percent.

With 99 percent of Fox viewers believing that the election was "legitimate," only the constant propaganda of Rupert Murdoch's disinformation campaign stands in the way of a majority of Americans coming to grips with the reality of two consecutive stolen elections.

That *The New York Times*, *Wall Street Journal* and *Washington Post* finally ran coverage of problems with electronic voting machines this week is itself big news. It says the scandals surrounding computer fraud and financial illegalities at Diebold and other electronic voting machine companies have become simply too big and blatant for even the bought, docile mainstream media (MSM) to ignore.

The gaping holes in the security of electronic voting machines are pretty old news. Bev Harris's *blackboxvoting.org* has been issuing definitive research since Florida 2000. *Freepress.org* warned of the impending electronic theft of Ohio 2004 with Diebold machines eight months before it happened.

After that election, Representative John Conyers (D-MI) issued a report confirming that security flaws could allow a single hacker with a wi-fi to shift the vote counts at entire precincts just by driving by. Then the Government Accountability Office reported that security flaws were vast and unacceptable throughout the national network of electronic machines.

Despite overwhelming evidence that George W. Bush has occupied the White House due to the fraudulent manipulations of the GOP Secretaries of State in Florida and Ohio, none of this has seeped into "journals of record" like the Times and Post.

Until this week. *The Times* was sparked out of its stupor on May 11, after officials in California and Pennsylvania warned that Diebold touchscreen machines, slated to be used in upcoming primaries, were hopelessly compromised. Michael Shamos, a professor of computer science at Pittsburgh's high-tech Carnegie-Mellon University, called it "the most severe security flaw ever discovered in a voting system."

Douglas W. Jones, a computer science professor at the University of Iowa, says "this is a barn door being wide open, while people were arguing over the lock on the front door."

The Times refers to the uproar as "the latest concern about touch-screen machines" while having completely ignored dozens of complaints in Ohio 2004 that voters who selected John Kerry's name saw

George W. Bush's light up, or saw the light on Kerry's repeatedly go out before they could complete the voting process.

The *Wall Street Journal* ran the following kicker: "Some former backers of technology seek return to paper ballots, citing glitches, fraud fears."

The WSJ could have run that story last year after the bipartisan commission on federal election reform, co-chaired by President Jimmy Carter and former Secretary of State James Baker, noted in no uncertain terms that: "Software can be modified maliciously before being installed into individual voting machines. There is no reason to trust insiders in the election industry any more than in other industries."

Indeed. There's every reason because of the unprecedented power and money involved in U.S. politics to trust them less than anybody else.

In its March 2006 primary, it took a week to tally Chicago's votes because of technical problems in Sequoia Voting Systems equipment. In Maryland, electronic voting scandals prompted a unanimous vote by the State House of Delegates demanding that touchscreen machines be scrapped. The Maryland Senate effectively killed that bill, which is certain to come back.

Citizen lawsuits are being filed in Arizona, California, New York and New Mexico by the nonprofit Voter Action organization.

The new concerns about Diebold's equipment were discovered by Harri Hursti, a Finnish computer expert who was working at the request of Black Box Voting. The new report forced Diebold to warn of a "theoretical security vulnerability that could potentially allow unauthorized software to be loaded onto the system."

In other words, one of the prime manufacturers of the machines on which America casts its votes has admitted those machines can be hacked.

But as *The Times* has finally reported, the company, in one of the new century's most truly laughable letters, has claimed that "the probability for exploiting this vulnerability to install unauthorized software that could affect an election is considered low."

A company spokesman has admitted the flaw was actually built into the system to allow election officials to upgrade their software. But Diebold is apparently confident that those officials would never, ever cheat. "For there to be a problem here, you're basically assuming a premise where you have some evil and nefarious election officials who would sneak in and introduce a piece of software,"says Diebold's David Bear. "I don't believe these evil elections people exist."

The *Times* has thus far chosen not to report on the staggering history that frames such statements. As *freepress.org* reported in 2003, Diebold CEO Walden O'Dell promised in a GOP fundraising letter to "deliver Ohio's electoral votes to George W. Bush."The election chief in Florida 2000 was Katherine Harris. In Ohio 2004 it was J. Kenneth Blackwell. Both controlled access to their state's electronic voting machines, and are widely believed to have exploited their now obvious flaws. Both served simultaneously as secretary of state and as state co-chair of the Bush–Cheney campaign. As of today, the electronic access cards for Ohio's electronic voting machines have been ordered into Blackwell's personal office, despite the fact that he is the GOP nominee for governor in the upcoming November election.

Recently passed House Bill 3 in Ohio does not mandate post-election audits of electronic voting machines, nor does the Help American Vote Act (HAVA) of 2002. The rush to electronic voting machines was fueled by the passing of the HAVA Act, which authorized more than $3 billion in federal funds to purchase new voting equipment. HAVA's principal architect was Rep. Bob Ney (R-OH), whose financial ties to Diebold, through disgraced lobbyist Jack Abramoff, have yet to be fully exposed.

Blackwell personally negotiated a no-bid contract for Diebold touchscreen Direct Recording Electronic machines (DREs) while holding stock in the company. Under HB3 Blackwell will decide whether the machines will be audited or not in an election where he is running for governor.

"We're prepared for those types of problems," said Deborah Hench, the registrar of voters in San Joaquin County, California, according to *The Times*. "There are always activists that are anti-electronic voting, and they're constantly trying to put pressure on us to change our system."

Aviel Rubin, a professor of computer science at Johns Hopkins University, did the first in-depth analysis of the security flaws in the source code for Diebold touchscreen machines in 2003. After studying the latest problem, *The Times* reported Rubin said: "I almost had a heart attack. The implications of this are pretty astounding."

More coverage from the mainstream corporate media may surface as the machines malfunction in the 22 primary elections scheduled in May and June. The next major e-vote meltdown should occur during the May 16 primaries in Kentucky, Oregon and Pennsylvania.

There's still time to move to hand-counted paper ballots for the November 2006 election. And if current trends continue, some of the mainstream media may actually start reporting on the issue.

Reprinted with authors' permission; first published on the Online Journal, May 16, 2006 © Freepress.

Bob Fitrakis is Editor and Publisher of the Free Press *and* freepress.org, *is an award-winning investigative reporter and holds a Ph.D. in political science and a J.D. He co-authored and edited the international election observers' report on El Salvador's first free and fair election in 1994. He is co-author, with Harvey Wasserman, of* Did George W. Bush Steal America's 2004 Election? Essential Documents *and the forthcoming* What Happened in Ohio: A Documentary Record of Theft and Fraud in the 2004 Election *(New Press).*

Harvey Wasserman is an award-winning journalist, columnist and author of a dozen books on politics, history, the environment and energy. With Bob Fitrakis he helped break many of the key stories in Ohio 2004, with the Rev. Jesse Jackson calling them "the Woodward and Bernstein of the 2004 election." Their books, What Happened in Ohio? *(New Press) and* How the GOP Stole America's 2004 Election and Is Rigging 2008 (www.freepress.org) *are at the core of the controversy. Wasserman's* Solartopia: Our Green-Powered Earth, A.D. 2030 *and Harvey Wasserman's* History of the United States (www.harveywasserman.com) *are cult classics in the alternative history and energy movements.*

The Truth About Elections
from an Election Judge

May Schmidt

MY NAME IS MAY SCHMIDT and I am 60 years
old. I live in Austin, Texas, and I have served as
an election official in Travis County for 35 years. I
started my election career when my mother became an alternate
election judge in 1960. I began work as an election clerk in 1970,
when we still used paper ballots. I have also worked elections using scantron ballots, punch cards and the current electronic system. I have worked as a clerk, alternate judge and as a judge, primarily in Precinct 250 in Central Austin. Travis County is a large
county and includes most of the City of Austin (the Austin metro-
politan area has a population of more than 1,000,000 people.) Our
precinct rolls list about 2,700 registered voters, of which about 2,000
are active voters. We tend to have a very high percentage turnout.
I have missed only a handful of elections in 35 years and I work
the same precinct so I am dealing with my neighbors. We hold our
elections in the hall of the local public elementary school. The ex-
periences I am about to share about voting and elections are similar to those of other local election officials.

Most people are unaware that the entity holding the election
largely determines what election system is used. It is not uncommon
to use one method in one election and a different system in the next
election. In addition, the rules and procedures change with almost
every election due to changes in the law or legal interpretations at

the state and/or federal level. Because of all this, election judges and alternates are required to attend training before every election.

In anticipation of the March 2006 primary elections, I attended judges training and one of the first sentences uttered was that voters are now comfortable with electronic voting systems but that they increasingly distrust election officials (the inference being that the most distrust occurs with local, i.e., precinct level). This is not my experience. I have just the opposite experience at my precinct. People appreciate us working elections and regularly make a point of telling us so.

At every election, I receive numerous complaints, questions and remarks regarding the safety of the ballot, secrecy and so on from my voters. Many of the voters question ballot secrecy because they are skeptical about the electronic voting system and its honesty: how do we know it records the votes as voted and can it be hacked into? They all want their vote to be recorded and counted properly. I feel voters have a right to know whether their vote is being counted properly.

I am very concerned about the new electronic voting systems, their reliability generally and the sanctity of the ballot. Even with my 35 years of experience, I still do not know how these machines work and whether they are recording votes properly. That really disturbs me.

I consider that one of the most important parts of my job as an election worker is to provide citizen oversight and accountability with voting. Yet because of electronic voting, local oversight and accountability are effectively removed.

With paper ballots we never left the precinct until every single ballot was accounted for. Any ballots that were unreadable or had problems were put in a separate envelope to be reviewed at officials at election central. Yet with electronic voting, hundreds, even thousands of ballots may have problems and vendors and some election officials glibly pass off these massive problems as "user error" or a "glitch."

With paper ballots, we sometimes had difficulty determining voter intent but these ballots were reviewed by other election officials to try to determine how the voter meant to vote. This meant that two teams of election officials viewed the ballots. Even today we have to account for access codes as to how many people signed in and how many voted.

However, with electronic voting, I am not allowed to view my own precinct totals. How can I properly do my job?

What disturbs me the most is all the stories I hear in Texas and around the country of hundreds of thousands of lost votes that have occurred with the recent use of computerized electronic voting equipment. This includes undervotes (fewer votes than voters); overvotes (more votes than voters); and machine malfunctions and breakdowns. *Every vote must be accounted for.* There needs to be a paper trail. We need to see our precinct totals. We could then follow the tallies to the central counting station for that election.

Until we get rid of all electronic voting and go back to paper ballot elections, handcounted with oversight and with totals available at the precinct level, I don't see how we will ever restore true accountability and true integrity to the election process.

Some of the Types of Problems I Have Had

Technical problems

In Travis County, we use the Hart InterCivic electronic voting machines. The machines have to be daisy chained together and to the Judge's Booth Controller (JBC) like old-fashioned Christmas tree lights. This means that if you have a nonfunctional machine in the chain, all the machines that follow are out of order as well. We were told initially that all we needed to run the machines was one electric outlet. This is easier said than done when you are holding your election in the hall of a school in session. Not only are most halls wired only for the occasional outlet, but the wall lengths are chopped up with classroom doors, science exhibits, bulletin boards, and so on, making it difficult to string together more than about five booths safely.

In addition, I discovered in the November 2004 presidential election when I was sent ten booths, that I do not have sufficient electric power to run more than five machines. This was my only experience with this number of machines. The Travis County troubleshooters had to bring out a power booster, take the system down (at that point, people were waiting in line more than one hour to vote), and then restart the system.

Before a recent election, we had widespread and prolonged electrical blackouts in Austin. I asked the Travis County trainers about getting sufficient paper ballots to use in the event of a blackout on election day because paper ballots are the backup plan. For most elections, we are provided about 30 paper ballots regardless of the type of election—local, state or federal. The county would not give me assurance we would have more ballots in the event we needed them. I could not get information about how long the batteries would last in the voting system if the power went out. I was told simply to think positive. I should be provided sufficient supplies of paper ballots to run my election efficiently regardless of the circumstances so everyone can vote.

Now that we have used the machines for a couple of years in Austin, most of our voters are familiar with using Direct Recording Electronic voting systems (DREs). However, we are getting more comments that people do not believe that their vote is being counted properly. We still have some non-technical folks who need assistance and some new voters as well. We are having more downtime and technical problems; perhaps this is due to the age of the system. The cables for connecting machines have been replaced once and still we have some stripped threads and sometimes we have a machine out of service for part or all of the day. When the threads are stripped we cannot connect or disconnect the machines properly.

In the 2006 primary, I started the day with a disabled access machine which had to be replaced before the polls opened. I had a second machine malfunction during the day. I was able to shut down the second machine without affecting the string until the troubleshooters could arrive. This was a very low turnout election. Had it been a high turnout election, this breakdown would have greatly slowed down the voting process. It occurred to me as I struggled with equipment problems that 2–3 years is about the length of time computers last these days before they have to be replaced. I foresee that we will be getting new machines shortly. Who knows at what expense? How many millions of dollars? In my opinion this is a waste of taxpayer dollars that could go to education and health.

One logistical problem not foreseen by the experts (although I foresaw it) is that the number of voters voting at a given moment on machines is limited by the number of machines. Paper ballots can be marked by many voters at once and on any type of surface.

Our machines produce no receipts or paper trail so that all you can do to check results is rerun the discs you just ran. This cannot be done at the precinct level. In addition, we at the local level never see our own box totals; we are not allowed to run totals on the JBC before turning it in, so if changes were to be made at the central counting station, we would never know it. The newspapers, by the way, used to publish the precinct totals usually the day after the election.

With paper counts, the local election judge kept one of the three tally sheets. We would keep the tally along with our other records for a period of time prescribed by law (currently 60 days to 22 months depending on the type of election). The judge's copy provides a backup in case other records are damaged or destroyed.

In Travis County, the electronic machines are delivered to the precincts within the week before the election. We have followed this procedure in every type of election since 1976. The machines sit in a corner of the hall until set up. They are cabled together with a lock for security purposes, so that people cannot tamper with them. However, in the March 2006 primary election, I went to the school the evening before to set up the booths (not unseal them, just set them up on their legs), and found that this task had already been done for me, even though the machines were still cabled together. I asked the custodian about it and he said, "Someone from the county" had come by. I had the key to the lock in my possession. I was not notified in advance that someone was coming by. In the May election of 2006, I asked if the county could notify us when they were coming so we could also be there. I was told this was a service they offered if they had time and there was no way to let us know a time.

The election judge has the key to uncable the machines in a similar manner to the olden days when the election judge kept the keys to the ballot box. This way the judge could remove the ballots and count them. This is supposed to limit access to only the judge or their alternate in his/her absence.

Each machine has a seal to indicate that it has been closed at Election Central. I break open the seals (I can actually do this with my fingers) and I have to account for all seals. Sometimes, I find a seal broken when I start to set up, which I find disturbing because that may imply that someone has tampered with the voting machines.

The Hart InterCivic has a memory card in each machine on which the votes are recorded; the JBC also has a copy. There is talk of having election workers download the cards over the Internet (although typically we do not have access to an Internet connection) into a central tabulator on election night before hand delivering the cards to the substations for counting. This would supposedly make results quicker for the media. But, of course, any hacker could cause mischief with the votes from anywhere. I consider this a considerable security breach.

One of the chief problems I see is that this process is not transparent to the users or the workers. We constantly hear in the news about hackers and what they can do and have done to computers. The voters in my neighborhood are typically well-educated and technologically savvy, and I think perhaps they are more aware of potential problems than some other voters. But many voters still are unaware of the risks and problems with these machines.

As a local election judge who has worked for many years, I am well aware of problems that can interfere with getting the polls open and keeping them open. We have had school personnel whose cars broke down on the way to unlock the building. One presidential election, we had the water main break in front of the school and had no water or sewage all day. Portable toilets had to be brought in. We had a power outage in a recent election.

I want a system that is easy, can be executed with minimal equipment and that the voters can understand easily. For me, the answer is hand-counted paper ballots. This system is cheaper, efficient and more transparent for the voter and election workers. I think voters trust paper ballots more. In my opinion if someone wanted to throw an election, one would have to have a group of complicit people in several precincts. With electronic voting it only takes one hacker to tamper with an election. It is the difference between NFL football and a pickup soccer game! With hand-counted paper ballots, we can literally vote on the curb, if necessary. We can carry materials to the nearest window and use natural light to vote.

As for accountability and oversight, during general elections in Texas, we are required to have Republicans and Democrats represented on our work teams. We now have combined primaries in Travis County, so we have Democrats and Republicans present. Texas also allows poll watchers (appointed by candidates, parties, or groups sponsoring issues) and the Texas Secretary of State has inspectors that periodically visit polling places. The Secretary of State's toll free number, by law, is posted at the polling place so that anyone can call them with a question or complaint. Speaking for myself, I have worked many elections when the inspectors and poll watchers were present.

There are a few things that the machines do well: they allow the blind to vote in privacy, they are wheelchair accessible (so are some other systems), and they allow those with fine motor skills problems to vote independently. If there was a safer way to accommodate handicapped voters other than electronic voting, then I would support it.

Curbside voting is much more cumbersome with these machines since we must unhook the last booth (the handicapped one), take it to the car, vote the individual and then hook it back up.

One efficient procedure that could be done has not been implemented for election day voting (although it is in place for early voting): the provision for a ballot for those voters who have moved outside the jurisdiction but are still eligible to vote for some candidates.

In closing, I believe that the basis of our system of government rests on the belief that we have a "government of the people, by the people, for the people," as Abraham Lincoln said in the Gettysburg Address. To me, this means that any citizen should be able to fully participate in our government. Elections, of all governmental functions, need to be an open process that can be physically verified. Electronic voting does not provide this. It is a system that must be accepted wholly on trust. We, as voters, cannot observe a ballot being placed in a box. No one sees the cast ballot. A fresh set of eyes cannot recount the results. A historian cannot examine past original documents. There is no physical assurance that the vote has been cast as the voter marked it or, for that matter, that it has even been cast at all. Reading daily news articles about computer viruses and hackers does not reassure me about the sanctity of the ballot box, it does not help me answer voter questions about the process, nor does it allow me, as an election judge, to reassure them that their sacred vote was truly counted as intended. This, to me as a public servant, is unacceptable.

———————————————

May Schmidt has been working elections in Travis County, Texas, since 1970. She has been a clerk, alternate judge and election judge. She was born in Austin (Travis County), Texas and graduated from the Austin Public Schools and the University of Texas at Austin. After serving in the Peace Corps in El Salvador, she returned to Austin and earned a Master of Arts in Latin American Studies and a Master of Library Science at the University of Texas at Austin. After a career at the Austin Public Library, she retired in 2000. Currently she is employed part-time at the University of Texas at Austin at the Texas Archeological Research Laboratory. Her hobbies are archeology and sewing. She is married to Jim Schmidt and has two children and one grandchild.

Votescam: The Stealing of America
The Radical Legacy of James and Kenneth Collier

Victoria Collier

'If we give up Votescam,' Jim told Ken, 'when we're old men we're going to look back and ask why we didn't fight the bastards. We're going to add up the plus and minus columns and all we'll have is money. I don't want to spend the rest of my life with this seething anger because I know I let them get away with it without going the last fucking inch.'

—*Votescam: The Stealing of America*

BECAUSE THEY WERE OUTSPOKEN, radical and contemptuous of undeserved authority, my father and uncle, James and Kenneth Collier, are usually left out of "official" discussions about how to reform and safeguard our elections system. But despite how uncomfortable they (often) made some people, they really should not be ignored. The Collier brothers were pioneer vote fraud investigators long before the 2000 election fiasco catapulted the issue to public awareness. They were warning Americans about the widespread use of computers to rig elections more than a quarter century before ballotless touchscreen voting systems began rolling into precincts like Trojan Horses. Their book, *Votescam: The Stealing of America* is more important today than ever before.

Jim and Ken were unusual men with tremendous personal strength, keen political understanding and great heart. They were *real* patriots, sacrificing their financial security and physical safety in order to bring the truth to the American people about why we're losing our democracy. They expected to win the Pulitzer Prize for their work—and they should have. Instead, they were dismissed and often vilified as "conspiracy theorists." Now, in 2006, when it's finally clear to millions of Americans that our votes *are* being stolen, manipulated and discarded, the Collier brothers' groundbreaking investigation is still carefully ignored by many new vote reform leaders who are afraid of being labeled "conspiracy theorists" themselves.

Why is this a problem?

Because election fraud *is* a conspiracy. It's a treasonous, tragic and so far *extremely effective* conspiracy to undermine, control and destroy democracy. We cannot win this fight by pretending that vote fraud began yesterday—or even worse, pretending that it has not yet begun.

I have heard Representative Rush Holt (D-NJ) say as much. On Amy Goodman's alternative news show "Democracy Now," Holt was unwilling to discuss any past incidence of fraud, even in the 2000 election. He inferred that it's enough to view vote fraud as a *potential threat* posed by the new ballotless, touchscreen voting machines.

Apparently, the over-hyped problem with "butterfly" ballots in the 2000 election provided a handy excuse for doing away with the ballot altogether. In 2002, George W. Bush signed into the law the Help America Vote Act, providing billions for states to adopt the use of these totally unnecessary, secretly programmed, unreliable, unaccountable, insidious machines, manufactured by an incestuous handful of corporations with strong political ties to the Republican Party.

Rush Holt's widely supported bill, H.R. 550, would allow for the continued use—and ongoing expense—of these machines, requiring the addition of printers to generate ballots. But according to Holt and his top supporter, David Dill, professor of Computer Science at Stanford University, those ballots need not be counted by hand. Only minimal "random audits" would be required; an extremely inadequate safeguard leaving loopholes wide enough for vote rigging insiders to walk right through. Worse, these "voter verified paper ballots" provide a totally false sense of security to voters who have not taken the time to inform themselves about this issue.

I would like to say to all journalists, election reform activists, elected officials and all others new to this issue: if you truly care about democracy, learn the history of vote fraud in America. Face the truth about how we came to this dark place where we have all but lost control over our government. We cannot win this fight without understanding what we're up against, and we cannot win if we are afraid to speak the truth.

❖ ❖ ❖

One of the most mysterious, low-profile, covert, shadowy, questionable mechanisms of American democracy is the American vote count.

—James Collier, *Votescam: The Stealing of America*

I don't want to get caught in this thing.

— Joyce Deiffenderfer, former president of the League of Women Voters.

You'll never prove it. Now get out.

—Elton Davis, channel 7 computer programmer in Dade County responsible for the impossible feat of projecting 100% accurate vote totals on election night, 1970.

The original FBI documented Votescam investigation began in Dade County, Florida in 1970, where Jim and Ken uncovered massive election fraud involving over 250 congressional candidates. The local television networks reported false election results to the public on election night, based on "projections" that later on proved to be almost 100% accurate—a statistical impossibility made more ridiculous by the network's claim that they based their results on the returns from one solitary voting machine somewhere in Dade County. In fact, the "official" results were falsified to match the phony results given out by the press. This incredible crime was made possible by forging the poll workers signatures, which were on record weeks in advance of the election, most likely by using a Rapidograph device.

Since then, evidence of similar vote scams have been uncovered by citizens running for office in other parts of the country. It is reasonable to believe—given the total lack of meaningful electoral oversight—that this insidious form of fraud has been taking place with regularity for decades throughout the nation. However, Jim and Ken did not believe it was possible to rig elections *on a national scale*, until they discovered the existence of News Election Services.

News Election Services (NES) was a consortium of all the major corporate news networks: ABC, NBC, CBS, AP, *The New York Times*, the *Washington Post*, and later, CNN and Fox. After its creation in 1964, NES operated in near total secrecy, gathering raw vote results funneled into their heavily guarded headquarters from precincts and counties on election night. The results were then disseminated to the individual news networks who reported them to the public—falsely claiming all the while that they were "competing" for results. Jim and Ken were the only reporters to ever investigate NES, but all questions about their processes and procedures were deflected with one company statement: "This is not a proper area of inquiry." When questions were pressed, the company representative would simply hang up the phone.

Given what Jim and Ken uncovered in Dade County, they strongly believed that election results were being manipulated by NES before they were ever disseminated to the networks. With no citizen, media, or government oversight, NES was perfectly positioned to rig elections *without detection*.

And remember this: it is fundamentally impossible to succeed in widespread election fraud without the complicity of the press.

This information is shocking, upsetting, even infuriating for most Americans to hear. Many simply *cannot* or *will not* hear it.

Yet, it is this refusal to face corruption that has allowed it to spread like a cancer deep into the bones of our nation. Why do we insist on believing that the mainstream corporate press cannot be thoroughly corrupted? It is controlled by an increasingly small handful of extremely powerful, super wealthy, highly politicized individuals—are they immune to corruption? No. They are more susceptible than any of us. Because *they alone* have the power to expose the crimes of government and industry to the world—to bring down entire criminal empires—they will be targeted, threatened and seduced until they are destroyed or they succumb to the corruption.

Then the censorship begins. Vitally important stories are not aired, and the editors and reporters who want to cover them are fired. New editors and reporters who *don't* rock the boat are hired. Fluff pieces replace real reporting, hard questions are rarely asked of officials, and the evening news becomes little more than a regurgitating of police reports and White House press releases. Meanwhile, the façade of a free press is rigorously maintained; small crimes are investigated and petty criminals paraded mercilessly for our viewing pleasure. However, the truly powerful criminals upholding the existing power structure are shielded. When this goes on for decades, the media becomes something like a bandage masking and perpetuating the infected wounds of our society.

What Jim and Ken uncovered in their twenty-five year investigation is that the next step in this degenerative process has been taken—the press is now *actively* complicit in government corruption. The most insidious form of corruption, in fact; vote fraud.

The most concise statement in the *Votescam* book regarding the relative power of the major networks came from ABC News Supreme Court correspondent Tim O'Brien. When ABC refused to air video that Jim and Ken had obtained that showed some members of the League of Women Voters illegally punching holes in cast ballots in one precinct in Florida, O'Brien apologetically explained:

"When you're dealing with the networks, you're dealing with a shadow government."

NES definitely operated in the shadows. Later on it changed its name to Voter Research and Survey (VRS) and then to Voter News Service (VNS). You might remember VNS from the 2000 election, which was likely the first time you ever heard their name. VNS was the organization that "called"the election for Al Gore in Florida. George W. Bush's refusal to accept that result sparked the two-month long fiasco that ended with his illegal appointment to the presidency.

Whether Gore had actually won or not (and subsequent vote tallying and additional evidence of Republican vote fraud show that he did), VNS had made the call and I believe they were not expecting to be challenged. *They had never been challenged before.* Given their requirement of operating in the strictest secrecy, the spotlight that shone on VNS after the 2000 election must have required serious damage control. How fortunate for them that Representative Billy Tauzin (R-LA), who headed the subsequent Congressional investigation into the role of VNS on election night 2000, refused to allow me to testify at the hearings, despite over 400 phone calls to his office on my behalf.

I had been granted an extremely unusual, spontaneous telephone interview with the former head of VNS, Bill Headline, just before the 2000 election. You can read my interview at *www.votescam.com*. Toward the end, I questioned Mr. Headline about his organization's total lack of public accountability. I asked why it is such a problem for VNS to allow journalists or citizen monitors inside their headquarters on election night.

> **Headline:** There is no problem. This is a. . . we're private organizations, and you know, uh. . . Mobil Oil doesn't invite people in to see how they send out credit card bills. . .
>
> **V. Collier:** But of course, this is different. This is the national vote count.
>
> **Headline:** It isn't different.

V. Collier: It is different.

Headline: It's not.

When VNS called the election for Gore, I believe that the Bush family and their extremist far-right backers staged a coup that surprised everyone, upending the existing balance of power in America permanently. If you think my use of the word "coup" is extreme, let's take a closer look at the 2000 presidential election. In a matter of weeks, Bush and his cronies pushed the court case *Bush v Gore* through the court system at unbelievable speed, all the way to the Supreme Court. For the Supreme Court to hand down the decision giving the presidency to Bush without a complete and thorough investigation and recount of the ballots in every state in question, was, in reality, a coup—and a complete breakdown of our democracy and of the right of citizens to have their votes fairly and thoroughly counted. Bush and his cronies influenced the court system to stop the recounts that were ongoing in various states at that time. This was successful due to the influence of key individuals, some of whom figured heavily in the Votescam investigation.

One notable player is Antonin Scalia, the Supreme Court Justice who helped illegally end the Florida recount and appoint Bush to office. Scalia was also responsible for quashing one of Jim and Ken's most important vote fraud lawsuits back in the 1980s while he was an appeals court judge. Justice Scalia is what Jim and Ken called a "stopper in the bottle" of vote fraud evidence. Janet Reno is another. Though I don't have proof that she participated in the 2000 Bush regime coup, Reno had paved the way for future fraud in Dade County. When she was Assistant State Attorney in Florida in the 1970s, Reno served the state by refusing to prosecute the Collier brother's extensive vote fraud evidence—falsely claiming that the statute of limitations had run out on the crime. Some time later, Reno had Jim arrested for stealing vote fraud evidence which he brought to her. She promptly threw the evidence out.

Without these corrupt people—and others like them—in positions of power for decades, widespread election fraud would be impossible.

❖ ❖ ❖

The Votescam investigation proves beyond doubt that computerized vote fraud did not become possible with the advent of ballotless, touchscreen voting machines. Much furor is being raised over these machines, which are more accurately the final product of decades of vote-rigging technology development. The ubiquitous Optical Scanners, computerized counters which are used with paper ballots, are often named as "safe and accurate" replacements for the touchscreens—but they are also computers that can be manipulated without detection. Sure, the scanners count real ballots, but what use are ballots if they are not counted by hand, in public, with totals posted at the precinct level, on election day? Yes, the ballots can be used for a recount, but have you ever tried to get a recount? It's easier to get a Green Card. Most States have statutes that make the candidate questioning the election pay for the recount, at costs that range in the hundreds of thousands of dollars. They frequently have to sue for the right to a recount, if they can afford one.

However, for election thieves, it's best to just get rid of ballots altogether. Hence, the paperless touchscreens.

This rapid evolution and promotion of computerized vote rigging technology supports the Votescam premise that our elections are rigged *from within*, with the complicity of corrupt voting machine vendors, certain secretaries of state, key elections officials, a portion of the membership of the League of Women Voters, leaders within both major parties, powerful individuals in every branch of government and the controllers of the mainstream media establishment.

It doesn't take a conspiracy of thousands. All you need are a few key people within each supervising organization who have a vested interest in maintaining the status quo, a few computer savvy criminals for hire, a tightly controlled and complicit mainstream press and hundreds of millions of apathetic, disinterested citizens who would rather do just about anything than spend time monitoring the vote count. You've got a recipe for election rigging that cannot fail!

And that's what we've got.

❖ ❖ ❖

Both Jim and Ken Collier died in the 1990s. I would like to share with you these words, from the final page of the *Votescam* book:

> *Now we understand why things have gone so terribly wrong in this country. It is due to the corrupted vote. It is the stolen vote that perpetuates corrupt city, state and federal governments.*
>
> When those corrupt power brokers in your town weed out that up-and-coming politician, they are looking for a person who is willing to "play ball."
>
> Politics is playing ball.
>
> Suddenly, you find property decisions going against nature; land and water needed for the perpetuation of life on our earth, suddenly disappears. A handful of developers get richer while the land, and the quality of life, gets poorer.
>
> But those paid- off officials need judges to further their ambitions. Judges are either elected or they are appointed by elected officials. Judges make the final decisions on property. They also rule on probate; they can steal yours or your children's inheritance. Often, corrupt attorneys, working with corrupt judges, become the beneficiaries of your life's work, not your heirs.
>
> In the same way, jobs evaporate, money inflates or deflates based on some political vote. You try to stop what you perceive as insanity by "voting the bastards out."
>
> But when they get reelected, and reelected, the press tells you that it was your fault . . . "you voted for them."
>
> You know that you didn't.
>
> *Who did?*

So where do we stand today? As I write this article, in the early years of the twenty-first century, there is barely a pretense of government accountability left in America. Members of Congress habitually ignore the needs of their constituents yet they miraculously get "voted"back into office again and again. This discourages the democratic process—including voter turn-out—paving an even smoother path for a corrupt incumbent.

Though a few good apples do remain in Congress, there is nothing left of the executive branch. The White House is now occupied by a terrifying cabal of extreme right-wing, super-wealthy corporate criminals and "end times"religious fanatics with blatantly fascist, militant tendencies and delusional imperialist goals. They stole the 2000 election by force, and when the mountain of evidence finally stands clearly on history's horizon, we will be able to look back and know exactly how they stole the 2004 election—using a variety of methods, including the manipulation of computerized voting machines.

In the meantime, they are in control. Waving the American flag and brandishing the Christian cross, they are waging a catastrophic war based on a complex web of lies. Why? Well, besides being the ultimate Orwellian double-speak, the "War on Terror"is also a convenient excuse for just about anything these lunatics want to do.

And what are they doing?

They are openly looting the civilized world, murdering tens of thousands of innocent people, demoralizing and wasting our military forces, torturing unnamed prisoners held in secret gulags, destroying our global reputation and strategic alliances, illegally spying on millions of innocent American citizens, threatening global nuclear war, obliterating vital social services and environmental protections, filling our government agencies with their inept cronies who are pocketing billions in illegal and mismanaged contracts, bankrupting our nation and dismantling our Constitution—and that's just what we *know* about. They are treasonous, immoral war criminals the likes of which this nation has never even imagined. Neither true Americans nor true Christians, they have commandeered leadership of both bodies and are using this unprecedented power to turn large parts of the world into living hell.

What can we do? We can't vote them out of office—we tried that. We have not been able to get Congress to stop handing them nearly every power they demand, let alone consider impeaching them. We can't get the mainstream press to expose their web of lies—or the vote fraud that got them into office in the first place!

Every square on the board has been covered. What is our next move?

❖ ❖ ❖

I just happen to have some ideas. The following are my thoughts on some step-by-step actions we can take to shift the balance of power on this chess board before We the People are finally check-mated and find ourselves carted off in the night with a bag over our head labeled, "National Security Threat."

#1. Stop kidding yourself. The situation is *really* bad. You need to turn off the T.V., cancel the ski trip, put down the latte, get together with some friends and start planning your part of the non-violent revolution. If you are already a revolutionary, skip to #3.

#2. Get educated. You don't have too much time for reading in the hammock, but understanding some real history is helpful. So while you're gathering a group of like-minded folks, here are some good resources:

For General Understanding of the Power Structure
   A People's History of the United States—by Howard Zinn
   Indispensable Enemies—by Walter Karp

For Understanding of How Elections are Currently Rigged
   Votescam: The Stealing of America—by James and Kenneth Collier
   Black Box Voting—by Bev Harris

Fooled Again—by Mark Crispin Miller

The Best Democracy Money Can Buy—by Greg Palast

#3. Make a decision. What are your politics? Do you support democracy? Not everyone does. Maybe you're an anarchist, or a communist, or something else. Just because you live in America doesn't mean you believe in representative government. But *if you do*, then you must believe in the vote, and *you have the responsibility to fight for it right now.* You have no right to turn away from that fight, or expect someone else to fight it for you.

#4. Join the existing organizations and individuals fighting for hand-counted paper ballots. This is the only acceptable method of voting. The ballots must be cast in see-through plastic boxes to prevent stuffing. All votes must be counted in public, at the precinct level, with the results posted on the wall before the ballots ever leave the room. The vote count can be filmed and aired live on public access T.V. Multiple citizen watch dog groups can help monitor the count, the transfer of ballots to the county level and the reporting of results to the public.

#5. Join existing activist groups and educate them about the need to expose and fight election fraud. Immeasurable resources and manpower already exist within these organizations. Direct action environmentalists who currently spend time bike-locking their necks to bulldozers and redwoods would serve their own cause just as well—if not better—by locking down on voting machines. The millions of activists who march against the World Bank, WTO and IMF should turn their attention to the organizations aiding and abetting vote fraud—rigging in the politicians who are selling our country's sovereignty to these international corporate extortionists.

Top Targets for Direct Action:
- All mainstream press offices. ABC, NBC, CBS, Fox (*especially Fox*), CNN, *The New York Times*, the *Washington Post*, NPR, and so on. No matter how "liberal"some of these corporations might appear, they all are routinely lying to the public and covering up government fraud and corruption, including vote fraud. The mainstream American press is the most

powerful force in the nation right now. It has been co-opted by super wealthy controllers who need to be ousted immediately by an engaged and enraged public.

- Secretaries of state. The buck stops with these guys. All forms of public pressure must be brought to bear on them, as they approve the form of voting technology used in their state.

- Precincts on election day. Marches, sit-ins, lock-downs and general boycotting of elections need to take place on election day. We cannot allow the charade of democracy to continue. Be creative.

#6. Contact "alternative" media and demand that they cover this issue extensively and repeatedly. It's time to make this issue #1! All other issues are affected by this one issue—vote fraud.

❖ ❖ ❖

When I was a teenager, I used to sit in front of the fireplace playing chess with my father and talking about Votescam. We both figured that if the country didn't wake up and take back the vote, the Republic would fall. And it would be ugly.

It's ugly now. And I wish he were here.

Victoria Collier is the daughter and niece of James and Kenneth Collier, authors of the groundbreaking book, Votescam: The Stealing of America. *This book chronicles the brothers' two-year investigation into how elections are covertly stolen using electronic voting machines, with the complicity of the major media networks and both major political parties.*

Since the Collier brothers' death in the late 1990s, Victoria has continued to keep this vitally important information alive through radio and public speaking. She also runs a variety of projects promoting sustainable living and organic agriculture in Taos, New Mexico.

Victoria can be reached at: editor@votescam.com; http://www.votescam.com.

E-voting Horrors from the Buckeye State

Bob Fitrakis

I COULD BARELY BELIEVE MY EYES. It was 6:30 in the morning at the Model Cities Neighborhood facility polling site on East Broad Street in Columbus, Ohio, and the longest line of voters I had ever seen snaked well into the parking lot. Hundreds of voters crammed into the halls inside the building that housed the predominantly African American Ward 55B. As the former elected Democratic Party Ward Committeeperson (1996–2000) for the 55th in Franklin County, I knew the turnout was unprecedented. Yet, the line did not appear to be moving. As I worked my way through the crowd with my black and white Election Protection T-shirt and white Legal Team member jacket, I was startled to find only three electronic voting machines inside—of which one was a provisional voter machine that was seldom used. In the spring presidential primary there had been four machines and in prior presidential elections, there had been five machines. It was now THE high stakes 2004 presidential election. . . and the lack of voting machines stunned me.

The missing machines took an immediate toll on the voters. Between 6:30 and 7:00 A.M., I documented 20 voters leaving the line for various reasons. The reasons most frequently given were that they would be late for work, or that they had to get their kids to school. One elderly handicapped man said he was going home to get a chair because he couldn't stand that long. I couldn't help but think things would be moving faster if there were paper ballots that could be distributed for voting instead of forcing people to wait hours in line to vote on the e-voting machines. The Columbus-based *Free Press* that I publish and edit would later break a story that Ohio's Secretary of State, J. Kenneth Blackwell, Co-Chair of the Bush–Cheney Re-election Campaign, had turned down a request from Franklin County Board of Elections officials to allow voters to use paper ballots to expedite the voting process.

But this was not the first time I had witnessed problems in Ward 55B involving the e-voting machines manufactured by Danaher. In 1992, I won the Democratic primary as a candidate in the 12th Congressional District. I'd received the endorsement of both the Franklin County Democratic Party and a group of black independent activists not tied to either party supporting the candidacy of south side environmentalist Roberta Booth. So while I was looking at my numbers throughout the inner city of Columbus, where I won every precinct over Ralph Applegate of rural Licking County, I found that my official vote in my home Ward was a statistically impossible 80–20 loss to Applegate. As a political scientist, trained in statistics, with a Ph.D., I knew immediately that the computerized voting machine had flipped the vote.

Although I won the primary with 60% of the vote, I still lodged a formal complaint with then-Franklin County Party Chair Fran Ryan, who served on the Board of Elections. I still remember her words: "Oh honey, does it really matter? You won anyway."Ryan never pursued an investigation of the obviously flipped votes in the '92 primary.

Later, in 1998, underfinanced and little-known Democratic challenger Ed Brown, in the same 12th District Congressional race, picked up an undeserved 6% of the vote when 3% of incumbent Representative John Kasich's votes were flipped to Brown through a software glitch in an electronic voting machine. With Kasich losing in his home base of Westerville, an investigation followed by the Franklin County Board of Elections at the Representative's request which proved the e-voting machine had wrongly programmed votes away from Kasich and to Brown. In part, this is caused by an Ohio law that requires candidate's names to be rotated on the ballot from precinct to precinct so none will have an advantage being first every time.

But, back to this fateful election day, 2004: between 7 and 10 A.M. I visited all eight polling places containing nine precincts in Wards 55 and 5 in the central city. All of them had long lines, and all but one had people standing outside in the cold rain. One of the most chilling scenes of the day occurred at the Douglas Alternative Elementary School polling site. Upon arriving, I was directed by Election Protection workers to speak with an elderly black woman who had fainted from standing in line for over two hours. (Election Protection is a citizens' group which had membership nationwide, committed to monitoring elections and reporting any voting and election irregularities they witnessed.) The lady explained to me that she was undergoing chemotherapy and couldn't stand any longer. I approached the presiding judge at the polling site and asked that the woman be accommodated as handicapped and be allowed to move to the front of the line. I was emphatically told that **no handicapped individuals would be accommodated at Douglas**. I threatened the standard legal action and pointed out that the people in line were willing to let her move forward, yet the presiding judge would not budge. After explaining the situation to the ailing woman, I watched her slowly walk away, cane in hand, giving up on voting that day. At that point I swore that the events I saw would be made public.

As I made my rounds and ended up back at Ward 55B, a young black woman who I had directed earlier to the Board of Elections to cast a provisional ballot, told me "Don't send anyone else down there, it's awful." I asked her what she meant and she said, "There's cops everywhere." I decided to make a trip a mile or so down Broad Street into Columbus' downtown area to the Board of Elections to demand more machines and investigate the report of police presence there.

In a scene reminiscent of my time as an international election observer in El Salvador, I found the Franklin County Board of Elections resembling a military bunker, surrounded by city buses and large concrete barriers. After I negotiated the concrete maze I came upon a large phalanx of armed, overwhelmingly white deputy sheriffs with a metal detector. Inside the building I observed additional security, as I demanded to see Matt Damschroder, County Election Director. To my surprise, the woman informed me that Damschroder was meeting with J. Kenneth Blackwell and President Bush and could not be interrupted. I continued to insist that I speak with an election official to lodge a formal complaint regarding the lack of voting machines in the inner city. Finally, Marlene Wirth, a longtime Board employee and Democratic Party operative was sent out to speak to me. Noting my Election Protection clothing, the first words out of her mouth were: "It's you people who are the problem."

She curtly informed me that there were no extra machines anywhere and I should quit bothering her. Later investigation by the Columbus Free Press revealed that 125 machines were held back on election day, all of them in the Democratic-rich city of Columbus. **Machines were missing in 74% of the majority African American wards in Columbus, costing John Kerry an estimated 17,000 votes.** Chris Wilson, who left his job at the Franklin County Board of Elections after the 2004 election debacle, told me that, "Matt (Damschroder) spent way too much time talking to the FBI and Homeland Security. He was like a little kid envisioning terrorist attacks." Wilson also supplied a document from former Franklin County Deputy Director Ed Leonard, a Democrat, who had warned the Board after the 2000 election that there was a potential for problems with long lines at the polls in future elections if there was a high voter turnout and not enough machines.

The Franklin County Board of Elections admitted they needed 5,000 machines for the turnout in the 2004 presidential election. They had in their possession 2,866, of which they only put out 2,741 on election day morning. It's much cheaper to buy paper ballots and pencils than to buy computerized voting machines. Had the voters in Ohio voted on paper ballots, like 95% of all the voters in the Democratic counties—an estimated 20% of the voters would not have had to leave the lines in the inner cities of Columbus. **The lines averaged between 3–7 hours in the inner city wards, while in white affluent suburbia, the average voter was spending 15 minutes in line to vote.**

The Danaher Direct Recording Electronic (DRE) machines were notorious for their unreliability. Their security problems were so bad that even Secretary of State Blackwell refused to allow Franklin County to purchase any more of the machines. The Danaher machines were originally called Shooptronics, named after their maker, Ransom Shoop, who was indicted twice for election tampering in Philadelphia.

In 1988, George H. W. Bush, the former CIA Director, was losing by 8 points in the presidential primary polls to Bob Dole just prior to the election. But, Bush won with a surprising 9% victory margin after then New Hampshire Governor John Sununu introduced the Shooptronic DREs into the state's largest city, Manchester. The *Washington Post* dutifully reported that pollsters failed to detect this unprecedented last second groundswell for Bush the Elder. Unexpected last minute groundswells, not predicted by pollsters, would become a habit for the Bush family. Bush the Elder, as CIA Chief, oversaw operations in the Third World, which rigged elections and toppled governments. Since it was merely election rigging not involving violence, these were referred to as "benign operations."

In early 2004, Athan Gibbs, founder of TruVote—a company that manufactured voting machines that provided paper ballots for recounts or audits had warned me of the vulnerability of e-voting machines to hacking and election rigging. "Why does every ATM machine that Diebold makes have a paper trail and the ability to be audited, but their election machines lack both features?" Athan asked.

Gibbs was in Columbus demonstrating his TruVote machine, which simultaneously allowed voters to push the button for a candidate and see their vote recorded on paper under plexiglass before being deposited in a lockbox. The paper ballot became the paper trail of record that could be hand counted or scanned independently from the DRE machine. In a *Free Press* interview, Gibbs told me to follow the money trail on the e-voting machines and to take a look at the Urosevich brothers—the siblings who were running the top two electronic voting machine companies at the time, Electronic Systems & Software (ES&S) and Diebold.

"It should bother you that so few people control all the voting in the U.S.," he said. After talking to Gibbs and interviewing Bev Harris of Black Box Voting, Harvey Wasserman (Senior Editor of the *Free Press* and co-author of many of my journalistic pieces) and I wrote an article for *motherjones.com* and I wrote a cover story for the *Free Press* entitled, "Diebold, Electronic Voting and the Vast Right-Wing Conspiracy." Within three weeks, Gibbs died tragically in a freeway accident with a semi truck. Some people likened the event to the Karen Silkwood incident.

As I drove around in the early afternoon on election day 2004, I heard the pollster John Zogby predicting an electoral landslide for Kerry. *The Harris Poll*® was likewise predicting a Kerry victory. Certainly I'd witnessed the largest turnout of voters in Democratic areas in the history of Ohio—at least in the central city. Like everyone else I was stunned when I saw the final vote result early Wednesday morning. It was as if somebody had flipped the 51% to 48% Kerry lead in Ohio with an electronic switch to give Bush a victory by the same margin. As a political scientist, it was inconceivable that for the first time, long lines in the inner cities did not equate with a Democratic winner. The exit polls, which are known for their startling accuracy, were suddenly off by implausible margins. What was the likelihood of Bush winning in Ohio with that margin of vote given the exit polls?—3 in 1,000.

Similarly, Bush was beating the odds *and* the exit polls in 10 of the 11 swing states. In Iowa, Nevada, New Mexico and Ohio, predicted Kerry victories vanished into the night. Only in Wisconsin, which had same-day voter registration and voting, did the exit polls come out within the margin of error. During that night, some of the strangest voting irregularities occurred in U.S. history. The U.S. General Accountability Office (GAO) would later assess: "some of [the] concerns about electronic voting machines have been realized and have caused problems with recent elections, resulting in the loss and miscount of votes." Yet, we in Columbus knew almost immediately of massive problems with the voting machines.

Ohio Secretary of State Blackwell immediately went on the offensive, writing a column in the Reverend Moon-owned *Washington Times*, calling the election a "model" and constantly stating in public that there wasn't a single act of irregularity on election day. Technically, he was correct because he was referring to the singular; in reality there were tens of thousands of irregular occurrences throughout Ohio. The Columbus Institute for Contemporary Journalism would document hundreds of them at two hearings on November 13 and 15, 2004, in Columbus where voters and potential voters who were turned away on election day, testified under oath.

On Thursday after election day, Earl Wurdlow of the First Unitarian Universalist Church invited me, as a political scientist, to participate on a panel dissecting the election with four other Ph.Ds. My approach was to simply reiterate all the irregularities that I had witnessed at the polling sites. Following the meeting, a man I've never seen before (or since) came up to me, looked me straight in the eye and said, "You're an attorney. If what you say is true, you ought to hold public hearings and put people under oath." Within minutes, two members of the League of Pissed off Voters (LOPV), Jonathan Meier and Amy Fay Kaplan, approached me and told me they were even more pissed off about the election, and wanted to know what to do. I told them we were going to have public hearings.

The next day, Meier and Kaplan arrived in my office and began making phone calls to get various voting rights groups to consider buying into the hearings. As attorney Cliff Arnebeck, would later explain, "This young woman Amy called me and she said, 'You're not doing ANYTHING! You're letting them get away with this!' and I thought to myself, 'you know, she's right!' "Arnebeck would later serve as the lead attorney in the *Moss v Bush* election challenge to overturn Ohio's election results.

The first hearing was held at New Faith Baptist Church in the heart of the 55th Ward. As the Director of the Columbus Institute for Contemporary Journalism, I decided that we would sponsor the hearings. When I called the court reporter with my credit card, I assumed I would be donating the $3,000 or so for the transcripts. But we were picking up allies quickly: the Alliance for Democracy, Common Cause, NAACP, CASE–Ohio, Greens, Libertarians, Democrats, Republicans, church members, local politicians and the LOPV, who had agreed to organize the event. My old political ally Michael Moore even promoted the hearings on his Web site's front page.

We didn't know whether to expect 5, 50 or 500 people as we drove to the church. People came out in droves. We had attorneys taking written affidavits in the church basement while we heard sworn testimony in the sanctuary from 1 to almost 6 P.M. We had to extend the time by two hours to accommodate the more than 500 people in attendance. And the media! There were independent documentary crews in every corner of the building and Pacifica radio network broadcasted the event. More than 200 people provided affidavits or testified at the church and two days later, a standing room only crowd of 250 people jammed the Franklin County Courthouse auditorium to provide further testimony. The coalition sponsored more hearings in Cincinnati, Cleveland, Toledo and Warren, Ohio.

Reoccurring testimony describing strange voting machine activity sparked my interest. Primarily coming from Mahoning County, there were reports of votes hopping from Kerry to Bush on electronic voting machines. In Franklin County, we heard repeated stories about the Kerry vote fading away after being pushed. These became known simply as the "Mahoning County Hop" and the "Franklin County Fade." While the vast majority of counties in Ohio used punch cards, Mahoning and Franklin were among the few that used e-voting machines. Also, the mainstream press had documented already the miracle of the "loaves and fishes" precinct—Gahanna Ward 1B at New Life Church. There, 638 people had cast votes and Bush, by the grace of God, received 4,258 votes. The Franklin County Board of Elections would later call this a "transmission error." A computer expert we consulted said it was more likely a hack that occurred on site at the church, which was affiliated with Reverend Jerry Falwell. Documents from the Board of Elections showed that the voting machines were put out up to a month ahead of time and left unguarded at polling sites.

After hearing all the testimony and looking at the official election night voting results, including the miraculous 131% voter turnout in Clyde, Ohio, and two precincts in Perry County with 124% and 120% voter turnout, Arnebeck suggested we challenge the election results. Susan Truitt of CASE–Ohio (Citizens' Alliance for Secure Elections) also signed on as an attorney, as well as Peter Peckarsky, a Washington D.C.-based attorney. The legendary Columbus School Board member, Bill Moss, who had served as a panelist at the New Faith Baptist Church hearing, volunteered, along with his wife Ruth, to serve as lead plaintiffs. **Both of them had witnessed the long lines at the polls, including the arrest of a mother who had allowed her daughter to hold her place in line while she went home to cook dinner for her family and then returned.**

The election challenge named Ohio Secretary of State J. Kenneth Blackwell, George W. Bush, Dick Cheney and Karl Rove as parties responsible for the incorrect election results. The Republican strategy was readily apparent—simply drag out the election process until Bush was inaugurated. Both Blackwell and Ohio Attorney General James

Petro refused to comply with any discovery requests from our 37 plaintiffs. Petro went so far as to claim the Ohio Rules of Civil Procedure trumped the statute, which gave us only 10 days for discovery; bear in mind most trials allow months for discovery. Under Petro's version, he could wait a week and ignore our discovery while Blackwell would get full discovery.

We served notice to Bush, Cheney, Rove and Blackwell for depositions, which they ignored. We also sought data from Rove's laptop computer in the discovery request. Representative Tom DeLay would famously attack this request on the floor of Congress claiming, correctly, that we thought Rove was manipulating the election through his laptop computer—a real possibility, according to the GAO report.

The lawsuit met with resistance, not only from Republicans, but from the Democratic Party that didn't want to be seen as sore losers. So, while Franklin County Democratic Party Chair Bill Anthony would publicly denounce me as a conspiracy theorist, he told me privately that he thought the election was stolen blind in southwest Ohio counties, dominated by the Republicans. We discovered he was correct.

Through our investigations we found that Bush's entire margin of victory occurred in Ohio's southwestern counties of Butler, Clermont and Warren. Blackwell's numbers suggested Bush won Ohio by 118,000 votes. He won those three southwest counties by 132,000 votes. Warren became nationally known for calling its own Level 10 Homeland Security Alert on election day, which usually means Osama bin Laden is in the neighborhood. The media and independent election observers were banned from witnessing the vote count. The FBI later claimed that there was no Homeland Security Alert issued in Warren County. Newspaper accounts attributed the "alert" to county officials. Employees from the Warren County Board of Elections, who promised to testify if subpoenaed, provided maps and an account of how the ballots had been diverted to an unauthorized warehouse under the control of "a Republican Party hack." In the wee hours of the morning after election day, a 14,000 vote surge occurred for Bush.

Our theory on Butler County, suggested by the State Supreme Court Chief Justice candidate C. Ellen Connally, was that someone had altered the vote count on the central tabulators, the computers where the final vote totals reside. Despite false information put forth by Secretary of State Blackwell, most of the rural counties counted their votes not at the precinct level, but by precinct at the county's central tabulator. This saved the county money by only having to buy one centralized counting machine. It also makes it easy for electronic fraud to occur since the final totals are tabulated outside the oversight of precinct election judges or any public oversight.

Connally received 5,000 more votes than Kerry, despite being a vastly underfunded African American civil rights advocate from Cleveland. Kerry received 112 fewer votes than Al Gore did in 2000, despite the fact that Gore pulled out of campaigning in Ohio with 6 weeks left to go, while Kerry and his supporters were campaigning and spending record funds. As a general rule, down ballot candidates for local and state offices, and particularly African American candidates, should not out-poll the Democratic presidential candidate in rural southwest Ohio. Kerry votes seemed to be missing in Butler County.

In Clermont County, the official results would have you believe that 10% of the people who voted for Connally then voted for Bush. Also, more than 10,500 voters in the area appeared to vote pro-gay rights *and* pro-Bush. These so-called Log Cabin Republicans may have been created by vote switching in these rural counties. Most voters in Ohio, particularly in strong party areas like the southwest Republican counties, will go to the polls with their Republican Party or conservative group sample ballots. It is extremely unlikely they would vote for gay marriage, for a retired African American female judge from Cleveland **and** for Bush.

The news accounts of the Ohio election irregularities reached U.S. Representative John Conyers who subsequently held a hearing on voting problems in Ohio in Washington D.C. and Columbus. The *Free Press* reports became a crucial part of his staff's report: "What Went Wrong in Ohio?" The Reverend Jesse Jackson came in to Ohio to assist in the election challenge lawsuit and Congressional challenge to Ohio's electoral votes for president. On January 6, 2005, an historic challenge by Cleveland Representative Stephanie Tubbs Jones and California Senator Barbara Boxer went forward during the certification of Ohio's electoral votes. This was the first time in U.S. history that a challenge occurred to a state's entire electoral delegation. **Once the U.S. Congress certified Bush's electoral votes, we withdrew the election challenge to overturn Ohio's election results. The lawyers determined there was no remedy to remove Bush under Ohio law, making the case moot.**

Blackwell, represented by Petro, filed sanctions against Arnebeck, Truitt, Peckarsky and me for our election challenge. The sanctions asked that the attorneys be fined and penalties be placed against their licenses to practice law. We hoped it would go to a hearing so we could present our evidence. We had three expert witnesses including Dr. Richard Hayes Phillips, a geomorphologist trained to investigate statistical anomalies, Dr. Ronald Baiman, an economist and statistician and Dr. Werner Lange, a sociologist. Dr. Phillips would have testified under oath that the official election results, as certified under Blackwell, were fraudulent and statistically implausible. Dr. Baiman would have testified that the exit polls were a reliable indicator that Kerry had, in fact, won, and that the Bush numbers were statistically impossible. The Ohio Supreme Court ruled that the threat of sanctions be dropped.

The Green and Libertarian Parties raised money to recount Ohio's 2004 election. The recount was more openly and visibly corrupt than the election itself, with technicians from Triad Systems, which runs the tabulation software that counts 41 of Ohio's 88 counties, showing up to make sure a true random recount did not have to occur.

A nonscheduled visit by a Triad technician led to the replacing of the hard drive on a 14-year-old Dell computer, which served as Hocking County's central tabulator. The county actually had an identical backup machine they could have used. Instead, a new hard drive was brought in, along with what Deputy Election Director Sherole Eaton described as a "cheat sheet" from Triad. Eaton was fired for blowing the whistle on Triad's suspicious activity. Frequently, this seems to be the reward when honest election officials come forward to expose corrupt election practices.

In Hocking County, instead of randomly selecting 3% of the county for a recount, the Republican Board of Elections Director Lisa Schwartze picked one precinct because its number of voters was exactly 3% of the county's total. The number of voters and convenience was more important than complying with the legal meaning of "random." Random means every voter in the county all must have an equal chance of inclusion.

The Board of Elections Director and the entire board in Lucas County were forced to resign by Blackwell due to massive election law violations in the Toledo area after the 2004 election. The precinct boundaries were never set and the Diebold opti-scan machines throughout the heavily pro-Kerry inner city precincts malfunctioned, leaving thousands of uncounted votes. During the recount, an eyewitness swore under oath that the Diebold technicians got to choose the precincts to be recounted in Toledo and even reprogrammed a memory card when they couldn't find the election day results from one precinct.

In 2006, three election officials in Cuyahoga County were indicted for violating recount laws. Recount observers filed complaints of violations of Ohio Election Code. At the time of this writing, their cases are still pending. **According to the indictment, these election officials pre-counted precincts and they did not randomly select the precincts that would match election day results. Their excuse?** *They wanted to save time.* Michael Vu, Cuyahoga County BOE Director, has vigorously defended their recount actions. His boss, Board of Elections Chair Robert Bennett, is a good friend of George W. Bush and is the Chair of Ohio's Republican Party.

In the November 2005 elections in Ohio, with four election reform initiatives on the ballot, the problems with electronic voting grew worse. New Diebold machines were placed in 41 Ohio counties. The final *Columbus Dispatch* poll, completed on Thursday prior to the election, showed reform issues two and three passing with about 60% of the vote. Both were unexpectedly defeated with the projected passing percentage of the vote becoming the massive margin of defeat. It was as if somebody had flipped the vote.

Usually if a poll is off by the monumental and disgraceful margins of this *Dispatch* poll, one looks for some historically intervening cause. None were really present over the weekend prior to the election. Next, one looks to see if the measurement, in this case the vote, was properly implemented. Throughout the state, the voting process resembled more of a train wreck than an election in a democratic society. Pollworkers didn't know how to set up, tear down or use the Diebold machines. A total of 187 memory cards from the voting machines went missing in Montgomery County. Keep in mind, each memory card is like an entire ballot box, containing all the votes from a precinct! In Carlisle, Ohio, a continuing levy to fund their city's fire department went down to defeat when another miraculous election event occurred: 250 voters voted against the levy in a precinct where 150 people voted. The City of Carlisle sued and gained the right to a re-vote.

The *Dayton Daily News* reported that 12 machines miraculously recalibrated themselves, which flipped the vote. In Toledo, scores of day laborers, including a Republican mayoral candidate, were missing for hours as they went out and hand collected the memory cards, according to the *Toledo Blade.*

While these bizarre and unacceptable e-voting problems plagued the whole state of Ohio, the mainstream press, led by *The Columbus*

Dispatch, refused to consider any possibility other than they had gone from being the best pollsters in the state, to the most incompetent polling operation in the state. To admit otherwise would be to concede that private, partisan, secret electronic voting runs counter to the principles of democracy.

By primary election day 2006, new ES&S machines were added in central Ohio counties. In Franklin County, the ES&S machines had problems and needed to be recalibrated during the voting process—meaning they were recording wrong results. In 160 precincts, which represent 20% of all the precincts in Franklin County, the voting started late because the pollworkers did not know how to work the machines. State Elections Director Damschroder admitted in *The Columbus Dispatch* that at least 50 voters walked away without voting. School levies were left off of the electronic ballot in three suburbs. In Delaware County there were recalibration problems as well. In Cuyahoga County, memory sticks from the Diebold machines turned up missing and one voter in a fit of rage attacked and took down two e-voting machines in Cleveland. Representative Tubbs Jones got a court order to keep one polling place open until 9:30 P.M. because it hadn't opened on election day until 1:30 P.M.

The hundreds of millions of dollars spent in Ohio on private, nontransparent, proprietary voting machines is perhaps the greatest waste of taxpayers' money in the state's history. **There's a simpler fail-proof technology that exists and is used in 95% of all democracies, including parts of the United States and our neighbor, Canada. It's called hand-counted paper ballots.** I've seen it work firsthand in El Salvador when I was an official international election observer in 1994. I witnessed how representatives from all the political parties, joined by members of the media international election observers, and any interested community members simply gathered around the table when the ballots were unlocked and hand counted. Everyone agreed on the vote count. There were no suspicious cyber-votes, bizarre recalibrations, "Mahoning County Hops," "Franklin County

Fades"or mysterious computer glitches that produce miraculous vote totals. It was simple and straightforward vote counting and it was done, counted twice, by 10 P.M.

Hand-counted paper ballots are the obvious antidote to the poison of secretive, privatized, proprietary e-voting machines. But, as the Republicans say in Ohio, it's never over until the cyber-vote comes in.

❖ ❖ ❖

What's Wrong With Legislative Attempts to Fix Election Problems?

Cynthia McKinney
with Abbe DeLozier and Vickie Karp

SEVERAL PROPOSED LEGISLATIVE bills attempt to solve problems with fraudulent voting systems; others just pretend to. None of them will succeed in securing Americans a guarantee that their votes are being counted as cast, even if they are passed. To understand why, it is necessary to first understand the real problem with the majority of our new streamlined, computerized voting systems: documented research indicates that two of the four major electronic voting machine vendors' software can be manipulated to "throw" an election; the "secret" software of the other two has prevented them from being carefully researched by non-vested parties; and most disturbingly, we are asked to "take it on faith" that our votes are safe with these systems.

Why should we?

The proposed legislation, deadlocked in Republican-controlled committees in Congress, takes the form of proposed amendments to the 2002 "Help America Vote Act" or "HAVA," another federal mandate which does anything but help Americans vote. It's helpful to also understand the implications of HAVA in the Big Election Picture: it offers a tantalizing $3.86 billion in federal funds to the states, in exchange for their upgrading old punch-card and lever voting machine systems for newer, improved voting systems and for thereby (supposedly) insuring the disabled the right to an unassisted vote.

As detailed in another chapter in this book, HAVA was passed as a supposed fix to the "hanging chad" problem in Florida in the 2000 presidential election. But what HAVA has done, rather than solve problems with elections, is create a demand for the most insecure, unauditable, problematic voting systems ever introduced into U.S. elections: Electronic voting machines, which were presented as "the" way that the states could comply with HAVA's federal mandate. (This is also not true, as electronic voting is NOT mandated as the only way the states can comply with HAVA requirements.)

Ironically, or perhaps not, four major electronic voting machine vendors were ready with their products to help the states comply with this Act—ES&S, Diebold, Hart InterCivic and Sequoia, as well as a few other smaller vendors. The problem is, their products involve secret, proprietary software that cannot be reviewed either by citizen oversight committees, or election officials; a significant portion of the machines they sell are DREs (Direct Recording Electronic) touchscreen machines which produce no paper, making it impossible to do recounts; and the record shows that tens, if not hundreds of thousands of problems, have arisen with voting on these systems and with the election results themselves.

Before I go into detail about why various proposed legislative solutions to "fix" these machines will not work, I'd like to go into a little more detail about the glaring security problems that they pose.

Bev Harris of the nonprofit organization, Black Box Voting, has devoted the last several years to researching the problems with electronic voting, as detailed in her book, *Black Box Voting: Ballot Tampering in the 21st Century*. For a litany of examples of highly suspicious problems with electronic voting during real election conditions, one need only read the appropriate chapters in her book, which is posted on her Web site, *www.blackboxvoting.org*, or to visit another election reform Web site, *www.votersunite.org*. By contracting with computer programming experts and security engineers to examine the Diebold software, Bev Harris's efforts have produced the best documented evidence available that these machines are highly susceptible to fraud.

Bev and her expert "computer security team," consisting of Dr. Harri Hursti, world class computer programmer and security engineer from Finland, and Dr. Herbert Thompson, author or co-author of twelve books on computer security, of Security Innovations of Florida, were invited by two county election officials to examine real Diebold election equipment and software. Ion Sancho of Leon County, Florida, invited them in 2005 to examine Diebold Optical Scan counters which are used to count paper ballots, and Bruce Funk of Emery County, Utah, invited them in March 2006 to examine the Diebold TSx touchscreen voting machines which are equipped with printers for the purposes of providing the voter with a "voter verifiable paper receipt or trail" which voters can (supposedly) use to verify that their vote was cast accurately by the computer.

I was one of a very few witnesses to Harri Hursti's exploits in Leon County, Florida, in the summer of 2005 and I got to watch firsthand as Hursti and Dr. Herbert Thompson actually examined the Diebold election software and optical scan counters. Shockingly, they quickly found multiple ways of "hacking in" via undetectable entries in 60 seconds or less that even a novice could execute, resulting in "flipping" election outcomes!

Though I was not present when the Black Box Voting "Hacking Team" went to Utah in March (of 2006), I am aware from the report on their findings. Harri Hursti reported that even more disastrous security issues were discovered by this exploit than what they found in Florida!

Another computer expert, Jeremiah Akin of Riverside, California, found the Sequoia company's election software; he downloaded and researched it, and found that built-in to the programming was the ability to manipulate the results of the Spanish ballot: Whoever accesses the language settings for the election programmer actually has the choice of loading the program to cast the vote for the candidate actually voted for; OR for a different candidate! Many other security problems with the Sequoia election software have also been identified by Akin.

Why would any election software program designed with integrity even have such features? The answer is, it wouldn't! All evidence points to one conclusion: these election systems were designed to be hacked.

I attended the Washington, D.C., press conferences in September, 2004, where Bev Harris, Jeremiah Akin, Herbert Thompson, and other computer experts demonstrated the six simple hacks that could flip an election in less than 60 seconds. I was absolutely astounded at what I saw! I was invited to be a "guest hacker"! I was reluctant at first to try this novel experience, but was taught in mere moments to successfully hack a mock election set up on a laptop, using real Diebold election software. The same version that has been used in numerous counties across the country. It took less than a minute! With three clicks of the mouse, I was in! The implications of this were, and still are, frightening in terms of the threat these machines pose to U.S. election integrity!

Though most of the mainstream media were represented at these D.C. press conferences, the tone of the stories reporting the day's events was dismissive of the threat to elections represented by electronic voting machines. For those of you who have trouble believing negative reports and documentation about these machines because you "don't see it on CNN," it's time for you to wake up to the fact that mainstream media ownership is concentrated in the hands of just a few players, and in the end, stories such as that which occurred at those press conferences in D.C. may never get the intense, comprehensive and honest coverage they deserve. If you want the truth, you have to go out and look for it!

Considering that the Help America Vote Act is the excuse being used to encourage states to buy these dangerous elections systems, it is ironic to learn that electronic equipment is *not even necessary to meet the HAVA requirements* as they relate to the disabled voter! Ellen

Theisen, founder of election reform group VotersUnite (.org), and a team of other election activists have created a non-electronic voting system for the disabled which DOES offer them the ability to vote unassisted; does NOT have to be certified in many states because it is considered a *device*, as opposed to a voting *system*, and is extremely affordable compared to any of the electronic systems being offered as HAVA compliant. Freddy Oakley, the County Clerk of Yolo County, California, just purchased the first order of Ellen's creation, the Vote-PAD, and has set an excellent example for other election officials around the country: Election officials do NOT have to buy electronic equipment in order to fulfill the HAVA mandate for the disabled voters! The state of Wisconsin has also recently purchased the Vote-PADs for some of their counties.

Sherry and David Healy of Mill Valley, California, have also devised a non-electronic voting system for the disabled called "Equalivote" (*www.equalivote.com*). Either the Vote-PAD or the Equalivote will provide compliance with HAVA without costing taxpayers millions of dollars invested in highly suspect, insecure voting systems.

❖ ❖ ❖

So with that background, let's take a look at some of the proposed legislation to amend HAVA:

H.R. 550, sponsored by Representative Rush Holt of New Jersey: this is widely viewed by election activists as the best of the proposed legislation.

Rep. Holt wrote the first version of this bill in 2003. H.R. 2239 would have required printers be added to electronic voting machines, still ensuring a method for the disabled to vote privately. However, the bill never made it to the House Administration Committee since we now know that is was likely blocked by this Committee's head at that time, Rep. Bob Ney of Ohio. Ney has since stepped down from his position due to his connection with the Abramoff lobbyist scandal. Ney was also the author of the aforementioned Help America Vote Act, and was lobbied by several of the major e-voting system vendors for that purpose.

The revamped version of H.R. 2239, H.R. 550, has many voting activists fired up once again over its mandate for paper trails for elections. The language mentions "voter verification and mandatory paper record audit capacity," as well as accessibility and voter verification of results for individuals with disabilities. This just sounds wonderful, but it totally misses the mark for the reasons stated below.

The biggest problem with this approach is that instead of simply requiring real paper ballots, H.R. 550 allows for a vaguely defined "paper record," which could be anything from a thermal paper receipt to a printout tally. Even if printers are added to provide a voter verifiable "audit trail," we must still rely on the small likelihood (and the integrity of) a recount or audit to determine problems with the electronic system's recording of the vote. H.R. 550 would authorize the HAVA-created Election Assistance Commission (EAC), a federal body charged with creating uniform federal standards for voting systems and elections, to conduct random hand counts of the voter-verified records for each federal general election in at least 2% of the precincts in each state.

Holt's bill would *not limit* audits to 2%, therefore allowing the states to decide if they would prefer to audit a higher number of the votes.

As so aptly pointed out by Nancy Tobi, of Democracy for New Hampshire (*www.democracyfornewhampshire.com*), in her recent article, "What's Wrong with the Holt Bill?"(parts 1 and 2, February 2006, listed in our bibliography), the Election Assistance Commission is an executive branch commission whose members are appointed by the sitting president. While designed as a bipartisan commission, the president has the power to make recess appointments without the checks and balances of Congressional oversight and approval. In

January 2006, President George W. Bush, against the bipartisan recommendations of senior Congressional leaders, made three recess appointments to another commission, the Federal Election Commission, at least two of which were highly controversial.

The EAC, Tobi explains, is equally vulnerable to this type of crony appointments, and is a *nonrepresentational body with extraordinary power over the nation's elections*. H.R. 550, in Sec. 4a, "gives this Executive entity blanket authority to conduct recounts in any state of their choosing and, 'at the option of the State or jurisdiction involved; to conduct recounts of state and local elections." Do we really want the only safeguard to electronic voting, audits and recounts to be in the hands of a federally controlled, crony-appointee commission, with the power and authority to contract out this sacred duty and preempt state and local control in the process?

To take a closer look at a recent critical recount in Ohio in 2004 and the evidence of how this crucial recount was mishandled, see Rep. John Conyers' *What Went Wrong in 2004?*, and Bob Fitrakis and Harvey Wasserman's book, *Did George W. Bush Steal the 2004 Election? A Collection of Critical Documents*. (Another excellent account of vote fraud documentation is the Sundance award-winning film, *American Blackout*, which follows voter disfranchisement in the 2000 and 2004 presidential elections.) **Here's what Americans need to really understand: When the stakes are high, recounts and audits are manipulated and stolen, just as elections have been.**

Other proposed legislation:

H.R. 704, Voting Integrity and Verification Act of 2005, sponsored by Rep. Jim Gibbons of Nevada. This bill would amend HAVA to create a paper trail by which the voter could use to verify his vote before it was cast and counted. H.R. 704 would require the voting system to produce a permanent paper record for each ballot cast which meets specific requirements relating to manual audit capacity.

All comments made regarding H.R. 550 related to "voter verifiable paper trails" and the unlikely possibility that audits will ever be conducted in a manner that would actually prove vote fraud apply to this bill as well.

H.R. 939, Count Every Vote Act of 2005, sponsored by Rep. Stephanie Tubbs Jones of Ohio. I applaud my fellow Congresswoman for the comprehensive approach she is taking with this proposed legislation. It covers a lot of ground in trying to expose and eliminate the weaknesses and problems with electronic voting, much more than many of the other proposed amendments to HAVA. In addition, it goes a long way toward addressing prevention of the rampant voter discrimination that has been especially evident in the last two presidential elections.

Like the other proposed bills listed before it, it would also:

- require a voter-verified paper record which would be considered the official recording of the vote in the case of an audit or recount;

- provide for mandatory random, unannounced audits of 2% of the vote, to be conducted by none other than the federally appointed Election Assistance Commission; and at the option of the state or other jurisdictions, a 2% audit of elections in those jurisdictions when held concurrently with federal elections;

- provide that electronic voting systems use only open source code (software that is revealed to the public) and includes the prohibition of wireless communication devices in voting systems (present in much of the Diebold equipment);

- requires certification of software and hardware used in electronic voting systems;

- require security standards for manufacturers of voting systems used in Federal elections;

- study, testing and development of best practices to enhance accessibility and voter verification mechanisms for disabled voters;

- voter verification and audit capacity funding; impartial administration of elections; standards for purging voters; election day registration and early voting;

- voting rights of individuals convicted of criminal offenses; election day as a public holiday;
- study of the use of the Internet for voter registration and also voting in federal elections;
- other provisions designed to tighten up election integrity and eliminate voter discrimination.

When it comes to her approach regarding electronic voting, Rep. Tubbs Jones' H.R. 939 has the same weakness as the other proposed legislation: Paper records that are only to be used in the case of a 2% audit, which still allows for electronic voting systems to be used; gives the federal entity, the Election Assistance Commission (EAC), the task of conducting those audits; in fact, it would strengthen the EAC. Along with the suggestion of studying how the Internet can be used for both voter registration and voting in federal elections, this bill moves into very risky territory as far as security goes.

Regarding the Internet being used for voter registration and even for voting, Bev Harris and many other election researchers agree that putting any sensitive components of an election (of which voter registration is one, and voting itself is THE big one) on the Internet is one of the highest risks to election security possible. There are limitless ways that votes and election results can be manipulated through the Internet! Teenagers with laptops could be deciding elections for us from Internet cafes anywhere in the world!

H.R. 3910—Verifying the Outcome of Tomorrow's Elections Act of 2005, sponsored by Rep. Tom Feeney of Florida. Key components of this amendment would prohibit an election official from providing a ballot to a voter who lacked a current valid, state-issued photo identification. The bill imposes similar requirements for voting by mail. In addition, the bill states the following requirements:

- Requires criminal background checks for anyone who is to tabulate or certify the tabulation of votes.

- Requires a permanent, individually verifiable paper record of each vote cast.

- Requires each state to conduct regular tests of the equipment used to tabulate votes in voting systems to ensure that a system meets error rate standards and is working correctly.

- Requires a state to permit a representative of each political party with a candidate on the ballot used at a precinct during an election to observe the tabulation of the votes cast on the voting system and the certification of such tabulation.

Weaknesses of this amendment, as regards to electronic voting, are the same as each of the other cases: Not only does this version propose the same old verifiable paper record of each vote, it does not even provide for the paltry 2% mandatory audit that is mentioned by each of the others (irrelevant as that would actually be). **Also, it is important to note that testing of voting machines referred to above is not reliable for a variety of reasons, as the election software can be put into "test" mode when election officials are checking the machines just prior to an election, and the software can be programmed to operate a different way in real election conditions.**

Mr. Feeney should know. He is named in an affidavit by a computer programmer, Clint Curtis, for having solicited Mr. Curtis's software company employer, the Yang Corporation, in October of 2000 to design election software that could be rigged undetectably to manipulate an election. Feeney requested "a vote fraud software prototype" that was touchscreen capable, and which would have a hidden hacking function that would be concealed even if the source code was inspected.

Curtis told the company owner, Mrs. Yang, that hiding such a function would be impossible if the source code was inspected, and she said, "You don't understand. In order to get the contract, we have to hide the manipulation in the source code. This program is needed to control the vote in South Florida." Curtis never provided the program Feeney requested, but one must speculate if someone else did.

S.B. 2437: Senator John Ensign of Nevada introduced this proposed HAVA amendment in January of 2005, which has a clearly defined requirement for "Voter Verified Paper Ballots" in Federal elections, and where the "VVPB" and electronic voting co-exist, in the case of conflicting results, the paper ballot becomes the ballot of record. It is called the "**Voting Integrity and Verification Act of 2005 (VIVA).**"

Key aspects of S.B. 2437 (VIVA) are as follows:

- Voters would be able to verify the accuracy of their ballot "in a private and independent manner" by allowing the voter to review an individual paper version of the "voter's ballot" before the "voter's ballot" is cast and counted.

- All electronic records produced by any voting system will be consistent with the paper records.

- In the event of any inconsistencies or irregularities between any electronic records and paper records, the voter verified paper record is considered the true and correct record of the votes cast.

- The paper ballots will be used as the official record for the purpose of any recount or audit, conducted with respect to any election for Federal Office.

As good as this sounds, it still doesn't really go far enough. It gives the paper ballot priority over the electronic ballot in cases of conflicting totals, which is great, but then we just get back to the problems with getting a fair, honest recount or audit done—of 100% of the paper ballots! And if the paper ballot is going to have priority over the electronic total, we must ask, why use the machines in the first place?

Starting with federal elections makes sense from a logistical standpoint. However, working from there to infuse this bill into state and local elections, it allows those state and local elections to be subject to the consequences of electronic voting systems without the safeguards proposed in this bill. Election reform activists concede, "Without some provisions to require mandatory, manual audits of those paper trails, they won't do anything to provide great verifiability of election results." (National Ballot Integrity Project commentary from Robert Kilbrick of Verified Voting.)

❖ ❖ ❖

So there you have it, the major attempts to modify the Help America Vote Act, with the stated intention to either provide more election integrity, to provide more ability for all voters to cast a ballot, or both.

As well-intentioned as most of the sponsors of these bills are, if we have to rely on mere mandatory 2% audits or recounts only in close races (where paper ballots are still used, which is a shrinking percentage of all elections), especially when recounts are handled by the Election Assistance Commission, election results will continue to be called into question as they have been for the last several years, going back to at least 2000 and earlier.

Our current voting systems have taken the citizens out of the counting and accountability.

Relying on recounts is not a safeguard for several other reasons: The expense of holding recounts is in many cases cost-prohibitive, and some states, like Ohio, are raising the cost to conduct them. And when a supposed "winner" demands a concession from his/her opponent, and a quick and decisive declaration of victory, as we saw in both the Bush versus Gore and Bush versus Kerry races, the option of a recount quickly fades into the background. Additionally, the courts have offered no support in response to demands for fair and extensive recounts in the case of a close election, as we saw in 2000 when the Supreme Court actually ruled for STOPPING the recounting of paper ballots in Florida. **This Florida state legislature, incidentally, has recently passed a law against the hand counting of paper ballots!** But besides all of these reasons, in many of our largest population centers where touchscreen voting has taken hold, real recounts are impossible anyway, because there *are* no paper ballots.

Because of the recent Black Box Voting computer experts' demonstrations to election officials on certified voting equipment showing the ease of tampering, manipulation, reprogramming and alterations of vote tallies in seconds, there is reason to suspect that even adding printers to electronic voting systems could still permit us to be using software that records our votes one way, while printing paper records that show something else. Without the transparency of paper ballots that are hand counted in public view, how can we ever trust the results of electronically run elections with secret software and no ability to have a meaningful recount?

In my unique position as both a voter and an elected official, and as an invited guest to both execute and witness election hacking on the software of the second largest provider of election software in the United States, I, Cynthia McKinney, can come to no other conclusion than this: Electronic voting in any form cannot be trusted as long as the powers who control the technology cannot be trusted. Private vendors who now control our elections also are secretly gaining the political advantages of controlling candidates, policy and billions of dollars. Citizens must take back control of elections, with careful oversight and thoughtful legislation that provides checks and balances with close citizen monitoring throughout the election process.

In conclusion, there is only one perfect voting system: Elections held with paper ballots, hand counted in public view. That is our best chance to restore fair elections to this country. As Bev Harris says, a paper ballot, hand-counted election has about five or six "attack vectors"; with electronic voting, there are 50 or 60.

How would YOU rather vote?

———————————————

In just nine years, Cynthia Ann McKinney, Georgia's first African American Congresswoman and the only woman serving in the state's congressional delegation, has emerged as an internationally renowned advocate for voting rights, human rights and the strengthening of business ties between Africa and the United States. She is known as a passionate, intelligent, charismatic and effective member of the House of Representatives.

As a Georgia state legislator from 1988 to 1992, Congresswoman McKinney gained national attention because of her determined struggle for a fair and just reapportionment plan in Georgia. Elected to the U.S. House of Representatives by a decisive margin in 1992, McKinney has continued that struggle. Congresswoman McKinney's increasing influence on Capitol Hill was acknowledged with her appointment to the powerful and prestigious Armed Services Committee. She is also a key member of the International Relations Committee, serving as Ranking Member on its International Operations and Human Rights Subcommittee.

Election Reform in the Eyes of a Citizen, Through the Lens of a Camera

Kathleen Wynne

I REMEMBER IT WAS A HOT, sticky night in McKinney, Texas, a small town outside of Dallas. Even though I grew up in Texas, being away for over 30 years helped me forget how hot it gets there in July. But I quickly forgot about the heat when, around midnight, Bev Harris and I took a ride to the Diebold Election Systems' offices to check out the dumpster located behind their offices.

I have to admit I felt a little strange in the setting I found myself—sitting in a car with Bev, across from Diebold's parking lot and scoping out the lighting situation around their large dumpster. We also noticed police cars driving by often enough that we figured a police headquarters must be just down the street from Diebold's offices. That certainly made things more interesting. While we sat there, I thought, how did a 51-year-old woman end up in a situation like this? Nonetheless, despite all the doubts running through my head, Bev convinced me that this specific dumpster might contain some crucial information about Diebold and their voting machines and it was well worth the risk of getting caught in an embarrassing situation to find out whether it did. This was the day I took my first dumpster dive.

Our luck was holding out; the lighting was dim in the back where the dumpster was located. We considered this a *sign*. (My advice to anyone who someday may want to dumpster dive for democracy— the first time one *dives*, it should be in as subdued and private setting as possible. At least, until you get the hang of it. I guarantee it's an experience you'll never forget.) Anyway, we parked the car beside the dumpster. I took a deep breath, jumped out of the car and then climbed right inside the dumpster. It was one of those types of dumpsters you usually find next to an industrial site—HUGE.

Inside it, I found myself surrounded by a sea of trash—large white and black bags bursting with paper and Lord knows what else, cardboard boxes scattered everywhere, miscellaneous trash coupled with the acrid smell of thrown-out lunch waste. I started digging through it and grabbed any bags filled with papers and started throwing them over the side to Bev, who immediately put them in the car. I worked fast rummaging through the dumpster trying to choose the *right* bags because there were so many to choose from. It wasn't long before the car was filled to the brim with bags both inside the car and the trunk. There was barely room left for us and the car stunk to high heaven. . . but *we didn't care*. We could hardly wait to get back to the Motel 6, where we were staying, and open up the bags and see what was inside.

When we arrived, there were some people standing outside the motel. They watched us unload the car of all those bags and take them to our room. On the last trip to the car, we innocently looked at them and said, "inventory" and left it at that. We spent well over an hour going through the bags separating the various documents. This job required rubber gloves and perfume. The perfume was for cutting the rank smell of the leftover food that rotted in the hot Texas sun all day. It was immediately evident that we had hit pay dirt or *pay trash*. Incredulously, Diebold had thrown away completely intact internal memos and e-mails; planning information; problems with equipment and customers; price bid worksheets; staff bonuses; and even financial statements! After we quickly went through the bags, I looked at Bev and said, "Let's go back"! There were still a number of bags left in the dumpster which we thought might have more important stuff and we had to get it. Considering what we found from the first dive, it was worth taking a chance to go back.

It was about 3:00 A.M., and we parked the car at a parking lot in front of some other offices so that I could work up the nerve to take a second dive. At this hour, our car was conspicuously the only one in the parking lot. After we sat there for about 15 minutes, Bev looked over at me and said, "We'd better think of something to say, if a cop stops by to check out why we're parked here at this hour."

Not wanting to take a chance of being questioned by a Texas policeman prompted us to go for it. I climbed in the dumpster a second time. We got another six or seven bags and then high-tailed it out of there. We didn't realize it at the time, but what we had in our possession would prove to be very important to our future investigations. You know what they say: "One man's trash is another man's treasure." Following are some examples of those "treasures" found in the Diebold dumpster, along with Internet links to the documents, and how they helped our investigations: Diebold financial documents revealing questionable payments, and showing that some payment items may have been untruthfully reported to government authorities.

One document, first published online by Black Box Voting in July 2004, exposes large payments to entities that were under investigation for making unusual payments to political figures. Black Box Voting has identified a $144,000 payable to "Lottery Services of Georgia," which was one of 16 companies found to have received pass-through payments from GTECH in a 1995 probe. The same document, and others, show payments of $20,000 per month to a Juan Andrade, Pat Gallina's partner in the Diebold-funded ACG Group. Some details on these characters and companies:

- In May 2005, Black Box Voting broke the story of ACG Group, LLC, which has been funneling money from Diebold into the pockets of . . . someone. A principal of ACG Group, LLC is Dr. Juan Andrade, Jr. (the "A" in ACG). Andrade told Black Box Voting on videotape that Diebold money is paid to him directly, and that Diebold money also goes through ACG Group, for purposes that are largely for "persuasion."

- The "G" in ACG stands for Gallina—Pasquale "Pat" Gallina. According to the *Columbus Dispatch*, Gallina was caught giving $10,000 to the Franklin County Republican Party, handed off through the Franklin County Director of Elections. The *Dispatch* also contains a report of a $50,000 donation by Gallina to Ohio Secretary of State Ken Blackwell's political interests. Remember Mr. Blackwell—the one who "oversaw" the highly questionable presidential election Ohio recount in November 2004?

  Accounts payable documents: *http://www.bbvdocs.org/diebold/accts-payable1.pdf*

- Documents also show payments to California lobbying firm, Rose & Kindel, whose executive recently popped up with an appointment in new California Secretary of State Bruce McPherson's administration. Incidentally, it is the secretary of state's office that oversees elections in all states in the United States. One of the payments made, over $45,000, does not match the amount reported by Diebold for the same period (around $7,000). See *http://www.bbvdocs.org/moneytrail/rose-kindel-pymts.pdf*.

  Copies of Diebold disclosures to California can be found here: *http://www.bbvforums.org/forums/messages/1954/4447.html*

In another document, an executive memo, Diebold execs admit to a culture of ethics problems. You can sense the gnashing of teeth as they describe trying to explain to the Diebold audit committee about the lying and obfuscating that went on during California Secretary of State Kevin Shelley's administration. His term began in November 2002 and later resulted in Shelley's banning the use of Diebold's touchscreen voting systems in four counties and decertifying all touchscreen systems in California on April 30, 2004, until security measures were put into place to safeguard the November vote.

The memo states that this cost the company dearly, resulting in a $3 million loss for the year.

❖ ❖ ❖

Cleveland, Ohio

Of course, I'm getting ahead of myself here. Let's go back a couple of years when this journey began. It was around the winter of 2003 when I took notice of this election reform movement, still in its early stages. I was living in Cleveland, Ohio at the time, working as a legal secretary in the Intellectual Property Department of one of Cleveland's many law firms. I knew nothing about electronic voting. I had voted either on lever machines or punch cards ever since I was old enough to vote. It never occurred to me that America would end up voting *electronically* and the concept of it kind of "snuck up on me." So, when I stumbled across an article on the Internet about the fast growing electronic voting method, which went so far as to describe it as "FAST, EASY AND FUN!", I knew something was up, but I wasn't exactly sure just what.

One thing that rang true to me about this article was that it was an extremely one-sided view about electronic voting and was worded pretty much like a carefully crafted PR piece prepared to promote electronic voting. Perhaps this was an effort to wind its way into the American psyche convincing us that electronic voting was good for America! Any American knows when they hear hype and this sure sounded like it. And where there's hype, there's usually a lot of money at stake.

In fact, the hype reminded me of an old Texas saying—"I can tell when someone's pissin' on my boots and calling it a rainstorm!" Without really understanding why, I knew we were headed in the wrong direction, letting machines count our votes, and I immediately set out to learn more about this thing called "electronic voting." I wanted to know when it began, how it worked, who manufactured these machines, and most importantly, WHO decided this was how America should vote and WHY.

Like most people, I have absolutely no computer background whatsoever, but I have been blessed with a lot of plain ole common sense—something I learned while growing up in a small town in Texas. To this day, I still believe common sense is the best "BS" detector there is. You just need to rely on it as often as you can and learn to trust it.

The first voting expert I called was Dr. David Dill, Professor of Computer Science at Stanford University and founder of VerifiedVoting.org, a California-based organization founded in 2004, which acted as a citizens' watchdog-type of organization in response to his lack of confidence in electronic voting machines.

I asked Dr. Dill for advice about this issue. I was a neophyte and everything he said about these machines and how they worked just sounded like a bunch of techno-babble to me. Because of my lack of computer background, I knew that this wasn't going to be a quick learning experience. I began obsessively searching the Net and collecting articles about anything related to electronic voting that explained this issue in plain English and steered clear of the techno-speak. The big picture was beginning to take shape.

After careful research, the one thing that struck me as extremely dangerous, and part of the core problem of what we were dealing with, was the *privatization of* our election process. Citizens had virtually handed over their voting process to the manufacturers of these voting machines and the experts for *safekeeping*.

Ever since people began voting in America, bipartisan teams of election judges and precinct workers carefully hand-counted paper ballots. They then matched the ballots they collected to precinct sign-in sheets. The results of elections were posted on the precinct door as well as in the local newspapers. If even one vote was missing in comparison to the number who signed in, the mistake was carefully tracked down. We are missing that citizen participation with electronic voting technology. Thousands of votes disappear into thin air! What has become of our democratic voting process? As it stands now, technically, these vendors not only owned the machines, they also owned our votes, thanks to trade secret laws which protected their best interests over that of the citizens.' To complicate matters more, I learned that every state, and every county within each state, uses a different type of electronic voting system. The reality of what we had allowed to happen to our election process was, at first, overwhelming and then it became very frightening. Where do we begin to fix this?

Another problem I soon discovered was that the federal voting standards meant to scrutinize and oversee the performance and help protect the security of these voting systems were curiously written *before* these systems came into use. This meant there were no meaningful, up-to-date federal or state regulations in place to adequately measure the security of these systems. **Who was in charge of that plan?**

Another interesting fact about these machines is that before an election there's a legal requirement to run Logic and Accuracy (L&A) testing. The purpose of this testing is to check the software and to test the operation of the machine as it accepts manual votes; to verify that votes entered on the machine are reported correctly on a summary report printed by the machine; and to make sure accumulated totals are correct. But there's a problem with this: this test is done in *test mode*; during an election, however, they are running with an entirely different program with the machine functioning in *election mode*.

What this means is that these tests only test a point in time, not an election. They can only *verify* the test. Also this means that there is no way to do a meaningful recount that shows how the voter intended to vote. When vendors tell you they can perform a recount from the machine's audit log they are giving you false information. The audit log simply shows how the machine recorded the vote. Were the machine to have been corrupted, tampered with, or errantly programmed, we could never account for the voters' intended vote. The only *verification* possible for an election is a rigorous 100% hand audit of all the paper ballots.

I then reviewed certification hearings and minutes of meetings of election officials from various states and was shocked to find that **state and county officials rely almost exclusively on the vendors'**

word alone to certify these machines for use by the public, rather than relying on independent stringent testing guidelines. In fact, in a videotaped interview with the Supervisor of Elections of Leon County, Florida, Ion Sancho, Mr. Sancho told us that election officials become so dependent upon the vendors for technical assistance, implementing machine upgrades and replacing of broken machine parts that they begin to treat them just like *family*. And that it is commonplace for some election officials to have vendor representatives helping them run the election itself, something that obviously gives access to sensitive machinery, software and the ability to manipulate vote totals to private interests without any citizen oversight. Mr. Sancho said this has been going on from the very beginning since voting machines became a big part of our elections.

Which leads to the most disturbing thing I've learned about the election process: that the American people have been systematically taken out of the process altogether and relegated, whether they like it or not, to trusting these for-profit companies—Diebold, ES&S, Sequoia and Hart InterCivic (the big four)—to make certain our votes are secure and counted accurately. Of course, we forgot to take into consideration that by virtue of being a for-profit business, each one of these voting machine vendors has a legal obligation *first* to their stockholders' best interests—profits, profits, profits, *not* the American peoples' best interests—by sparing no expense in guaranteeing the security of their machines that count our votes.

An aside: On the 1st, 2nd, and 17th of March 2006, respectively, Black Box Voting (BBV) was asked by Emery County, Utah County Clerk, Bruce Funk, to come to Utah and help him analyze his newly acquired Diebold TSx touchscreen voting machines (as mandated by the state). He had found some anomalies and wanted us to help him find out whether there were more. After several conference calls with Mr. Funk discussing the matter and what should be done, BBV decided we should move forward with his request and proceeded to bring in and underwrite Finnish computer security expert, Harri

Hursti's, and Security Innovation's testing of the voting machines. The lack of security found through the testing process was astounding. Both Mr. Hursti and the security expert from Security Innovation were stunned with what they found. Mr. Hursti's report is the most devastating report of a voting system *ever*. (See *http:// www.blackboxvoting.org/BBVtsxstudy.pdf*.)

❖ ❖ ❖

Back to Cleveland

For the first time in my life, I was actually afraid for my country and what this meant for a democracy *by*, *of* and *for* the people. The big question in my mind was could a working democracy survive being privatized? America had to have been asleep at the wheel to let this happen. America was headed for a rude awakening. I just prayed we'd wake up in time before we were literally taken over by these machines. (Sounds like a movie plot, doesn't it?)

Whenever I brought up the subject of electronic voting to friends in Cleveland, I was met with blank stares. In 2003, no one seemed to think much about this growing, new phenomenon called electronic voting in Cleveland. Besides, most political activists in Cleveland were more intent on getting out one of the largest voter registration drives ever in the city's history. They were convinced this was the way to win elections and didn't think electronic voting was a problem; at least, not yet.

I knew I'd have a better chance of being listened to, and getting the message out about the dangers of electronic voting, if I could get involved with an organization in the city that was aligned with some of the major powerbrokers in Cleveland. The name of the organization that had those connections was the Greater Cleveland Voter Registration Coalition (GCVRC). The GCVRC was a coalition of unions and a few nonprofits. It was a start. The GCVRC is a 501(c)(3) organization whose mission was to register under-represented members of the Cuyahoga County population and to advocate for proper handling of those registrations.

After joining this organization, I promptly went out and purchased a video camera. Looking back now, I really couldn't tell you what possessed me to make that purchase, but I do remember that I was compelled to do so. For some reason, I knew that I would need to document people and events every chance I got and that this was going to become an important tool for the election reform movement someday. To be honest, I don't know how I knew, I just knew. Not a very "scientific" way of thinking, true, but I'm not a scientific kind of person. I've learned to trust my intuition and I'm glad I did.

After many frustrating months of trying to get the GCVRC to focus on the voting machines and not just voter registration, they finally agreed to support my efforts to organize a Town Hall Meeting in Cleveland so that we could *finally* discuss the issue. I wasted no time organizing this meeting. It would showcase citizens and politicians who were familiar with this issue and were as concerned as I was. I had to get well-known people to speak who would have the drawing power to bring people in and who could persuade them to listen and learn about this issue.

Invited to attend were a number of state reps from Cleveland including Claudette Woodard and Shirley Smith; Rep. Michael Skindell from Lakewood, Ohio; and Toledo State Senator Teresa Fedor, one of the state legislature's leading advocates for election reform. Senator Fedor was instrumental in pushing for a law requiring voter verified paper audit trails (VVPAT) to be added to all voting machines in Ohio. At that time, the VVPAT idea was thought to be *THE* solution because citizens would be able to verify their votes before being counted by the machine. That was thought to be all that was necessary in protecting the integrity of the final machine count. (It was only later that we realized that the paper trails were not the answer to safeguarding our votes. When Leon County, Florida's Supervisor of Elections, Ion Sancho, allowed BBV and Finnish

Computer Security Expert, Harri Hursti, access to one of his memory cards and Mr. Hursti was able to re-program the memory card in such a way that the "paper trails" generated by the voting machine could be falsified, we knew we had to come up with another solution to safeguarding our votes.)

However, I do consider my greatest coup as convincing Bev Harris to agree to speak at the Cleveland event. I had read about Bev and knew that she was the woman who literally started the election reform movement. She was this grandmother who had discovered Diebold's 40,000 confidential files on an unprotected FTP site and exposed this to the country and subsequently "wrote the book" on the subject, *Black Box Voting: Ballot Tampering in the 21st Century.* I knew there had to be a greater power involved if Bev Harris was willing to come to Cleveland to speak about electronic voting at a Town Hall Meeting in the Midwest.

❖ ❖ ❖

The Town Hall Meeting—April 23, 2004

I immediately found a person willing to videotape the entire event, as I was going to be involved with moderating and keeping the event running smoothly and couldn't do it myself. I knew this was going to be an historic event, having such a menagerie of politicians, election reform experts, election officials, vendors and citizens all in the same place discussing this basically unknown issue in Cleveland, Ohio—and we just had to get it on film, to at least remind us of how it was "in the beginning" of the election reform movement in Ohio. Also, I was hoping against all odds that it would be the spark that would cause the election reform movement to catch fire in Northeast Ohio and spread throughout the state. With an election just around the corner, we had no time to waste if we didn't want Ohio to become "another Florida." Little did we know how prophetic that feeling was in early spring of 2004.

One thing is for sure, with Bev Harris coming to town, I, along with Doreen Lazarus, set to work organizing every aspect of this Town Hall Meeting and making certain Bev would get as much exposure as possible. Doreen has a public relations business of her own and volunteered all her time in scheduling interviews with the media for Bev. She did a fantastic job and is one of the thousands of unsung American heroes doing good works all over the country on behalf of this cause. It was a full day of radio, TV and newspaper interviews for Bev.

We even managed to schedule some time for Bev, Senator Fedor and State Representative Peter Uvagi, to meet with the Director of the Cuyahoga County Board of Elections, Michael Vu. It was such an honor to have the opportunity to be with Bev and watch her in action. I remember after our meeting with Michael Vu, we looked at each other as we left his office and proclaimed simultaneously, "bought and paid for"! We came to this conclusion because Mr. Vu was so pro-Diebold throughout the meeting and wouldn't budge on that position no matter what evidence we brought forward about the company's past history with problems telling the truth. His mind was made up and I felt the meeting was just his way of going through the motions in order to give the impression he had taken our concerns seriously.

During the course of that day, I never imagined I would have so much in common with *Bev Harris*. Actually, I felt a little like Forrest Gump, ending up in the middle of something of this magnitude that would virtually change my life forever. From that point on, I was never the same person. My vocation had become election reform.

❖ ❖ ❖

The "Change"

Soon after the Town Hall Meeting, I made a life changing decision based on my newfound and continuous passion to work on the electronic voting issue: I quit my job and set about working in the election reform movement full time. I also began the habit of video-taping everything and everyone related to it. One of the most important things I got on film was an interview with two election employees of Cuyahoga County, Ohio, who were later indicted *for allegedly counting the ballots in private* prior to the 2004 recount in that county (Emphasis mine). They were Coordinator of Elections Jacqui Maiden and another lower-level elections employee, Kathleen Dreamer. I got them to say on film that they were going to use the same procedures in the 2004 recount that had been used in previous years by former election officials. A comfort to Ohio voters, no doubt!

While videotaping the Cuyahoga County recount, I also interviewed several of the observers. They voiced their concerns that the votes were coming out in "batches" of 50 or more at a time, and they couldn't see how that was possible if the ballots had been presented to them just as they were when they came out of the machines (in accordance with Ohio Election Code). The way the recount was being conducted didn't make sense to them or to me. This concern was never resolved and remains in need of an answer today.

I also videotaped the Certification of the Recount by the Cuyahoga County Board of Elections, in December 2004, wherein **Jacqui Maiden and Michael Vu both admitted they had indeed counted the votes in private prior to the recount!** Mr. Vu added that they had done so "to facilitate it for the observers"! Despite the loud protestations of a number of citizens of Cuyahoga County attending the meeting and pleading for them *not to certify* this recount, the Board promptly called for a vote to certify this legally flawed recount. The vote was *unanimous.* So much for citizen input and outrage.

Due to the concerns of these observers, a complaint was filed against the Cuyahoga County Board of Elections asserting they had violated Ohio Election Code by counting these votes privately prior to the recount. I also submitted copies of my videotape of those interviews, the recount and the Certification of the Recount meeting to.the prosecuting attorney investigating this case, Kevin Baxter. **So far, three people have been indicted on the basis of the evidence presented thus far.** (Jacqui Maiden, Kathleen Dreamer and Rosie Grier, an assistant manager with the board. All three still work at the board at the time of this writing.) The prosecuting attorney, Mr. Baxter, calls the videotapes I submitted the best evidence in the case. (At the time of the writing of this chapter, the trial for these three women is about to take place; however, there have been reports that there may still be more indictments of the higher-ups in the Cuyahoga Board of Elections.)

Questions have been raised by concerned citizens of Cleveland pertaining to the investigation, including allegations that Mr. Baxter may be less than vigilant in his efforts to get all the evidence relating to what really happened and everyone who knew about it. They are questioning why only mid-to-lower level election employees have been indicted, while those in positions of authority, such as County Elections Director Michael Vu and Deputy Director Gwen Dillingham, have been bypassed completely in having any responsibility for what their subordinates allegedly did in counting the ballots in private. Isn't it possible that these three women were only doing what they were instructed to do? What procedures used in past recounts were these women talking about? How could these same procedures be known only to these three women but not by the Director or Deputy Director? Would these three women conspire on their own to count these votes in private, without the knowledge of their superiors? Why would they take such a risk?

These are questions that should be answered to the satisfaction of the citizens of Cuyahoga County, who are not only paying for this investigation with their hard-earned tax dollars, but deserve nothing but the most thorough, honest and fair investigation Mr. Baxter can muster. These three women certainly deserve nothing less, as they face jail time and a felony charge permanently on their record if convicted. Time will tell if this investigation plays out to be just another "dog-and-pony show" to appease the people of Cuyahoga

County. It's up to all of us who are concerned about justice being done to make certain that doesn't happen and all of the appropriate people are held accountable.

❖ ❖ ❖

The Road Trip to Pick Up Public Records and More Dumpster Diving

There was another occasion when I was particularly happy that I had remembered to bring my video camera along for the ride. It was our visit to infamous Volusia County, Florida. I had been given the opportunity to travel along with Bev and Andy Stephenson, another Black Box Voting investigator at that time, throughout the country during the summer before the November 2004 Presidential Election, as well as after. During these trips, we conducted interviews with election officials and citizens, did a little "dumpster surveillance" and collected as many of the public records Black Box Voting had requested on election night from counties throughout the country as we could.

One of the most unforgettable and eventful episodes of this road trip was when Bev and I drove out to Volusia County, Florida and ended up making an unexpected side trip to Volusia County's elections warehouse early one morning in December 2004.

Right after midnight of the November 2004 Presidential Election, we had sent out by e-mail over 3,000 Freedom of Information Act requests for election records. One for each county in America. Our goal was to collect as many election documents as possible and scour them for irregularities or signs of nefarious activity. This was the first massive records request of its kind and would also prove to be the first steps in our learning how to conduct an effective citizen audit of an election. We were breaking new ground in what is meant by *meaningful citizen oversight* and we knew it.

Deanie Lowe, Volusia County's Supervisor of Elections at the time, told us that the election records we'd requested were there, *but for us not to go there, that they would bring them to us the next day.* Well, the first thing you learn in investigating election anomalies is when an election official in a problematic county tells you NOT to do something, as in this case, that's exactly the thing you must do, if at all possible!

The warehouse was located far off the beaten path, behind a sheriff's office, near a swampy looking area. Besides not being easily accessible, it also had signs that read "Authorized Personnel Only." Hmmm, what does one do in such a situation? We thought about it for about a minute and then decided to drive onto the premises, in spite of those signs, and made our way to the warehouse.

Bev and I were determined to find out what was going on in that warehouse and decided we would explain to them when we arrived that we wanted to save them the time and just come by the warehouse and pick up our public records. As soon as we arrived, we noticed that there were a lot of out-of-state cars parked in front of the warehouse. Wonder where they were from and why they were there? We also noticed a large, black plastic bag sitting on a concrete platform outside of the warehouse. It was open wide enough that one could see poll tapes and what looked like ballots sticking out of it. After we parked, we made our way to the entrance of the warehouse.

Inside, we found three election workers sitting at a table filled with poll tapes and pen in hand. When we asked if we could pick up our records, we were immediately told to leave and to return to the main elections office. It was quite evident from the shocked looks on their faces that they did not want us there. If only I'd had my camera with me then!

On our way back to the car, Bev told me she was not leaving without that black bag filled with potential evidence of wrongdoing. Whatever the risks involved in taking it, we knew it would be worth it. (Don't forget, the warehouse was right behind a sheriff's office). So, to make a long story short, Bev walked up to the bag and grabbed it. At the same moment that she was dragging it toward the car, an election employee by the name of "Pete" was walking towards her from behind. As he got closer I heard him ask, "What are you doing, you can't take that bag!" He then snatched the bag out of Bev's hands and put it back on the platform. Realizing that this was definitely going to be a "Kodak moment," I immediately grabbed my camera, got out of the car and started filming. Having the presence of mind to bring my video camera that morning gave me an opportunity to document on film, forever, a moment that can neither be forgotten nor rewritten in history.

A tug of war ensued over the garbage bag between Bev and Pete, resulting in the bag ripping open. Bev immediately began going through the documents, identifying them to the election employees who were standing around watching this event. Moments later, Bev grabbed one of the papers and hastily scribbled a public records request for the garbage bag, which she announced to my camera.

In the midst of all this activity, Pete told Bev that she couldn't take the bag and yelled out to someone to "call the sheriff's department." One thing is for certain, had I not had that video camera with me, we may well have been arrested and there's no telling what their story would have been regarding our exchange with them.

They knew it too. As I captured the event, I could see through the camera's lens that they were not comfortable being filmed. Getting the event caught on film during such a controversial confrontation with election officials does put you, the citizen, on equal ground with them. **With a video camera, you now have a witness to the event that can't be accused of being mistaken or lying. Now *that's* citizen empowerment!**

Ultimately, the Sheriff was called and one of his deputies did show up to check out the situation. In retrospect, I believe he decided not to detain us partly because we were two middle-aged women who clearly didn't seem to be a threat, AND because I had a video camera in my hand. After quietly explaining what had just transpired and telling the deputy that I had filmed the entire event, he decided to let us go. Happily, we made a clean getaway with the contents of the garbage bag! To this day, I think we avoided being arrested because of my new best friend—my video camera. To this day, I never leave home without it when I'm on a mission for BBV.

What we found was exactly what we had suspected: poll tapes (one of them signed by election officials) and sample ballots. There is no excuse for this. These election officials had to know that, by law, they were obligated to maintain and store all election records for 22 months. Clearly, Volusia County election employees were violating federal law by throwing away these records. Videotaping made it possible for us to prove this and to expose election officials flaunting election laws.

By simply taping the event as it occurred, the truth of what really happened was able to be told. It captured on film Bev's powerful display of patriotism in "real time," as it was happening. There's a special inspiration that comes from seeing one citizen standing up to several intimidating election officials and holding her ground in protecting her civil rights. Showing such moments to the public is one sure way to keep this movement alive and growing.

This is only the story of Volusia County, Florida; but reports from citizens around the country are telling many stories of wrongdoing by election officials. That is not to say that there are not thousands of election officials in America who are doing a wonderful job and are dedicated to what they do—administering fair and honest elections. It IS to acknowledge that many election officials are not following election procedures and laws.

❖ ❖ ❖

Citizens Getting Involved

Now that I am a full-time investigator for Black Box Voting and have been traveling around the country with Bev attending public meetings regarding election reform, voting machine security, or meeting with election officials, citizens and election reform advocates of all walks of life, and getting most of it on film, I would like to share with you some observations and thoughts about what we should do with what we've learned along the way.

By capturing all those events, I've created a virtual archive of a large cross-section of what's happening in the election reform movement. I believe that this film will be our memory of one of the most important times in our nation's history since the Revolutionary War. It will give us a way to go back in time and bring back to life those citizen patriots who have made great sacrifices and never gave up on democracy in spite of the overwhelming odds. It will be a gift from us to the next generation to guide them in not making the same mistakes we did when we abdicated to voting machine vendors our civil right as American citizens to oversee and manage our own elections. We must do everything we can to put elections back in the hands of citizens where they belong.

In an effort to help make that happen, Black Box Voting has launched an action alert to all citizens to take their video cameras with them to:

- public hearings/meetings;
- meetings with voting machine vendors;
- board of election meetings;
- election reform conferences;
- testing of voting machines (Logic & Accuracy tests required by every county); and
- elections

This would be one of the greatest collections of evidence showing the state of our elections in the most comprehensive way. It would be a powerful educational tool for citizens to use in winning this Herculean effort to achieve *meaningful election reform*. I hope citizens heed this call to action. It would really be something to see—a united citizenry gathering evidence and documenting elections throughout the nation. It would not only be an unprecedented display of patriotism, but a testament to the greatness of the American people when faced with extreme challenges: how they rise to the occasion.

If anything, citizens would learn, as I did, that seeing these events through the lens of a camera keeps it all in perspective like nothing else. In discovering this wonderful tool, you will see a side of human nature you would never have seen otherwise. Putting anything on film changes the way you see things. You get to see people up close and personal, and the camera's eye sees things the human eye can't. When filming a person, you find you really listen to what they have to say and listening opens all kinds of doors that bring people together on common ground.

It is in the capturing of thousands of these intense and sometimes special moments, along with the many wonderful patriots that are the life and breath of this country—moments that would otherwise be fleeting and pass unnoticed—that I feel I have found my niche in this noble fight. Through the lens of my camera, I can help create an historical quilt weaving together the many and varied stories that make up this movement and what we are trying to achieve. Through the neverending life of film, the truth will always be there when we need it to push us forward and to inspire us. Through this tapestry of labor and love, we can know the truth, and it is this truth that will set us free.

❖ ❖ ❖

Who We Are and What We Want to Achieve

Black Box Voting is a 501(c)(3) nonprofit, nonpartisan organization. We are a consumer protection for elections organization that investigates and provides hard evidence that would stand up in a court of law to support any claims we make relating to any and all aspects of flawed voting machines, insufficient certification procedures, insufficient election procedures and any violations of elections laws. We report these findings and post them on the BBV Web site so that other citizens can learn about these findings and benefit from them. Citizen oversight is best served by an informed citizenry.

Most importantly, BBV believes that there should be citizen oversight of the highest form in every phase of the election process. We cannot compromise on this requirement if we intend to achieve the kind of election reform we've been fighting so long and hard for—*period*. We cannot accept only peripheral oversight, but *real* oversight in which every average American citizen can participate, and a process they can understand without needing a Ph.D. or having to trust one.

This brings me to the kind of solution that, I feel, would embrace the kind of citizen oversight BBV wants to see. Being a non-technical person, I believe I speak for a large number of my fellow citizens when I say, **"we should return to hand counting paper ballots at the precinct level."** It's a simpler, more citizen-friendly method of voting that is totally transparent. Citizens advocating this method of voting can accomplish this only if they work together in developing a realistic, well-considered plan that addresses all the issues expressed by election officials and politicians, the majority of which are resisting changing back to hand counts. One must remember that many of them backed the very expensive decision to purchase electronic voting equipment. To admit that the purchase was a mistake, and that the simple solution of hand-counted paper ballots is a superior way to hold an election, would take some serious swallowing of pride.

Such a plan should also spell out the reasons why election officials and politicians *should* support hand counts, as well as how this method of voting could be implemented throughout the country and still meet all the various standards and laws that exist in the 50 states. Successful models for hand-counted paper ballot elections exist now and are still in place in many areas of our country, as well as parts of Canada, Australia and other countries as well.

One thing's certain: I don't think *trusting vendors* should be part of the equation any longer, considering **we've proven that at least two voting systems certified for use by the Independent Testing Labs have some of the worse security flaws ever found in a voting system,** and because the certification process itself has been proven to be totally broken. A broken certification process calls into question all voting systems recommended for certification. It doesn't get much worse than this. It's clear we need to change everything about how we're currently voting, from top to bottom. (See the following link to read a short briefing report on the testing labs certification failure: *http://www.blackboxvoting.org/itahearing.pdf.*)

Based on all the evidence uncovered by *Black Box Voting.org*, other election reform groups and organizations, and literally hundreds of citizens throughout the country, we can no longer accept on blind faith from the vendors, experts, politicians and election officials that our election process is working just fine and continue to outsource our elections to them. *Citizens must be involved in the election process at every level* and take back the oversight and management of our elections. It's our civil right, it's the way our forefathers meant it to be and it's the way it should be.

I borrow these words from poet and activist June Jordan, "We are the people we've been waiting for." So, people, let us unite with the same commitment and passion as they did in 1776, and take back our elections and our country!

Kathleen Wynne, Associate Director, Black Box Voting, has been a full-time investigator with Black Box Voting since the organization was founded in 2004. Wynne mentors citizens, teaching them how to monitor local elections and consults with public officials. She has testified at numerous public hearings and has provided evidence to members of the U.S. Congress, the EAC and other public bodies. Before coming to Black Box Voting, Wynne spent 20 years as a senior administrator with major New York City law firms. Her extensive legal experience has been invaluable in helping to teach citizens how to document elections problems with evidence that can stand up to scrutiny.

Wynne's videotapes documented recount breaches in the 2004 Ohio election which have since led to two indictments in Cuyahoga County. Her investigations into the money trail resulted in the first documented chain of money between Diebold and public officials. She also videotaped as elections records were pulled out of the Volusia County, Florida, garbage shortly after the November 2004 general election and other obstructiveness by election officials. She videotaped all four of the Black Box Voting "hack" studies by Harri Hursti and Dr. Herbert Thompson in Leon County, Florida, and Emery County, Utah.

Company Information on Electronic Voting Systems Vendors
(What you won't find on the company Web sites)

Bev Harris
from *Black Box Voting: Ballot Tampering in the 21st Century*

IF ANYTHING SHOULD REMAIN part of the public commons, it is voting. Yet, as we have progressed through a series of new voting methods, control of our voting systems and even our understanding of how they work, has come under new ownership.

> It's a shell game, with money, companies and corporate brands switching in a blur of buy-outs and bogus fronts. It's a sinkhole, where mobbed-up operators, paid-off public servants, crazed Christian fascists, CIA shadow-jobbers, war-pimping arms dealers—and presidential family members—lie down together in the slime. It's a hacker's dream, with pork-funded, half-finished, secretly-programmed computer systems installed without basic security standards by politically-partisan private firms, and protected by law from public scrutiny.[1]

The previous quote, printed in a Russian publication, leads an article that mixes inaccuracies with disturbing truths. Should we assume crooks are in control? Is it a shell game? Whatever it is, it certainly has deviated from community-based counting of votes by the local citizenry.

We began buying voting machines in the 1890s, choosing clunky mechanical lever machines, in part to reduce the shenanigans going on with manipulating paper ballot counts. By the 1960s, we had become enamored of the poke-a-hole method (punch cards). In the early 1980s, we saw the advent of fill-in-the-oval ballots, run through a scanner for tabulation (optical scan systems). In the mid-1990s, we decided to try computers that mark votes using touchscreens or dial-a-vote devices (direct recording electronic, or DRE, systems). Then we began experimenting with Internet voting.

We first relinquished control to local election workers, who managed lever machines and punch card voting. With the advent of optical scan systems, local election workers gradually gave up control to private, for-profit corporations and their programmers and technicians. In a frenzy of mergers and acquisitions during the 1980s, local election services companies sold control of our voting systems to a handful of corporations. During the 1990s, these corporations engaged in a pattern of setting up alliances and swapping key personnel, which has given just a few people, some of whom have vested interests, far too much access to and influence over our voting systems.

This is not a computer programming problem. It is a procedural matter, and part of the procedure must involve keeping human beings, as many of us as possible, in control of our own voting system. Any computerized voting system that requires us to trust a few computer scientists and some corporate executives constitutes flawed public policy. It doesn't matter whether they come up with perfect cryptographic techniques or invent smart cards so clever they can recognize us by sight. The real problem is that we've created a voting system controlled by someone else.

During the 1980s, mom-and-pop companies sold election supplies. That changed when the dominant player in the elections industry, Business Records Corp. (BRC), embarked on an acquisitions blitz. You'd almost think they wanted to corner the elections industry.

Business Records Corp. (BRC)

Business Records Corp. was a subsidiary of a Dallas, Texas, company named Cronus Industries Inc.,[2] which was owned by a consortium of wealthy Texas powerbrokers.

July 1984: BRC acquired Data Management Associates of Colorado Springs, Colorado, a closely held concern that supplied county governments with computer software and services, and acquired David G. Carney Co., a closely held San Antonio firm that marketed records-keeping services. Then it purchased the assets of C. Edwin Hultman Co., a closely held Pittsburgh company that provided county government information services.[3]

November 1984: BRC acquired Western Data Services Inc., a firm that provided online computer services to several hundred county and municipal governments, school districts and other governmental agencies in Texas.[4]

November 1984: BRC acquired Contract Microfilm Services and Business Images Inc.[5]

February 1985: BRC acquired Roberts & Son Inc. of Birmingham, Alabama, a firm which provided voting equipment and election materials to county governments.[6]

April 1985: BRC acquired Frank Thornber Co., a Chicago firm specializing in election-related services, equipment and supplies.[7]

November 1985: BRC acquired Dayton Legal Blank Co.[8]

December 1985: Cronus Industries Inc., the parent company of BRC, completed the purchase of Computer Election Systems Inc. of Berkeley, California. At that time, Computer Election Systems was the nation's largest manufacturer of election machines and related equipment. It provided election computer programs and equipment to more than 1,000 county and municipal jurisdictions.[9]

January 1986: BRC acquired Integrated Micro Systems Inc. of Rockford, Illinois.[10]

March 1986: BRC merged with Computer Concepts & Services Inc. of St. Cloud, Minnesota.[11] During the same month, it acquired Sun Belt Press Inc. of Birmingham, Alabama, and merged it into Roberts & Son Inc. one of the election and voting equipment companies acquired by BRC in February 1985. It also bought the government operations of Minneapolis-based Miller/Davis Company. The government portion of Miller/Davis provided legal forms, election supplies and office supplies to local governments in Minnesota.[12] Business Records Corp. dominated the U.S. elections industry until 1997, when it was purchased by Election Systems and Software.

Election Systems and Software (ES&S)

Founded in Omaha, Nebraska, under the name Data Mark Systems by brothers Todd and Bob Urosevich, the company soon changed its name to American Information Systems (AIS). In 1984, the Uroseviches obtained financing from William and Robert Ahmanson, whose family piled up a fortune in the savings and loan and insurance industries.[13] Howard Ahmanson Jr., a younger cousin of the AIS financiers, has parlayed his fortune into extremist right-wing politics, pushing the agenda of the Christian Reconstructionist movement, which openly advocates a theocratic takeover of American democracy.[14] William and Robert Ahmanson appeared to be more moderate than Howard Jr. and invested money in theater and public broadcasting. In 1987, they sold their direct shares in the voting machine company to the Omaha World-Herald (which took a 45 percent stake in the company) and the McCarthy Group (35 percent).[15]

And here the fun begins—watch the bouncing ball. . .

It turns out that the Omaha World-Herald has also been an owner of the McCarthy Group.[16] The Omaha World-Herald was owned by Peter Kiewit, the head of Peter Kiewit Sons' Inc., until his death.[17] Before he died, Peter Kiewit set up the Peter Kiewit Foundation, requiring that at all times the foundation have a director from Peter Kiewit Sons' Inc. as a trustee. Kiewit arranged for the Omaha World-Herald stock to be purchased by its employees and the Peter Kiewit Foundation, which holds a special class of stock, giving it veto power over any sale proposal. The largest single stockholder in the World-Herald Company is the Peter Kiewit Foundation.[18]

Tracing ES&S ownership thus leads us to the *Omaha World-Herald* and then to the Peter Kiewit Foundation. It also leads to the McCarthy Group, which is headed by Michael McCarthy. He came to Omaha to sell Peter Kiewit's ranch when he died. Michael McCarthy assumed Peter Kiewit Jr.'s position as a director of Peter Kiewit Sons' Inc. in 2001.[19] The McCarthy Group shows up as one of the investments of a World-Herald subsidiary, in turn leading back to the *Omaha World-Herald* and the Peter Kiewit Foundation.

Dizzy yet?

I became interested in Kiewit because if anything is less appropriate than Chuck Hagel's ties to ES&S, it would be a Kiewit relationship of any kind to any voting system vendor. So who is Kiewit?

Peter Kiewit Sons' Inc. and its subsidiaries have been tied to a string of bid-rigging cases in as many as 11 states and two countries. In an antitrust case that involved charges of bid-rigging in New Orleans, Kiewit pleaded no contest and paid $100,000 in fines and $300,000 in a civil settlement. In South Dakota, a Kiewit subsidiary pleaded guilty to bid-rigging on road contracts and paid a fine of $350,000. In Kansas, a Kiewit subsidiary was found guilty of bid-rigging and mail fraud on a federal highway project. The firm was fined $900,000 and a company official was sentenced to a year in jail. A Kiewit subsidiary paid $1.8 million for bid-rigging on a state highway project in Nebraska, and a Kiewit vice president was jailed.[20]

The Army Corps of Engineers at one point decided to bar Kiewit from bidding on all federal projects but later changed its mind. Kiewit builds munitions plants and military airstrips. Does Kiewit have a political agenda? Absolutely. Kiewit's Jerry Pfeffer has spoken before Congress to ask for more privatization. "Kiewit, based in Omaha, built more lane-miles of the Interstate Highway System than any other contractor," he said. ". . . We're active in toll roads, airports and water facilities. . ."[21]

Pfeffer, advocating privatization of the highway system, has stated glibly that "American motorists will gladly pay market prices to avoid congestion." He goes on to suggest to Congress that Kiewit should get special tax treatment. Kiewit also owns CalEnergy Corp., has been involved with Level 3 Communications, and is a quiet giant in telecommunications; underneath its highways, Kiewit lays fiber optic cable and has been outfitting our roads with video surveillance cameras since 1993.

When the state of Oklahoma forbade Kiewit to bid anymore, Kiewit set up a different company called Gilbert Southern Corp. According to the *Sunday Oklahoman*, "Gilbert Southern Corp. recently submitted a sworn affidavit to the transportation department saying it had no parent company, affiliate firms or subsidiaries."[22] But Kiewit owned Gilbert Southern Corp. lock, stock and barrel. When the state of Oklahoma found out, it yanked the contracts.

In another obfuscation, Peter Kiewit & Sons took contracts in Washington State under the guise of a minority-owned firm. The government thought it was giving contracts to a company owned by African American women; actually, it was a bunch of white guys in Nebraska. Kiewit paid more than $700,000 in fines while denying liability or wrongdoing.[23] Kiewit's corporate papers indicate that investigations and litigation are normal, saying there are "numerous" lawsuits. This is a handy thing to know; apparently you can skip disclosure of pending litigation, if there's a lot of it.

This example illustrates why voting machine vendors should be required to provide full disclosure on owners, parent companies, stockholders and key personnel. Kiewit has connections with both ES&S parent companies and has a track record of hiding ownership when it wants to, it has a powerful profit motive for getting the people it wants into office and it has broken the law in the past to achieve its goals.

We should require enough disclosure so that we can at least ask informed questions next time we buy voting machines.

In 1997, the company that had called itself American Information Systems bought elections industry giant BRC and changed its name to Election Systems and Software. The Securities and Exchange

Commission objected on antitrust grounds, and an odd little deal was cooked up in which the assets of BRC were shared between two voting companies, ES&S and Sequoia.

Sequoia Voting Systems

Sequoia Voting Systems has nearly jockeyed its way into position to grab voting-machine dominance away from ES&S and Diebold. We are told to trust Sequoia's voting systems, along with the people who sell and service them. Well, come with me for a moment and let's do a little re-enactment. After this, you, the jury, can decide for yourself how much trust you want to offer Sequoia.

You be Philip Foster, Sequoia's southern regional sales manager and the project manager who oversaw Riverside County, California's first touchscreen election. I'll be your brother-in-law, David Philpot of Birmingham, Alabama.

I am going to hand you a manila envelope stuffed with $20,000 or $40,000 of kickback cash.[24] These envelopes are sealed, and I won't tell you what is in them. I instruct you to travel to Louisiana and place them in a drawer belonging to Louisiana State Elections Chief Jerry Fowler. You do so. And then you do it again. Five times. If we are to trust Sequoia Voting Systems, we must believe that Phil Foster had no idea what was in those envelopes. Foster said in an interview that he did nothing wrong. He continued to work for Sequoia after these allegations were revealed.

Peter Cosgrove, Sequoia's chief executive officer at the time, decided that the allegations against Foster (two counts of conspiracy to commit money laundering and one count of conspiracy to commit malfeasance in office) were "without merit," so he continued to employ him.

"As a company, we believe the allegations against him are without merit," said Cosgrove, "and we believe the statements against him were made by convicted felons."[25] Well that much is true. Both Foster's brother-in-law, David Philpot, and Louisiana's elections chief,

Jerry Fowler, pleaded guilty. Fowler went to federal prison. Another
participant in the scam, which reportedly cost Louisiana taxpayers
$8 million, was New Jersey's Pasquale Ricci, who pleaded guilty to
conspiracy to commit money laundering.[26]

When the charges against Foster were thrown out, the prosecu-
tor appealed. State District Judge Bonnie Jackson upheld the dismissal
of charges, ruling that prosecutors had failed to show the charges
resulted from evidence collected separately from Foster's grand jury
testimony. Because he had been immunized, prosecutors could not
use Foster's own statements against him.[27] "My investigation of the
charges reveals he hasn't done a thing in the world wrong," Foster's
Baton Rouge lawyer, Karl Koch is reported to have said.

OK. Let us assume that Foster really had no idea what was in
those envelopes. Forty thousand dollars is a minimum of four hundred $100 bills, a pile two inches thick. We are trusting these guys
with our vote. Do we really want someone around our voting machines who is so naive that he doesn't understand the implications
of sticking manila envelopes stuffed with two-inch-thick wads of
something shaped like money into desk drawers belonging to election officials?

Of the big four voting vendors, Sequoia currently has the tidiest
corporate ownership but the most recent indictment of an employee
and the most prolific habit of hiring its own regulators. Besides hiring former California Secretary of State Bill Jones, Sequoia hired
Kathryn Ferguson, the elections official who helped purchase Sequoia
machines for Clark County, Nevada, and Santa Clara County, California, as vice president, corporate communications.

In October 2003, she moved to Hart InterCivic.[28] Michael Frontera,
former executive director of the Denver Election Commission, went
to work for Sequoia after awarding it $6.6 million in contracts from
his own department.[29] Alfie Charles, former spokesman for Secretary of State Bill Jones, is now spokesman for Sequoia Voting Systems.[30] At the time of the bribery scandal, Sequoia Voting Systems

was owned by Jefferson Smurfit Group, a company based in Ireland. In May 2002, Sequoia was purchased by Great Britain's De La Rue PLC, and Phil Foster's loyal and trusting boss, Peter Cosgrove, was retained and promoted.

De La Rue is considered a blue chip company. Its fortunes are heavily affected by politics, and it has at least one politically active investor. It is the world's biggest commercial money printer. De La Rue was one of the first British companies to profit from the war in Iraq, earning a quick windfall when it received the assignment to print the new Iraqi bank notes. During the first Bush administration, De La Rue was called in toward the tail end of Sandinista rule in Nicaragua to create new money.[31] De La Rue is also involved in Britain's national lottery through its investment in Camelot Group plc. In this capacity, it enraged British citizens when they learned that Camelot had assigned its executives a 40 percent pay hike while reducing the funds allocated to good works.[32]

De La Rue would very much like to take Diebold's position, and not just in election systems. The firm also sells ATMs and smart cards and lists Diebold Inc. as one of its competitors.[33]

In July 2003, the U.S. Department of Justice launched an investigation into a U.S. division of De La Rue, alleging that it had engaged in an illegal price-fixing scheme in relation to the supply of holograms for Visa banking cards, violating U.S. antitrust laws. In a statement, De La Rue said the "individual implicated" in the price-fixing allegation had "left the business in October 1999."[34] One of the most aggressive investors in De La Rue stock is the hugely wealthy Australian Lowy family, who, by March 2003, had picked up 5.5 million shares (just over 3%) through their private investment vehicle, LFG Holdings. Frank Lowy is Australia's second richest man. He is highly political, particularly with pro-Israel issues, and has come under fire for his company's payments to Lord Levy (British Prime Minister Tony Blair's special envoy to the Middle East), which the Aussie billionaire authorized directly. At first, his payments raised suspicions of a cash for access intrigue at the highest level of British politics, but as the size of the payments (£250,000 or $460,000 USD) became apparent, the Australian media began raising questions of cash for foreign policy.[35]

The Lowy family contributes heavily to the Democratic Party.[36] On August 4, 2003, Sequoia Voting Systems quietly announced a partnership with VoteHere Inc. for electronic ballot verification on its touchscreen machines.[37] **It is amazing how much money the elections industry is willing to spend just to avoid giving us ballots we can read and use for audits.**

The VoteHere system provides a receipt with a code number on it, not a human readable ballot. You get to check your single vote using a secret code. If you believe this constitutes public counting of the vote then please meet me under the bridge at midnight and enter your special password into my PalmPilot, and I'll slip you a brown paper bag with some stock tips in it. Count on 'em. Trust me.

Instead of allowing the vote to be counted in the open, viewed by citizens, the VoteHere solution requires us to give control of our elections to a handful of cryptographers with defense industry ties.

VoteHere Inc.

Like a Timex watch, this company takes a licking but keeps on ticking. Launched by a cryptographer named Jim Adler during the height of the dot-com boom, VoteHere hoped to usher us into the brave new world of Internet voting. Adler picked up funding from Compaq Computer, Cisco Systems and Northwest Venture Associates, $15 million by November 2000.[38] He also did an honorable thing: He made his company's source code available for review.

Adler's Internet voting system did not fare well in a simple review titled, "Vote Early, Vote Often and VoteHere: A Security Analysis of VoteHere," a master's thesis by Philip E. Varner. After defining threats to the publicly available VoteHere system in such areas as completeness, privacy, verifiability, fairness and reliability and creating an attack tree, Varner identified several weaknesses in the VoteHere system and concluded it was not ready for use.[39]

Undaunted, the entrepreneurial Adler charged ahead with a plan to have us try voting on totable Compaq iPAQ hardware using VoteHere software and online polling sites connected to the Internet.[40]

But his Internet plans did not materialize, and Adler also stopped making his source code available for public review. VoteHere persuaded places like Swindon, England, and the city of Suwanee, Georgia, to try the system and conducted an online advisory election for the Conservative Party in Sweden. But by 2003, it had few sales to show for six years of work and $15 million in outside investments.

I have seen no more sources of funding for VoteHere, nor much in the way of sales revenues, but one thing I did find was a board of directors spiked with powerbrokers from the defense industries. For a long time, VoteHere's chairman was Admiral Bill Owens, a member of the Defense Policy Board and Vice Chairman of Scientific Applications International Corp. (SAIC), which performed the Diebold review for the state of Maryland. Robert Gates, former CIA director and head of the George Bush School of Business at Texas A&M, was another director. VoteHere may be trying to make a comeback with its Internet voting concept. It hired former Washington State Secretary of State Ralph Munro as its chairman. Pam Floyd, who had worked for Washington State Elections Director David Elliott, left to take a position with VoteHere for three years; she recently became Washington's assistant state elections director and she oversees Washington's Internet SERVE project.

Washington State is now leaving the door open (through legislation proposed by Munro crony and current Secretary of State Sam Reed) to arrange for more Internet voting in the state.

In 2003, VoteHere decided to go after the innards of other vendors' touchscreens, perhaps hoping to become the Good

Housekeeping Seal of Approval for electronic voting machines by claiming that its system verifies the integrity of the vote. This verification system is another way to avoid giving voters the paper ballots they are asking for.

I had always been a proponent of hybrid systems, combining voter verified paper ballots with computers. **Systems like VoteHere, though, make me wonder if we aren't safer going back to straight hand-counted paper ballots.** Every time we propose a solution to solve a problem with computerized voting systems, a new salesman pops up with a different cure, new techno-jargon, a fresh sales pitch and friends in high places, and starts lobbying our public officials. By the time we figure out the latest spin, it could be too late.

❖ ❖ ❖

VoteHere had its eye on a Pentagon project called SERVE, designed to convert our armed forces over to Internet voting. Despite its clout, VoteHere did not win the contract. Instead, the contract was awarded to *election.com* and Hart InterCivic.

election.com

This company is no longer in existence, at least in its original form. I am including it so that you can see just how slipshod our government procurement system, which originally awarded the SERVE contract to *election.com*, really is. According to its Web site, *election.com* was a global election software and services company, which provided election services like voter registration and Internet voting. *Newsday*'s Mark Harrington discovered that *election.com* had sold controlling ownership to an unnamed group of Saudi investors who, he reported, paid $1.2 million to acquire 20 million preferred shares, for 51.6 percent of the voting power. The investment group was identified as Osan Ltd.[41]

I spoke with Amy Parker, press contact for *election.com*, in February 2003.

Harris: "Is the *Newsday* article, which states that 51.6% of *election.com* is owned by Osan Ltd, accurate?"

Parker: "No, that is not true."

Harris: "Is Osan Ltd. involved?"

Parker: "Osan Ltd. became the largest shareholder of *election.com* in December 2002—that's an accurate statement—and after December 2002 Osan held 36.2% of all outstanding shares."

Harris: "Is Osan based in the United States, or where?"

Parker: "In the Cayman Islands."

Harris: "So when *Newsday* said they have controlling interest. . ."

Parker: "After December 2002, Osan held 36.2% of all outstanding shares. And that's equal to 58.2% of the voting power."

OK. So Osan actually owned *more* controlling interest than reported by *Newsday*. Why would we want our military votes counted by a Saudi-owned company? At least, if it's approved by the Pentagon, one would assume that it's a pretty solid operation. But for some reason, *election.com* pulled the names of its directors off the Internet. There are ways to find pages that have been removed, so I did and began contacting directors.

I soon received an e-mail from one of the directors, which said simply, "You should call me."

I did, and he spoke with me at some length but only after getting my agreement not to reveal which director he was when I printed this interview.

Harris: "I notice they've taken the names off the Web. Are you still involved?"

Director: "No."

Harris: "Tell me about your experience with *election.com*."

Director: It looked like a hot company, [was] featured in *Red Herring* as one of the companies most likely to affect the world and all that. . . What happened is that Joe—they had a CEO named Joe, Joe something. . ."

Harris: "Joe Mohen?"

Director: "That's it. He ended up loving publicity too much. They put those machines in on the Democratic Convention, a giant waste of money, over a million, so Joe could get on TV. When they wanted to start going that way I got concerned. If they were getting into public elections, the market wasn't as huge [as elections in the private market, such as stockholder votes and union elections].

"Of course, the reason I got into it was we wanted to run a business, we wanted to become profitable. . . . So, the 2000 election in Florida happens, and they change their philosophy and want to do public elections. I said 'this isn't going to work.'

"Finally we get Joe to resign as CEO and we got the Number 2 guy [Charles Smith] to resign also. By this time we were about out of money."(He explained that they brought in a new CEO, who pumped in new money and got some contracts in Australia, but it wasn't long before they ran out of money again.)

Director continuing: "Then, the guy we fired [Charles Smith] comes back with this Arab money. They wanted the board as well as the company. For $5 million, they bought the whole damn thing. At the time the Arab money came in, I made the motion to go ahead and dismiss our butts."

Harris: "What about Charles Smith? I hear he's the guy who represents the Arabs."

Director: "Charles Smith is the guy who we fired. He is sort of an Arab himself; I don't know why he has the name Smith."[According to his bio, Smith previously worked with Procter & Gamble in Saudi Arabia and with PepsiCo in Cairo.]

Harris: "Who else is in the group of investors?"

Director: "Nobody knows who this group is."

Harris: "How Saudi is Osan Ltd?"

Director: "Oh, it's all Saudi as far as I know. What do you know about the thing?"

Harris: "Just what I read in *Newsday*."

According to the *Newsday* article, Defense Department spokesman Glenn Flood, when asked how the department screens the background of contractors, said: "We don't look into that [country of origin] part of it... It's the process we're interested in, not the company, unless they screw up."

Penelope Bonsall, director of election administration for the Federal Election Commission, told *Newsday* that tracking issues like *election.com*'s change of control doesn't fall under the purview of any federal agency.

I decided to ask Amy Parker more about the Pentagon deal, but the conversation got derailed:

Harris: "With regard to the military contract, what will *election.com* be doing and what will Hart InterCivic do?"

Parker: "We're not the prime contractor on that project."

Harris: "*Election.com* is not the main contractor?"

Parker: "No."

Harris: "Who is, then?"

Parker: "That's Accenture."

Harris: "I spoke with Hart InterCivic, who has explained to me that Accenture does not make voting systems. What they do is procurement. They procured the contract and then subcontracted it to *election.com* and Hart InterCivic, is that true?"

Parker: "Yes."

Harris: "Accenture holds shares in *election.com* also, doesn't it?"

Parker: "No."

Harris: "No?"

Parker: "Accenture, we have a formal strategic marketing alliance and as part of that they took an equity position."

Harris: "So, Accenture holds shares in *election.com*, then."

Parker: "Yes."

On July 2, 2003, *election.com* announced that it had sold its assets to Accenture, turning the military SERVE project over to an Arthur Andersen spin-off and Hart InterCivic.

Hart InterCivic

You might get the impression that Hart InterCivic, a voting system vendor based in Austin, Texas, is a cozy little family owned operation, giving us real faces that we can hold accountable and trust with our vote. Not quite.

The chairman of Hart InterCivic is David Hart, whose family developed Hart Graphics, at one time the largest privately held commercial printer in Texas.[42] Internet growth and the ease of putting documentation on disks and CD-ROMs reversed the company's fortunes.

"We began to see, in the later part of the '90s, a crack in the strategy," David Hart said. "The presses weren't staying busy." In looking for other work to fill the void, "we just ran into a wall. We were singularly unsuccessful."[43] And it was here that the comfortable, family owned company turned into a venture-capital- and government-privatization-driven election vendor. Hart InterCivic sells the eSlate, a dial-a-vote variation on the touchscreen concept that uses a wheel instead of a poke with a finger to register your vote.

The finances and managerial control of Hart Graphics were at one time closely controlled by the family, but Hart took a different approach to its election business. They lined up three rounds of venture capital and formed an alliance with a gigantic social services privatizer. For initial funding, Hart went to Triton Ventures, a wholly owned subsidiary of Triton Energy, a firm that primarily exploits oil fields in Colombia. Triton, in turn, is a subsidiary of Amerada Hess.[44]

The $3.5 million awarded by Triton in 1999 didn't last long, but the Help America Vote Act, with its massive allocation of federal money, hovered just over the horizon. In October 2000, Hart picked up $32.5 million more from five sources.[45] In 2002, it raised another $7.5 million.[46]

RES Partners, which invested in Hart's second and third rounds, is an entity that represents Richard Salwen, retired Dell Computer Corporation vice president, general counsel and corporate secretary, who had also worked with Perot Systems and EDS. Salwen is a heavy contributor to George W. Bush and the Republican Party.[47]

Hart's most politically charged investor is an arm of Hicks, Muse, Tate, & Furst, which was founded and is chaired by Tom Hicks. Hicks bought the Texas Rangers in 1999, making George W. Bush a millionaire 15 times over. Tom Hicks and his investment company are invested in Hart InterCivic through Stratford Capital. They are also heavily invested in Clear Channel Communications, the controversial radio-raider that muscled a thousand U.S. radio outlets into a more conservative message.[48]

In Orange County, California, and in the state of Ohio, Hart InterCivic entered into a joint enterprise called Maximus/Hart InterCivic/DFM Associates, led by Maximus Inc. Maximus Inc. is a gigantic privatizer of social services. It cuts deals with state governments to handle child support collections, implement welfare-to-work and oversee managed care and HMO programs.

A Wisconsin legislative audit report found that Maximus spent more than $400,000 of state money on unauthorized expenses and found $1.6 million that Maximus couldn't properly document. These unauthorized expenses included a party for staff members at a posh Lake Geneva resort; $23,637 for "fanny packs" to promote the company, with the bills sent to the state; and entertainment of staff and clients by actress Melba Moore. Maximus settled for $1 million.[49] Maximus jumped into the smart card business and soon afterward entered the elections industry through an alliance with Hart InterCivic.

All this alliance building and venture capital seeking and political shoulder rubbing is very nice for the big boys in Texas. However, it fundamentally changes the way we run our democracy. Do we really need to bring in Maximus, Hart InterCivic, DFM Associates, Triton Oil, CapStreet Group, Dell Computers, Texas Growth Fund, and the owner of the Texas Rangers, just to count a vote?

The voting machine industry has created such a byzantine path to computerized voting that it cannot possibly be cheaper or more efficient than voting in a much simplified way.

What do we really know about the certifier, Wyle Laboratories?

Texas billionaires Sam and Charles Wyly were the ninth-biggest contributors to George W. Bush in 2000, and Sam Wyly bankrolled the dirty tricks that wiped out John McCain's lead during the South Carolina primary. I wondered if the Wyly brothers are involved in Wyle (pronounced Wyly). I found many Wyly companies, and at least two companies called Wyly E. Coyote, but never found a link between Texas Bush pals, the Wyly brothers and Wyle Laboratories. I did find a link between Wyle Laboratories and prominent, right-wing, monied interests: William E. Simon, who, along with Richard Mellon Scaife and the Coors family, has been one of the primary supporters of the Heritage Foundation and its derivatives.

And I did find conflict of interest. You would expect that a company that certifies our voting machines would not have its owners running for office. You would also expect that no one who owns the certification company would be under criminal investigation. You'd be disappointed.

Shortly after Wyle Laboratories split off from Wyle Electronics in 1994, controlling interest was acquired by William E. Simon & Sons, a firm owned by a former Secretary of the Treasury, William E. Simon, and his son, Bill Simon, a candidate for governor of California in 2002. Just before the election, in August 2002, William E. Simon & Sons was convicted of fraud and ordered to pay $78 million in damages. In what is surely record time for our glacial judicial system, the conviction was overturned in September 2002. The reason? William E. Simon & Sons had partnered up with someone who was a criminal and no one could tell who was the guiltiest.[50]

Recently, Wyle Laboratory shares held by William E. Simon & Sons were bought out. Now Wyle Laboratories is a wholly owned subsidiary of LTS Holdings Inc., an entity I can find no information about, controlled by individuals whose names are unavailable.

Diebold Election Systems

By now, Diebold Inc., the owner of what is now arguably the largest voting machine company in the United States, has become famous for its vested interests and an idiotic written statement made by its CEO. Diebold director W. H. Timken has raised over $100,000 for the 2004 campaign of George W. Bush, earning the designation "Pioneer." Bush supporters qualify as Pioneers if they raise at least $100,000, and Rangers if they raise $200,000.[51]

On June 30, 2003, Diebold CEO Waldon O'Dell organized a fundraising party for Vice President Dick Cheney, raising $600,000 and many of our antennas.[52] Julie Carr Smyth, of the *Plain Dealer*, discovered in August 2003, that O'Dell had traveled to Crawford, Texas, for a Pioneers and Rangers meeting attended by George W. Bush. Then Smyth learned of a letter, written by O'Dell shortly after returning from the Bush ranch and sent to 100 of his wealthy and politically inclined friends, which said, "I am committed to helping Ohio deliver its electoral votes to the president next year."[53]

Admitting that such candor was a mistake, O'Dell later told Smyth, "I don't have a political adviser or a screener or a letter reviewer or any of that stuff."[54] O'Dell described Diebold as "a model of integrity and reporting and clarity and disclosure and consistency" and said he hoped his company would not suffer because of his mistake. A model of integrity and—clarity? Disclosure, perhaps, if you count embarrassing leaks and the sharp hissing sound of security flying out the window. Wally O'Dell's statement was ill-advised, if not downright arrogant. But while Wally O'Dell can write about delivering the vote, Diebold's programmers may be in a position to actually do so. Where do they come from?

Diebold Election Systems was formed when Diebold Inc. of Canton, Ohio, acquired a Canadian company called Global Election Systems Inc., headquartered in Vancouver, British Columbia.[55] In some ways, nothing changed. The manufacturing body of the elections company continued to be in McKinney, Texas, under the same management, and the programming brain continued to be in Vancouver, Canada, with the same programmers.

Two of these programmers, Talbot Iredale and Guy Lancaster, have been designing and programming voting machines for Diebold Election Systems Inc. and its predecessors since 1988. Iredale and Lancaster developed the ES-2000 optical scan voting system currently used in 37 states.[56]

These two men worked for North American Professional Technologies (NAPT), a subsidiary of Macrotrends International Ventures Inc. Their assignment was to develop a computerized voting system. Macrotrends and NAPT were marketed by Norton Cooper, who had been jailed for defrauding the Canadian government in 1974.[57] This did not keep him out of trouble. He became a stock promoter who sold so much stock in flawed companies through Macrotrends that Jaye Scholl, a writer for *Barron's*, portrayed him as a "hazard" and cautioned the well-heeled to avoid him at the golf course.[58]

In 1989, members of the Vancouver Stock Exchange (VSE) ordered Macrotrends to cease any doings with Cooper because his deals went south too often and *Forbes* had written an article describing the VSE as "The Scam Capital of the World," causing an erosion of confidence in the entire exchange.[59]

Charles Hong Lee, a director of both Macrotrends and NAPT, was a childhood friend of Cooper's. In 1989, Lee was ordered to pay $555,380 in restitution when Lee was sued, together with Norton Cooper, by investors in a Macrotrends venture called Image West Entertainment. Cooper settled, but Lee failed to answer the complaint and also failed to list the lawsuit on his personal disclosure form with immigration officials. In 1994, Lee and his partner, Michael K. Graye, allegedly bilked 43 Chinese immigrants, mostly small businessmen, out of $614,547 more in fees than was authorized by the agreement. The unauthorized fees were paid to United Pacific Management Ltd., controlled by Graye and Lee.[60]

In 1991, NAPT and Macrotrends were reorganized, and the name was changed to Global Election Systems. At this time, Michael K. Graye became a director, a position he held for two years.

Earlier, Graye had misappropriated $18 million from four corporations, but the law had not yet caught up with him. In 1996, Graye was arrested on charges of tax fraud, conspiracy to commit tax fraud and money laundering, stemming from activities from 1987 through 1991 with four other companies.

For Graye to make bail, a Hong Kong-based shell company called Nexus Ventures Ltd. obtained $300,000 from unwitting investors in Eron Mortgage. Before Graye's sentence could be pronounced in Canada, he was indicted in the United States on stock fraud charges for his involvement with Vinex Wines Inc., a company he and Charles Hong Lee ran. Graye spent four years in prison on the charges related to Vinex Wines and was returned to Canada in May 2000; in April 2003, he admitted that he had misappropriated $18 million and committed tax fraud, and he was sent back to jail.[61]

These founding partners, along with Clinton Rickards (sometimes listed as C. H. Richards), set up Macrotrends, NAPT and then Global Election Systems. During these early years, Iredale and Lancaster nurtured the ES-2000 optical scan voting system into existence.

The company appears to have washed its hands of Cooper, Lee, and Graye. These criminals were involved a decade ago, so why is this relevant now? It's important because it tells us something about the ethics and due diligence of both Diebold and Global Election Systems. If you are asking people to trust you with their votes, but convicted felons hired and managed the programmers who are now your key people, you have some explaining to do. If criminals who were managing your company were written up in *Barron's* and *Forbes*, publicly embarrassing everyone, we would expect that you would rid yourself forever of such people. If you then hire two more convicted felons, you have just demonstrated that we cannot trust you with our votes.

One such felon, a 23-count embezzler named Jeffrey Dean who specialized in computer fraud, was made a director of Global Election Systems in 2000 and then was assigned to be the head of research and development, with access to all components of the most sensitive parts of the voting system. The other, a cocaine trafficker named John Elder, has directed the sensitive punch card printing for both Global and Diebold, and has had involvement with the processing of incoming absentee ballots. Elder is still running the printing division for Diebold.

By 2001, Global Election Systems had grown substantially, but had accumulated a pile of debt. Diebold Inc. began making arrangements to purchase the company in June 2001. Diebold made a sizeable loan to Global in 2001 and, according to securities documents, arranged to take over manufacturing of Global's voting machines when the Canadian firm could not come up with the cash to service its orders.

While Diebold was loaning money to Global, embezzler Jeffrey Dean remained a director of the company and, according to memos, was involved with the Windows CE system used in the touchscreens and the new 1.96 series optical scan software. He also was working on a project to integrate voter registration software with the GEMS central tabulation program, and he claimed to have developed a "ballot on demand" system which, he bragged to Diebold, could optionally connect a voter with the ballot—a feature which is certainly illegal and would remove voter privacy.

Global Election Systems was formally purchased by Diebold Inc. effective January 31, 2002, and at this time Jeffrey Dean became a paid consultant to Diebold Election Systems and John Elder took over Diebold's national printing division.

Six weeks later, Diebold landed the biggest voting machine order in history: The $54 million conversion of the state of Georgia to touchscreen voting.

Endnotes

1. *The St. Petersburg Times* (Russia), 23 September 2003; "Chris Floyd's Global Eye."

2. *The Wall Street Journal*, 27 December 1985; "Cronus Director Lowers Stake to 5.4% From 12%."

3. Dow Jones News Service—Ticker, 26 July 1984; "Cronus Indus announces several acquisitions."

4. *The Wall Street Journal*, 2 November 1984; "Cronus Unit Acquisition."

5. Dow Jones News Service, 8 November 1984; "Cronus Industries unit acquires two firms in Oklahoma."

6. Dow Jones News Service—Ticker, 22 February 1985; "Cronus Industries unit buys Roberts & Son Inc."

7. Dow Jones News Service—Ticker, 28 March 1985; "Cronus Indus unit acquires Frank Thornber Co."

8. Dow Jones News Service—Ticker, 27 March 1985; "Cronus Indus unit acquires Dayton Legal Blank Co."

9. PR Newswire, 16 December 1985; "Cronus Industries Inc. Acquires Computer Election Systems Inc."

10. Dow Jones News Service—Ticker, 8 January 1986; "Cronus Indus unit acquires Integrated Micro Systems."

11. Dow Jones News Service—Ticker, 5 March 1986 "Cronus Indus unit combines with Computer Concepts."

12. Dow Jones News Service—Ticker, 5 March 1986 "Cronus Indus unit acquires two businesses."

13. *The Omaha World-Herald*, 28 February 1984; "Election Year Boosts Fortunes of Omaha Firm."

14. *San Francisco Examiner*, 4 August 1999; "Conservative group gears up for 2000 vote in California."

15. *The Omaha World-Herald*, 3 June 1994; "Welsh Named Top Executive, Board Member."

16. *The Omaha World-Herald*, 10 April 1996; "McCarthy Transfers Acceptance Shares."

17. *Barron's*, 17 June 1996; "The Other Man From Omaha."

18. *The Omaha World-Herald*, 12 June 1984; "84,000-Acre Kiewit Ranch Fails to Attract Any Buyers."

19. *The Omaha World-Herald*, 15 July 2001; "Business People Lyman-Richey Names Officers."

20. *Newsday*, 25 March 1986; "Convicted Firm Got City Pacts."

21. Political Transcripts by Federal Document Clearing House, 18 July 1996.

22. *The Sunday Oklahoman*, 3 July 1983; "Public Agencies, Probed Firms Doing Business."

23. *Sunday Times* (London), 17 November 1996; "Rec bidder under fire."

24. *The Baton Rouge Advocate*, 16 August 2001; "Ala. businessman pleads guilty to role in election-machine scam."

25. *The Press-Enterprise*, 19 August 2001; "Louisiana charges are unrelated to work with Riverside County voting machines."

26. *The Baton Rouge Advocate*, 20 August 1999; "Fowler indicted in scheme, Audit led to malfeasance, laundering counts."

27. *Saturday State Times/Morning Advocate*, 15 February 2003; "Appeals court affirms decision to toss case. Immunity deal was in place, judge says."

28. Business Wire, 27 October 2003; "Kathryn Ferguson, Former California and Texas Election Official, Joins Hart InterCivic to Head Company's Voter Registration Group."

29. *Denver Post*, 30 December 1998; "Election chief takes job with department contractor."

30. *Los Angeles Times*, 15 November 2003; "The State; Elections Worker Is Transferred; A state employee involved with screening new voting machines is moved after it is revealed that. . ."

31. Datamonitor Company Profiles, 23 May 2003; "De La Rue PLC - Products & Services Analysis"; and *Business & Media*, 21 September 2003, "Business-Business Comment"; and *The Observer Ruelette*, 14 July 2003; "Observer Column."

32. Reuters News, 28 May 1997; "UK government outraged by lottery salary rises."

33. Hoover's Company Capsules, 4 September 2001; "De La Rue PLC."

34. Reuters News, 27 July 2003; "De La Rue investors gunning for Gough"; and *Print Week*, 17 July 2003; "Investigation at De La Rue arm."

35. *Citywire*, 11 July 2003; "Australia's richest family buys De La Rue"; and *The Sunday Times*, 16 March 2003; "Aussie billionaire goes for De La Rue

banknotes"; and *The Sydney Morning Herald*, 8 April 2002; "The $300,000 Lord Who Lobbed Westfield Into Tony Blair's Court."

36. *Australian Financial Review*, 26 October 2002; "Perspective—Westfield—The cut-throat corporate."

37. Business Wire, 4 August 2003; "Sequoia Voting Systems and VoteHere to Provide Additional Electronic Ballot Verification Options."

38. *The Seattle Times*, 22 November 2000; "Computer balloting gets a boost, Bellevue start-up gains new financing."

39. Master's thesis, 26 April 2001, University of Virginia, by Philip Varner: "Vote Early, Vote Often and VoteHere: A security analysis of VoteHere."

40. Business Wire, 3 October 2000; "Compaq Teams With VoteHere.net to Deliver Online Voting Pilots For Fall Presidential Elections."

41. *Newsday*, 27 February 2003; "Saudi Link to LI Start-Up / Unnamed investors take over voting Web site."

42. *Austin American-Statesman*, 28 February 2001; "Times of change at Hart; Founder reflects on end of an era for Austin institution."

43. Knight Ridder Tribune Business News, 28 February 2001; "Austin, Texas, Graphics Company to Close after 89 Years in Business."

44. Hoover's Company Profiles, 11 March 2002; Triton Energy Limited.

45. *InformationWeek*, 2 October 2000; "Cost Of Compliance."

46. *Austin Business Journal*, 8 November 2001; "Investors cast $7.5M vote for Hart InterCivic."

47. CN group Web site *http://www.thecapitalnetwork.com/advisory.php#* and *www.OpenSecrets.org*.

48. *Global Energy Business*, 1 August 2001; "CAES: Ready for prime time" 34 Vol. 3, No. 4."

49. *www.polarisinstitute.org/corp_profiles/public_service_gats_pdfs/maximus.pdf*.

50. *The San Francisco Chronicle*, 6 August 2002: ". . . Though Republican candidate for governor Bill Simon insists he knew nothing of his former investment partner's criminal background, an investigation ordered by Simon's accounting firm revealed four years ago that the man was a convicted drug dealer. . . . Even a quick Internet search would have shown that Paul Edward Hindelang's 1982 conviction for smuggling 500,000 pounds of marijuana into the country had been splashed over the front pages of Florida newspapers. . . . Simon and Sons. . . and their partners, as well as his attorneys and accounting firm, spent nearly $1 million in so-called due diligence research on Hindelang and others involved."

51. Common Cause report: "President Bush's Top Fundraisers"; source, Bush–Cheney '04 Inc. as of June 30, 2003.

52. *Akron Beacon Journal*, 1 July 2003; "Cheney cashes in for GOP at fundraiser; Fairlawn event brings in $600,000; critics try to get message out."

53. *The New York Times*, 9 November 2003; "Machine Politics In the Digital Age."

54. *The Plain Dealer*, 16 September 2003; "Diebold executive to keep lower profile; O'Dell says he regrets mixing politics with firm."

55. Canada Dept. of Corporations, *Financial Post* database: Moly Mite Resources Inc. (B.C. 1982 amalg.) Name changed to Macrotrends Ventures Inc. April 4, 1986; Macrotrends Ventures Inc. amalgamated with Racer Resources Ltd. to form Macrotrends International Venture Inc. effective Aug. 17, 1988; Macrotrends International Ventures Inc. name changed to Global Election Systems Inc. following amalg. with North American Professional Technologies B.C. Ltd effective Nov. 22, 1991; Global Election Systems Ind Plan of Arrangement with US-based Diebold, Incorporated and Diebold Acquisition Ltd. Effective Jan. 31, 2002.

56. Guy Lancaster resume, meeting with Guy Lancaster, Annual corporate information in the Canadian Survey of Industrials, which begins listing design of the ES-2000 in 1988.

57. *Vancouver Sun*, May 11 1991; "The Money Pit? Taxpayer's money marked for loans to western firms can disappear on VSE."

58. *Barron's*, May 1989; "Saga of an Unrepentant Tout—Meet Norton Cooper—and Why Investors Are Sorry They Did."

59. *Vancouver Sun*, 3 September 1993; "Two blasts from the past find new connection in Farm Energy company."

60. *Vancouver Sun*, 30 March 1994; "Unauthorized fees upset investors in fund."

61. *Vancouver Sun*, 20 May 2000; "Ex-Vignoble boss committed to trial: Businessman who borrowed money for his bail from disgraced Eron Mortgage Corp. facing fraud charges."

Why We Need Disclosure of Owners

Bev Harris
from *Black Box Voting:*
Ballot Tampering in the 21st Century

Elections in America—Assume Crooks Are In Control[1]

Only a few companies dominate the market for computer voting machines. Alarmingly, under U.S. federal law, no background checks are required on these companies or their employees. Felons and foreigners can, and do, own computer voting machine companies.

Voting machine companies demand that clients sign 'proprietary' contracts to protect their trade secrets, which prohibits a thorough inspection of voting machines by outsiders.

And, unbelievably, it appears that most election officials don't require paper ballots to back up or audit electronic election results. So far, lawsuits to allow complete access to inspect voting machines, or to require paper ballots so that recounts are possible. . . have failed.

As far as we know, some guy from Russia could be controlling the outcome of computerized elections in the United States.

—Lynn Landes

❖ ❖ ❖

This is the article that triggered my interest in voting machines. After all, how hard can it be to find out who owns these companies?

Chuck Hagel

Poster Boy for Conflict of Interest

He stunned them with his upsets. Nebraska Republican Chuck Hagel came from behind twice during his run for the U.S. Senate in 1996. Hagel, a clean-cut, crinkly-eyed, earnest-looking millionaire, had achieved an upset win in the primary against Republican Attorney General Don Stenberg, despite the fact that he was not well-known.

According to CNN's *All Politics*,[2] "Hagel hoped he could make lightning strike twice"—and he did: Hagel then defeated popular Democratic Governor Ben Nelson, who had led in the polls since the opening gun.

The *Washington Post* called Hagel's 1996 win "the major Republican upset in the November election."[3] Hagel swept all three congressional districts, becoming the first Republican to win a U.S. Senate seat in Nebraska in 24 years. "He won counties up and down the politically diverse Platte River Valley and topped it off with victories in Omaha and Lincoln," reported the *Hastings Tribune*.[4]

What the media didn't report is that Hagel's job, until two weeks before he announced his run for the Senate, was running the voting machine company whose machines would count his votes. Chuck Hagel had been chairman of American Information Systems ("AIS," now called ES&S) since July 1992.[5] He also took on the position of CEO when co-founder Bob Urosevich left in November 1993.[6]

Hagel owned stock in AIS Investors Inc., a group of investors in the voting machine company. While Hagel was running AIS, the company was building and programming the machines that would later count his votes. In March 1995, Hagel stepped down as chairman of AIS; on March 31, he announced his bid for U.S. Senate.[7] When Hagel won what *Business Week* described as a "landslide upset,"[8] reporters might have written about the strange business of an upstart senator who ran his own voting machine company. They didn't because they didn't know about it: On Hagel's required personal disclosure documents, he omitted AIS. When asked to describe every position he had held, paid or unpaid, he mentioned his work as a banker and even listed his volunteer positions with the Mid-America chapter of the American Red Cross. What he never disclosed was his salary from or stock holdings in the voting machine company whose machines had counted his votes.[9]

Six years later, when asked about his ownership in ES&S by Lincoln's Channel 8 TV News, Hagel said he had sold that stock. If so, the stock he says he sold was never listed as one that he'd owned.

This is not a gray area. This is lying. Hagel's failure to disclose his financial relationship with the company was not brought to the attention of the public, and this was a material omission. Reporters surely would have inquired about it as they researched stories about his amazing upset victories.

It is therefore understandable that we didn't know about conflicts of interest and voting machine ownership back in 1996. Had we known, perhaps we never would have chosen to herd every precinct in America toward unauditable voting. Certainly, we would have queried ES&S about its ties to Hagel before allowing 56 percent of the United States to count votes on its machines. In October 2002, I discovered that he *still* had undisclosed ownership of ES&S through its parent company, the McCarthy Group.

The McCarthy Group is run by Hagel's campaign finance director, Michael R. McCarthy, who is also a director of ES&S. Hagel hid his ties to ES&S by calling his investment of up to $5 million in the ES&S parent company an "excepted investment fund." This is important because senators are required to list the underlying assets for companies they invest in, unless the company is "excepted." To be "excepted," the McCarthy Group must be publicly traded (it is not) and very widely traded (it is not).

Charlie Matulka, Hagel's opponent in 2002 for the U.S. Senate seat, finally got fed up. He called a press conference in the rotunda of the Nebraska Capitol Building on October 23, 2002. "Why would someone who owns a voting machine company want to run for office?" Matulka asked. "It's like the fox guarding the hen house."

Matulka wrote to Senate Ethics Committee director Victor Baird in October 2002 to request an investigation into Hagel's ownership in and nondisclosure of ES&S. Baird wrote back, in a letter dated November 18, 2002, "Your complaint lacks merit and no further action is appropriate with respect to the matter, which is hereby dismissed."

Neither Baird nor Hagel ever answered Matulka's questions, but when Hagel won by a landslide, Matulka dug his heels in and asked for a recount. He figured he'd lost, but he asked how much he'd need to pay to audit the machine counts. It was the principle of the thing, he said. Matulka received a reply from the Nebraska Secretary of State telling him that Nebraska has no provision in the law allowing a losing candidate to verify vote tallies by counting the paper ballots.

In January 2003, Hagel's campaign finance director, Michael McCarthy, admitted that Hagel had ownership ties to ES&S. When the story was finally told, Hagel's staff tried to claim there was no conflict of interest.

"[Hagel's Chief of Staff Lou Ann] Linehan said there's nothing irregular about a person who used to run a voting-machine firm running for office," wrote Farhad Manjoo of *Salon.com*. "'Maybe if you're not from Nebraska and you're not familiar with the whole situation you would have questions,' she says. 'But does it look questionable if there's a senator who is a farmer and now he votes on ag issues? Everybody comes from somewhere.'"[10]

Two points, Ms. Linehan: A senator, who is a farmer, if he follows the law, *discloses* that he is a farmer on his Federal Election Commission documents. Then, if he votes oddly on a farm bill, people scrutinize his relationship with farming. Second, the farmer's own cows aren't counting his votes. Anyone with an I.Q. bigger than a cornhusk knows the real reason Hagel hid his involvement with American Information Systems on his disclosure statements. Hagel was reelected in November. An article in *The Hotline* quoted a prominent GOPer predicting that Hagel would run for president in 2008. The article then quotes Linehan: "It's abundantly clear that many people think that's a possibility for Senator Hagel."[11]

I called Victor Baird, counsel for the Senate Ethics Committee, beginning with a nonconfrontational question: "What is meant by 'widely traded' in the context of an 'excepted investment fund?'"

Baird said that the term refers to very diversified mutual funds. I asked why there were no records of Hagel's ties to the voting company in his disclosure documents. Was he aware of this? Had he requested clarification from Hagel? I knew I had struck a nerve. Baird was silent for a long time and then said quietly, "If you want to look into this, you'll need to come in and get hold of the documents."

Something in his tone of voice made me uncomfortable. I did not get the impression that Baird was defending Hagel. I rummaged through my media database and chose a respected Washington publication called *The Hill*, where I talked with reporter Alexander Bolton. He was intrigued, and over the next two weeks we spoke several times. I provided source material and he painstakingly investigated the story.

Unfortunately, when Bolton went to the Senate Public Documents Room to retrieve originals of Hagel's 1995 and 1996 documents, he was told they had been destroyed.

"They said anything over five years old is destroyed by law, and they pulled out the law," said Bolton.

But the records aren't quite gone. Hagel's staff told Bolton they had the documents. I located copies of the documents at *OpenSecrets.org*, a Web site that keeps a repository for FEC disclosures. In 1997, Baird had asked Hagel to clarify the nature of his investment in McCarthy Group. Hagel had written "none" next to "type of investment."

In response to Baird's letter, Hagel filed an amendment characterizing the McCarthy Group as an "excepted investment fund," a designation for widely held, publicly available mutual funds.

According to Bolton, Baird said that the McCarthy Group did not appear to qualify as an "excepted investment fund."[12] Then Baird resigned.

When Baird met with Bolton, he told him that Hagel appeared to have mischaracterized his investment. Then Hagel's staff met with Baird. This took place on Friday, January 25, 2003. Hagel's staff met with Baird again on Monday, January 27. Bolton came in for one final interview Monday afternoon, just prior to submitting his story to *The Hill* for Tuesday's deadline.

Baird had just resigned, it was explained, and Baird's replacement, Robert Walker, met with Bolton instead, urging a new, looser interpretation of Hagel's disclosures—an interpretation that did not mesh with other expert opinions, or even with our own common sense.

Where was Victor Baird? Could he be interviewed at home? Apparently not. Bolton was told that Baird still worked for the Senate Ethics Committee, just not in a position that could talk to the press. Could there have been another reason for Baird's resignation?

Maybe. Baird had announced in December 2002 that he planned to resign at the end of February 2003. But he changed his mind and left the position he'd held for 16 years, a month early and in the middle of the day.

In a nutshell:

- Hagel omitted mentioning that he received a salary from American Information Systems in any disclosure document.

- He omitted mentioning that he held the position of chairman in his 1995 and 1996 documents, but says he included it in a temporary interim 1995 statement. The instructions say to go back two years. Hagel also held the CEO position in 1994, but omitted that on all forms.

- He omitted mentioning that he held stock in AIS Investors Inc. and also did not list any transfers or sale of this stock.

- He apparently transferred his investment into ES&S' parent company, the McCarthy Group, and he disclosed investments of up to $5 million in that. He omitted the itemization of McCarthy Group's underlying assets. Under "type of investment," he originally wrote "none."

- When asked by Baird to clarify what the McCarthy Group was, he decided to call it an "excepted investment fund."

- Baird failed to go along with Hagel's odd description of the McCarthy Group as an "excepted" fund.

- Baird was replaced by a new Ethics Committee director who did support Hagel's interpretations.

- After this chapter was posted on the Internet, Hagel's staff sent a bulletin to the press saying that he did disclose his position with AIS. Several reporters simply accepted this misstatement at face value. In fact, Hagel's staff is referring to a temporary *interim* statement covering five months in 1995, which still omitted his stock holdings and salary from AIS and the CEO position. Somehow even the temporary disclosure of his ties to AIS disappeared from his final 1995 disclosure form. All of Hagel's 1995 and 1996 disclosure documents, including the temporary interim statement, contain material omissions and his final forms (the ones used by the press and the Senate Ethics Committee) omit *everything* about AIS.

Hagel has never been called upon to answer for these omissions.

Bolton told me that something had happened during his investigation of the Hagel story that had never occurred in all his time covering Washington politics: Someone had tried to muscle him out of running a story. Jan Baran, perhaps the most powerful Republican lawyer in Washington, and Hagel's Chief of Staff, Lou Ann Linehan walked into *The Hill* and tried to pressure Bolton into killing his story. He refused. "Then soften it," they insisted. He refused.

Bolton is an example of what is still healthy about the consolidated and often conflicted U.S. press. Lincoln's Channel 8 TV News is another example—it was the only news outlet that reported on Matulka's allegations that Hagel had undisclosed ties with the voting machine company scheduled to count their votes. The 3,000 editors who ignored faxed photocopies of Hagel's voting machine involvement, and especially the Nebraska press who had every reason to cover the story but chose not to inform anyone about the issue, are an example of what is wrong with the media nowadays.

Here's what Dick Cheney had to say when he learned that Hagel was also being considered for the vice presidential slot in 2000: "Senator Chuck Hagel represents the quality, character and experience that America is searching for in national leadership."

According to an AP wire report, Senator Chuck Hagel thinks he's capable of being an effective president and says he isn't afraid of the scrutiny that comes with a White House bid.

"Do I want to be president?" Hagel commented, "That's a question that you have to spend some time with. . . . I'm probably in a position as well as anybody—with my background, where I've been, things that I've gotten accomplished."[13]

Whether or not Hagel is in a position to run for president, the company he managed is certainly in a position to count most of the votes. According to the ES&S Web site, its machines count 56 percent of the votes in the United States.

❖ ❖ ❖

This is not, ultimately, a story about one man named Hagel. It is a story about a rush to unauditable computerized voting using machines manufactured by people who sometimes have vested interests.

Endnotes

1. Excerpted from article at *Common Dreams,* 16 September 2002; *Elections in America: Assume Crooks Are in Control,* by Lynn Landes.

2. *CNN AllPolitics,* 5 November 1996; "Hagel scores big upset for Republicans."

3. *The Washington Post,* 13 January 1997; "Brothers in Arms. . ."

4. *Hastings Tribune,* 6 November 1996, "Hagel savors upset win." *http://www.cnweb.com/ tribune/old/nov96/nov6/nov6_hagel.html.*

5. *The Omaha World-Herald,* 21 April 1992; "Omaha Firm Taps North Platte Native."

6. *The Omaha World-Herald:* 3 June 1994; "Welsh Named Top Executive. . ." Hagel took over as interim CEO from Bob Urosevich in November 1993. William F. Welsh III took the CEO position from Hagel in June 1994. Hagel remained as chairman.

7. "Fact Sheet" faxed from Chuck Hagel's office. Hagel resigned his chairmanship of American Information Systems on March 15, 1995, and announced his candidacy for the U.S. Senate on March 31, 1995.

8. *Business Week,* 10 July 2000; "Chuck Hagel. . . landslide upset."

9. United States Senate Public Financial Disclosure for New Employee and Candidate Reports: Chuck Hagel, 1995.

10. *Salon.com,* 20 February 2003; "Hacking Democracy."

11. *The Hotline,* 3 January 2003; "White House: Hagel cares about the U.S. and yes, all mankind."

12. *The Hill,* 29 January 2003; "Hagel's ethics issues pose disclosure issue."

13. The Associated Press, 31 January, 2003; "Hagel not ruling out run for White House," 2001.

Riverside County's Voting Machines
A Sea of Deception in the Desert

Jeremiah Akin

RIVERSIDE COUNTY, CALIFORNIA, was one of the first counties in the country to use paperless touchscreen voting machines. In 1999, the county purchased several thousand AVC Edge voting machines from Sequoia Voting Systems. As soon as the purchase was made the county's Registrar of Voters, who at the time was Mischelle Townsend, did everything she could to make her decision appear to be wise and well thought out. Unfortunately, Townsend's actions, as well as her successor's, Barbara Dunmore, have included repeatedly giving out misleading or outright false information in order to make the county's voting system sound more secure and accurate than it really is.

Mischelle Townsend stated under oath that Riverside County's voting machines record votes on "read-only" media. In a declaration for a lawsuit aimed at repealing California's requirement for voting machine paper trails, Townsend said, ". . . the ballot is stored on 'read-only' media."[12]

This sounds great. It sounds like the votes are recorded onto something that can not be changed. Unfortunately, this claim does not contain a shred of truth. Riverside's voting system stores votes on compact flash memory contained in removable PCMCIA cards. This type of memory is the same type of rewritable memory that many digital cameras use. Sequoia Voting Systems made it clear, in a report to Riverside County's RFP (request for proposal) for electronic voting machines that the votes are kept on flash memory PCMCIA cards,[3] in clear contradiction of Townsend's statements.

Members of the Riverside County Registrar of Voters office have even accessed voting information on the PCMCIA cartridges and manipulated it in order to provide audio ballots for the county's touchscreen machines.

The document titled, "Setting Up, Creating, and Validating Edge Audio Ballot Voting"[4] was given to me by Susan Maria Webber, who received a copy of it from Riverside County while she was in a lawsuit against the county. This manual details how to access the voting system's PCMCIA cartridges through a DOS prompt and use programs, provided by Sequoia, to manipulate information on the cartridges. The names of the programs are "reverse.exe" and "edge_bal.exe;" and **it should be pointed out that neither of these programs ever received a federal certification number.**

Riverside County used *reverse.exe* and *edge_bal.exe* to access and manipulate the rewritable memory on the PCMCIA cartridges—exactly what Mischelle Townsend testified couldn't be done.

Sequoia Voting Systems itself submitted information it knew to be false to the California Secretary of State's office, in a document titled "Responses to Questions Presented by California Secretary of State Kevin Shelley's Ad Hoc Touch Screen Task Force." In this document, Sequoia tells the secretary of state's office,[5] "The AVC Edge does not use any off-the-shelf software." The idea behind this statement is that if the public does not have access to their software, then no one can figure out a way to compromise the systems security.[6]

A test-report form, and the testing lab that Sequoia hired, both show that Sequoia used commercial off-the-shelf software in the AVC Edge. The 1999 Wyle test report states:[7]

The AVC Edge uses the following off-the-shelf software components:

- **pSOS** real-time operating system
- Phoenix **BIOS**
- Metagraphics graphics functions **I**
- Menuet windowing system
- Flash File System for ATA style **PCMCIA** Flash Rom and Compact Flash.

In addition, a 2003 study on touchscreen voting machines in Ohio shows the same information:[8]

> The following third party softwares are used in AVC Edge system: Phoenix BIOS, Metagraphics graphics functions, Menuet windowing system, Flash File System for ATA style PCMCIA flash ROM and CompactFlash.

One would like to think that a company that is intimately involved in counting our votes would not give false information to the secretary of state. But, just as the tobacco companies sent people to Congress to testify that they did not know that cigarettes were addictive, Sequoia management told the California secretary of state's office that they did not use off-the-shelf software in their voting system, though they were well aware that was not true.

The Riverside County Registrar of Voters Office tries to suggest, falsely, that touchscreen machines are mandated by law. The County put out a flyer titled "HAVA, Your Guide to the Help America Vote Act." This document does not have a date on it, but it was written when Mischelle Townsend was the Registrar of Voters. I was able to pick it up from the Registrar of Voter's Office in early 2006. The flyer states "HAVA requires that each polling place be equipped with a 'universally accessible' DRE (direct record electronic) device by Jan. 2006. Riverside County's touchscreen voting equipment already meets this requirement."

This makes it appear that there is a legal requirement for the county to have a DRE touchscreen voting machine. This is not true.

The HAVA act makes interesting reading. Sections 301–303 include the requirement to provide accessible voting systems for people with disabilities. These sections state that voting systems can satisfy the requirement for accessibility for individuals with disabilities "... through the use of at least one direct recording electronic voting system **or other voting system** equipped for individuals with disabilities at each polling place."[Emphasis mine.]

In other words, the HAVA act specifically states that machines other than DRE touchscreen voting machines can be used by counties. This is the exact opposite of what Riverside County's pamphlet stated.

From the start, Riverside County claimed that their voting system was secure, though they wouldn't let the public actually inspect the software to see whether their claim was true or not. Officials can make any claim they want if there is no way for the public to check up on it. Fortunately, we got a chance to test their accuracy when the Registrar of Voters' office accidentally leaked election management software online.

In October of 2003, election management and tabulation software (WinEDS), which had been used by Riverside County, was discovered on a publicly accessible ftp site on the Internet. This software is used for election management and vote tabulation. It was stored in an unencrypted file, which allowed anyone to install and inspect the voting system on his or her computer. WinEDS was downloaded by several people, including two reporters who wrote stories about the leaked software. Bev Harris posted the zip file that contained the software on the Web to ensure that people could examine the contents.

A quick note on version numbers: The software that was discovered is no longer in use by Riverside County. However, there is a lot that can be learned by examining code that was used in the past. The County claimed that this code was secure when they used it. If that claim is false, how can we trust the county's claims that the current version is secure? I recommend downloading the file yourself so you can verify what I have found.[9] If you do not have the technical skills required then I urge you to find someone who does.

How did Sequoia Voting Systems react to the fact that their software was left unprotected on an Internet site? A 2003 article in *Wired* magazine's story about the leaked software,[10] quoted Sequoia spokesman Alfie Charles as saying, "While this breach of security is grossly negligent on the part of the county's contractor, the code that was retrieved is used to accumulate unofficial results on election night and does not compromise the integrity of the official electronic ballots themselves."

In fact, WinEDS can produce both official and unofficial results. Imagine that the key to a bank's vault also happens to open its broom closet. Then it is discovered that the banker has been leaving that key under the doormat at night, and the embarrassed banker later declares, "The key found under the mat is the key to the broom closet" he would be making a statement that, while technically correct, is in fact, clearly deceptive. And if he went on to add, as Alfie Charles did, that security was not compromised, he would be lying. While Charles' comments where not technically an outright lie, they caused people to come to the same false conclusion that they would have if Charles did tell an outright lie.[11]

I once met Alfie Charles in Sacramento and I asked him why he did not reveal to the press that WinEDS also makes official results. He stammered for a second, and then said, laughably, that he failed to mention it because it was obvious and everyone already knew it! If he really thought that people knew what WinEDS was, then why did he give a description of it at all?

After I installed WinEDS on my computer it took me about 20 minutes to find the first major security problem. WinEDS uses a Microsoft product called Visio to manage ballot layout. Visio is a diagramming program, usually used for making flowcharts. However, WinEDS has extended Visio so it can be used to design the layout of ballots. This extension of functionality has been accomplished by using an interpreted scripting language called *VBScript*. The use of interpreted languages in voting software poses a major security threat because interpreted code can be modified by anyone who has access to the software. This means that a county insider could modify the software after it had been tested for accuracy.

The 2002 Federal Election Commission (FEC) Voting System Standards[12] specifically points out the danger of using interpreted code when it says *"This prohibition is to ensure that the software tested and approved during the qualification process remains unchanged and retains its integrity."*[13]

Not only does WinEDS allow someone to modify its code, WinEDS will clean up the modifications that the person made. Therefore, you can open WinEDS, insert malicious code into the program and run the program using that code; but the next time someone opens WinEDS, all the code you modified will be reset back into its original form. *Scoop News* published an excellent article exposing this problem.[14]

It should be noted that even though the interpreted code was found in an older version of WinEDS, Visio is still used in the current version of WinEDS. Visio by itself does not have the ability to manage ballot layouts, so Sequoia must have some code to extend Visio to get it to perform the functions they need. Although I doubt that it will happen, Sequoia needs to come out and tell the public whether they still use interpreted code in WinEDS. Sequoia did not inform the public of this problem in the past so I doubt that it will happen now.

Any experienced programmer who examines the Sequoia code, as I did, will notice something peculiar: A lot of the code is, by any standard, really, really poorly written. For example, there were whole sections of code that were *commented out*.

Here is an image of a piece of code from the LogModule of WinEDS's ballot management software, which is supposed to write errors to a log.

```
Public Sub WriteErrorLog(ByVal aiFileN As Integer, asErrSource As String, alE:
'    On Error GoTo ErrorHandler
''    Write #aiFileN, SCurrFunction, " Source " & Err.Source
''  ¯ Write #aiFileN, "Error N  " & Err.Number, " Description " & Err.Descript:
'    Write #aifileN, SCurrFunction, " Source " & asErrSource
'    Write #aifileN, "Error N  " & alErrNumber, " Description " & asErrDescrip'
'
' Exit Sub
'ErrorHandler:
''    Open sFileNameArray(aiFileN) For Append Shared As #aiFileN
''    SCurrFunction = "LogModule.WriteErrorLog "
''    Call WriteErrorLog(aiFileN)
' Exit Sub
' 'Write #aiFileN, InsertRow
End Sub
```

This piece of code has been modified so that no error message
will be written. The lines that start with the single quote are commented out, meaning that the computer does not use them.

In other words, a single keystroke—deleting a quote mark—
would now introduce a whole line of unintended code. Another single
keystroke would take it out again. At the very least, this invites the
introduction of virulent bugs.

This is a misuse of the comments. Comment lines were created
to allow a programmer to explain in plain English what the code is
doing. It is curious that such a basic rule is broken by Sequoia.

Here is another example of poor coding in WinEDS software.

```
Set msWord = CreateObject("Word.Application")
lResult = FindWindow(Null, "WinWord")
'Set msWord = GetObject("", "Word.Document")
msWord.Application.Documents.Open (sLogPath & lsFileN&
Set CurWDoc = msWord.Application.ActiveDocument
CurWDoc.PageSetup.PageWidth = msWord.InchesToPoints(Cc
```

You can see that the programmer commented out a line of code.
That commented-out line is an older method of opening a Microsoft
Word document in VBScript. The following line is a different way to
accomplish the same task. Clearly one method was dropped by the
programmer(s) working on this code, but it was still left in the file.
This is a sign of sloppy programming. One has to wonder how bad

Sequoia's internal code review process is to allow these kinds of mistakes to be included in their deployed production code.

I could easily fill a whole chapter just by showing images of poorly written VBScript code in WinEDS. Since I do not have the space to do that, I encourage the general public to look at the code themselves so they can see the extent of this mess for themselves.[15]

I also found problems inside WinEDS' database. WinEDS uses a Microsoft database called "SQL Server." The WinEDS database contains code in what are called *Stored Procedures*. When a Stored Procedure is called, a set of instructions is executed against the information in the database. If you install the WinEDS database software you can open up the Stored Procedures and see how WinEDS's database works.

Stored Procedures are not interpreted, like VBScript. Stored Procedures are compiled, meaning that they are changed from a human-readable form to a form that computers understand. Once code has been compiled it is much harder for a human to figure out what is really going on.

Unfortunately, since WinEDS ships out the code for the stored procedures with their product, it is just as easy to change the code (written in what is called T-SQL) in the database as it is to change the VBScript in WinEDS' ballot management software.

While examining the code in the database I found many problems, including the following.

In stored procedure bart_sp_earlyVoteTally one will see the following text:

```
SELECT t_EVTally.SERIAL_NUMBER,
t_EVTally.CANDIDATE_ID,
1, —*** this process only works for OFFICIAL ELECTION mode
@tally_type_id,
t_EVTally.SESSION_NUMBER,
t_EVTally.SELECTION_CODE,
COALESCE(rollup_precinct_id, V_PRECINCT.PRECINCT_ID),
t_EVTally.TOTAL
```

This shows us that the *test* mode does not test how the software will operate in a real election.

Before elections, Logic and Accuracy Tests (LAT) are run. The idea is to enter-in known numbers of votes for candidates, and if the numbers reported by the machine match the numbers entered, the software is said to have passed. However, since the control settings are changed from the test mode to the official election mode, the test only tests for another test—not a real election.

Imagine that you are playing poker and the dealer lets you inspect the deck before you play. You check it and it's fine, so you hand it back. Then he removes a few cards and replaces them with others, without letting you see their faces. When you object, the dealer says, "What's the problem? You inspected the deck before we started."

As you can see from the code above, a test run in the testing mode will not behave the same as a test run in official mode. Different code gets executed in the database when the software is in different modes.

Throughout the application, there are multiple instances like this. Code that remains non-active in test mode makes the public LAT test little more than a Public Relations show.

In stored procedure CreateViews I saw another problem. You will find the following code in the stored procedure:

```
— sometimes the comments magically exists
if not exists (select 1 from syscomments where id = object_id('V_'
+ @name))
Exec(@sql)
End
fetch cr_profile_tables INTO @name
```

This programmer found the code was not behaving as he thought it should, so he created a patch to fix the *symptom*—not the *cause*.

The proper way to deal with code that behaves in an unpredictable manner is to figure out why it's happening, and then to fix the system to make it behave in a predictable fashion. Comments that something "magically exists"should be red flags to anyone who is reviewing the system. One has to wonder how this comment got past both Sequoia's internal review process and the Federal Certification Process.[16]

Riverside County's current Registrar of Voters, Barbara Dunmore, has continued the tradition of public deception. In a March 2006 meeting in Sacramento, she told the California Secretary of State's office that the low number of people requesting paper ballots at polling locations showed that people in Riverside County don't want paper ballots.

In California, there have been a few elections in which people were supposed to be able to choose between voting on touchscreen voting machines and paper ballots. In Riverside County, it appears, the vast majority have chosen touchscreen machines. Dunmore stated, "When our voters go to the polling place, they expect to vote electronically, and this is demonstrated by the November 2004 elections, where less than one percent of the voters asked for paper at the polls, which was about 3,000 voters."

Dunmore also made a similar claim in an opinion piece published in the Press Enterprise. She wrote, ". . . Riverside County voters once again demonstrated their confidence in electronic voting by overwhelmingly casting their ballots on touchscreen machines."(Press Enterprise, Monday, November 29, 2004: "Election Choice: Paper or Plastic"by Barbara Dunmore.)

What Dunmore didn't reveal was that she had *ordered poll workers* **not** to offer people a choice. When a person walks into a polling place in Riverside County, they are automatically directed to the touchscreen machines; at no time are they told any alternative method is available.

But that is not all. Voters in Riverside who requested paper ballots on their own were in fact actively discouraged. I have had several people tell me about mistreatment by poll workers when they asked for paper ballots; one of them told their story to a a reporter from the *North County Times* who printed her story.[17] The report reads:

> Jean Eikelberger, a stay-at-home mom who lives in Corona, said she ran into a wall of resistance when she asked for a paper ballot.
> The response was like, "What? No, you do the electronic ballot," Eikelberger said.
> The female poll worker then got up and walked over to discuss the matter with other workers. Then she came back.
> She looks at me and says, "You know, you should have requested an absentee ballot. This is really causing a problem. This is really making things difficult."

The policies that Dunmore has created at the polling place are set up to generate more touchscreen votes than paper votes. If you conducted the poll another way you would have very different results. Imagine if voters walked into the polling place and were automatically assumed to want to vote on paper ballots. In addition, the poll workers have been instructed not to offer anyone the chance to vote on touchscreen computers. A person can vote only on one of them if they ask for it and if they put up with poll workers who tell them things like, "No, you do the paper ballot." The number of paper ballots cast versus touchscreen ballots would be dramatically different. However, it would be dishonest to say that you could measure the rate of acceptance of paper ballots by using the percentage of paper ballots cast that day.

In a March 2006 meeting with the California's Secretary of State office, Dunmore stated that Riverside's vote-tabulation software was not connected to the Internet, so it couldn't be tampered with from the outside. She told the California Secretary of State's office:

> I wanted to tell you a little bit about our Tally system—our Tally system, which runs when EDS (sic) is located in a glass-walled server room. And it's totally isolated within that ballot counting room, as we call it. There are no outside connections

to the Internet, to the intranet. Only electricity comes into that Tally server.[18]

The fact that Dunmore knew this to be false is revealed in a statement that she made to the *North County Times*:

> . . . the Board of Supervisors approved a pilot approach: Isolate the tally server from all outside connections until polls close on election night. At that point, the server can be plugged in to the county's protected computer network.
>
> Encrypted vote data from an Indio counting station can then be transmitted through a secure "tunnel" accessible only to those counting the votes in Riverside. The connection can then be unplugged after the final election-night transmission.[19]

Dunmore knew that the vote tabulation software is hooked up to the county Intranet, yet she told the Secretary of State's office exactly the opposite. To both the *North County Times*, and the California Voting Systems panel, Dunmore failed to mention the important fact that the county's "protected computer network" is, in fact, connected to the Internet.[20]

The Registrar of Voters is paid over $100,000 a year by taxpayers to represent *us*, and protect *our* interests. And yet, she is acting as if her real employer is Sequoia Voting Systems—lobbying for them, suppressing fair criticism of their product, covering up its weaknesses and vulnerabilities.

The facts cited above are just the tip of the iceberg. There is much, much more of the same, all of it pointing in the same direction, all of it painting the same picture: The Riverside County Registrar of Voters' Office has become little more than a rooting section for Sequoia Systems' flawed and vulnerable product, which has robbed Riverside's voters of the confidence we deserve in the security of our elections.

Election security is dependant on public observation. The best way to ensure that ballot boxes do not get stuffed is to have multiple people, with different political backgrounds and motives, watch the ballot box at the same time. If members of the public can not watch the votes get counted then the flood gates of election manipulation are opened.

It is impossible to watch a computer count votes. Even if you could see inside the computer case, and had eyesight powerful enough to see the microscopic inner workings of the computers components, computers add faster than humans can see. The closest that a person can come to observing votes get counted by computers is to watch election officials load cartridges into tabulation machines. This is the equivalent of watching people bring ballot boxes into a locked room that you can not see inside of and then later having someone come out and tell you the winner of the election. Under no circumstances is it acceptable to count ballots out of the public's view.

Replacing hand-counted paper ballots with invisible computer files is about as good idea as replacing natural human reproduction with cloning. Sometimes the old way is better.

Endnotes

1. *http://www.verifiedvoting.org/downloads/legal/california/benavidez/ 20040505.benavidez.townshend_declaration.pdf. (page 35). www.jeremiahakin.com/ RiversideChapter/2001_Wyle_Report.pdf - page 9 of the PDF.*

2. *www.jeremiahakin.com/RiversideChapter/programming_audio_ ballot_instructions.pdf.*

3. *http://docs.votetrustusa.org/sequoia/seqresptotf.pdf – page 10–11.*

4. In reality this does not work because you cannot hide the software from everyone. Company insiders will know the systems flaws and there is always the chance that the software will get leaked online. For the record, Sequoia uses encryption (SHA-1 and DES) that is open for public review. It is hypocritical for Sequoia to not open its software for public review, allegedly for security reasons, while they rely on public review to ensure that their encryption works. To see Sequoia's admission to using open encryption go here: www.sequoiavote.com/article.php?id=50.

5. *http://docs.votetrustusa.org/sequoia/Wyle_1999_Test_Report_ Sequoia_Edge.pdf - pg. 9 of the PDF.*

6. *www.jeremiahakin.com /RiversideChapter/compuware.pdf -page 207 of the PDF.*

7. The file can be downloaded here: *http://docs.votetrustusa.org/sequoia/ TX/Sequoia_Vote_Tally_software/WinEDS200.zip.* You can get instructions that

will show you how to modify the software here: *http://docs.votetrustusa.org/ sequoia/TX/.*

8. *http://www.wired.com/news/privacy/0,61014-1.html?tw= wn_story_page_ next1.*

9. As some people might have already determined, Alfie Charles' background is in politics. In fact, he used to work for the Secretary of State's office before he went to work for Sequoia Voting Systems. Charles is just one of many people who were in positions that could affect the profits of electronic voting companies who later joined one of them.

10. *http://www.eac.gov/election_resources/vss.html.*

11. The FEC standards actually do allow for interpreted code under some circumstances—see section 6.4 of the 2002 standards for details. None of the exceptions in section 6.4 apply to the WinEDS software.

12. *http://www.scoop.co.nz/stories/HL0404/S00024.htm.*

13. In addition to making the software available for download, I have extracted the VBScript code from WinEDS and posted it online. You can download it here: *http://www.bbvforums.org/forums/messages/2197/32953.html.*

14. The Federal Certification Process in notoriously weak. In fact, every major vendor has had voting systems that were given a federal certification that later turned out to contain significant security problems. A security audit done for the state of Ohio shows this. http://serform2.sos.state.oh.us/sos/hava/files/compuware.pdf.

15. *http://www.nctimes.com/articles/2004/11/14/news/californian/ 21_03_3011_13_04.txt.*

16. *http://www.ss.ca.gov/elections/voting_systems/hearing_ transcripts.pdf - pg 171 of the PDF.*

17. *http://www.nctimes.com/articles/2006/02/02/opinion/commentary/ 18_43_342_1_06.txt.*

18. This is not the only time that Dunmore has made statements she knows are false to the California Secretary of State's office. In January, 2005 Dunmore falsely claimed that she was providing audio ballots for members of a linguistic minority. However, these audio ballots had never been provided. See the following sites for information: *www.jeremiahakin.com/ RiversideChapter/cahuilla//Cahuilla.htm.*

19. *http://www.ss.ca.gov/elections/vsp_min_012005.pdf.*

Jeremiah Akin first got involved in electronic voting after observing a Logic and Accuracy Test in Riverside, California. Among other problems with the test, Jeremiah observed that members of the Riverside County Grand Jury had signed a statement saying that the test had successfully completed be-

fore the test was even finished. Members of the Registrar of Voters office tried to convince Jeremiah to sign the same paper even though they had conducted portions of the test outside the view of the test observers. Having seen firsthand how inattentive local government was when it came to ensuring that voting equipment was secure, Jeremiah decided to start researching the subject himself. His work has been featured in two books, Black Box Voting, *and* Steal this Vote. *Jeremiah has been quoted on the subject of electronic voting by* Newsweek, the Associated Press, Salon, Wired News *and many other news sources.*

Jeremiah grew up in Riverside, California, attended college at UC Santa Cruz, and is now residing in Austin, Texas, where he works as a senior level software developer for a Fortune 500 company.

Real Election Monitoring
Posted by Bev Harris on the Black Box Voting Website

Monday, June 05, 2006

Editors' note: This information was posted with reference to the primary elections and the mid-term elections that were upcoming at the time of this writing. BUT, this information survives 2006 and should be used by election reform activists for collecting evidence about election irregularities **anytime, any year!**

THE CALIFORNIA PRIMARY IS TUESDAY, June 6 (2006). As they say, "Democracy is not a spectator sport." Dive in and do your part to oversee and document this important election.

This coming November, control of the U.S. Congress will be determined in a nationwide general election. Primary elections are your chance to practice citizen oversight activities. With its massive population, California elections will play a particularly large role in control of the U.S. House of Representatives.

When there is a lot at stake, it is especially important to exercise your civil right to oversee and validate your own elections.

Here are some things that ordinary citizens can do:
First, a shift in thinking is needed this year. It is no longer enough to observe and tell stories about what you saw—even if you sign an affidavit. The sad fact is anecdotes don't produce change, even when they are very well organized. It's time to shift your thinking from watching elections to **collecting evidence**.

Evidence = audio recordings[1], video recordings, photographs and public records

Also: **Pick your observation point**. While it's important to observe the polls, it may be even more important to observe the chain of custody and the vote tallying that goes on after the polls close.

Here is a general laundry list of valuable things you can document. Fair elections are all about your right to oversee and validate. You should not have to "trust" in anyone else's word. You should be able to observe and document for yourself.

In some California counties, like Los Angeles County, you'll get a lovely tour and lots of speeches, but little opportunity to actually exercise meaningful oversight. If that happens to you, collect evidence to prove it.

Document any of the following obstructive behaviors:

- You are not allowed to watch poll closing activities
- You are not allowed to watch votes being counted
- You are not allowed to follow the ballot box, memory card, or cartridge chain of custody
- You are not allowed to watch the "depots" (regional transfer sites)
- You are not allowed to watch the processing of the absentee ballots
- You are not allowed to see the computer screens
- You cannot see who is in the counting room
- Some of the processing and tabulation takes place in rooms you cannot see
- They won't tell you where any other networked machines are or, they won't let you observe the area where other networked machines are
- You cannot see who is handling memory cards (or cartridges, or disks)

- They won't tell you the names (and/or who employs) the people who are tabulating and processing votes
- You are not allowed to watch pre-election voting machine preparation
- You are not allowed to watch pre-election voting machine testing
- You are not allowed to see all of the rooms where ballot box (memory card, cartridge) processing is taking place
- You are not allowed to watch check-in of cartridges, memory cards, etc.
- You cannot see all of the computers processing your vote
- They turn off the machine or blank the screen so you can't see what's on it (for example, hiding error messages)
- You are not allowed to have the all of the results reports
- You are not allowed to see the polling place results tapes at the precinct (end of day precinct results)
- They won't let you access public records, such as voting machine logs, reports, pollbooks
- They won't tell you the names of the people working there
- It's too dark to see handling of memory cards, cartridges, envelopes and election materials
- They won't tell you the chain of custody

Chain of custody problems

- Gaps in the accounting for (or your ability to see) handling of voting machines, memory cards, or ballots
- Handling memory cards by political party operatives or vendors
- Technicians working on voting machines during the election
- Technicians working on voting system during the count
- Machine does not print precinct results
- Voting machines, ballot boxes or memory/cartridges sent home with poll workers

Counting problems

- Modems can't connect
- Cards/cartridges won't upload
- Results don't match each other
- Results for a candidate go down when more votes come in
- Negative votes or machines count backwards

Auditing problems

- Things don't add up
- More votes than voters
- Votes show up in precincts with no registered votes
- Precincts results don't match central tabulator data
- Absentee votes co-mingled with polling place votes so you can't see which are which
- Precincts are missing

Other Actions You Can Take

Note: We, the editors, would like to add some other suggestions to the Action List:

1. Start an e-mail, calling and letter writing campaign amongst your friends and e-mail lists. On a regular basis, barrage your elected officials to change election laws banning electronic voting equipment and a return to safe hand-counted paper ballots.

2. Create actions around every election, produce press events and bring continuous attention to this issue.

3. Bring video cameras to every election; ask to be at the counting and tabulation areas at your precinct and county. Become an election judge and take your video camera to trainings, elections and certification hearings at the county and state level.

4. Demand an independent evaluation at the state level of voting systems and equipment, as well as demanding your secretary of state to appoint a bipartisan citizen panel to evaluate voting laws and equipment in your state. Study your state voting statutes (usually available online.) Seek legal counsel and consider taking legal action. Form a group or contact the ACLU or other appropriate citizen advocacy groups to help you.

5. Consider seeking legal counsel to evaluate any ideas you may have regarding taking legal actions against the vendors and manufacturers of these machines. As consumers, we have rights!

6. As consumers, consider organizing local and national boycotts of the corporations who manufacture and are affiliated with voting machines. Money talks! And the bottom line speaks to Boards of Directors of corporations.

7. Write letters to the editors of magazines, community newsletters, nonprofit publications, newspapers, call in to radio shows, buy billboard space on major roads across America, create a Web site to educate people and advertise your Web site, produce a documentary and take any action you can think of to bring attention to this matter. This is a NON-partisan problem. This issue affects everyone in America on both sides of the aisle and in any party affiliation.

8. Join the national Hand Count Registry—be on the national team to be ready to hand-count ballots in November 2006 (To sign up for the Hand Count Registry, go to: *http://www.bbvforums.org/cgi-bin/forums/board-profile.cgi?action=register.*

9. Use the Black Box Voting Tool Kit, a tutorial on a vast number of actions you can take. This Tool Kit is a Declaration of Independence for Citizens: *http://www.blackboxvoting.org/toolkit.pdf*

10. Demand that your county provide you with a paper ballot with which to vote on election day; they keep these on hand for absentee and mail-in ballots. Be sure to verify in writing that your ballot will not be fed into a computerized optical scan counter as occurred recently in Riverside County, California.

IF YOU DON'T DO ANYTHING ELSE AFTER READING THIS BOOK, consider donating money to the organizations working so hard to reclaim elections for our citizens: *www.blackboxvoting.org*, *bradblog.com*, *Voteraction.org*, and *Voterescue.org* are some of the best! Your donation, large or small, would greatly contribute to their work.

Endnote

1. California does not permit secret tape recording. It is a "two party consent state," meaning it requires the consent of both parties to take an audio recording. This is not necessarily true in a public space, such as the public area in an elections office. In these places it is generally assumed that anyone can hear what's going on and there is not necessarily any enforceable right to privacy in such settings.

There is no such prohibition against taking video without the audio. You can videotape to your heart's content in public places, except that you cannot videotape people's vote in a way that attaches it to the person who voted.

There is no prohibition against taking photographs. Many cameras that take digital photos also take Web quality video with audio. For options on equipment, see: *Citizen's Guide to Video and Audio Recorders* at *www.blackboxvoting.org*.

Reprinted with the author's permission from *www.blackboxvoting.org*.

Waste Archeology Watchdogs

This is a somewhat controversial suggestion. If you don't like it, skip ahead to another action. "Waste archeology" can be an effective way to counteract secrecy. (Just imagine what might have been learned about the phony homeland security lockdown in Warren County, Ohio, if waste archeology watchdogs had been active during the months preceding the election.)

WHAT TO DO: Pick a day once a week or once a month. Go with a friend. Scope the situation out ahead of time. Rescue documents destined for premature demise from the trash. Waste archeology projects: Local elections-related vendors, distributors and suppliers; elections offices; voting machine examiners and certifiers; ballot printers and mail processors. Note that many elections offices have multiple locations, therefore multiple opportunities.

Start now. Keep it up until after Election 2006.

Examples of important information gathered from waste archeology watchdogs:

100 pages of internal Diebold documents:

http://www.bbvforums.org/forums/messages/2197/7695.html
New uncertified "Vote Remote" software:
http://www.bbvdocs.org/diebold/voteremote.pdf

Triple Protection For Election 2006—Starting Now:

1) All American Paper Chase

2) Waste Archeology Watchdogs

3) Candid America Project

HOW TO DO IT: See Forums—Actions You Can Take Right Now

Reprinted with the author's permission from the Black Box Voting Forum on *www.blackboxvoting.org*.

How to Hold a Press Conference

Abbe Waldman DeLozier

_____

THE FOLLOWING INFORMATION is my simple guide to creating and producing a press conference or to publicize an event to the public.

First of all, let me qualify my credentials for writing this piece. I am not a media professional, but I have produced about 15 press conferences and most of them have been quite successful. They each received press coverage through one or more of the following mediums: radio, television and newspaper articles. Theoretically, a minimum of hundreds, perhaps thousands of people read, heard or saw the information and/or message of the event being covered.

I know this is something _anyone,_ including _YOU_ can successfully do.

This is a wonderful skill to learn and practice when you decide you want to become involved in your government.

The first thing I was told about producing a press conference is that you need a minimum of two weeks to organize the event. Luckily, I have proven this rule wrong on numerous events. Twice I had, out of necessity, to organize events in two days and one time I organized an event in 24 hours. Both events received coverage on the local news television shows on major network stations. So it can be done on short notice, too, though I don't recommend it due to stress levels.

The following are my recommendations on how to produce a successful political event that can receive coverage by the media.

1. Pick a public place to hold the event that has easy access, visibility, parking and electrical outlets. Ideally hold your event at the State Capitol while the State Legislature and Senate are in session. There will already be press present while the Legislature is in session. Churches or City Hall are also good places to hold an event. Pick a day when the City Council is meeting and hold your event while the City Council is in session. This exponentially increases your chances of press already being assigned to the area.

2. Hold your event between 10:00 A.M. and 1:00 P.M. Most news stories have to have time to go into production at the studio before the 5:00 evening news. Try to avoid events on Fridays and Mondays. There is too much other news going on before and after the weekend.

3. Keep your event brief and to the point. Have your speakers be elected officials, celebrities, or important business or community leaders in your town.

4. Limit each speaker to one to three minutes each to speak. Only invite a maximum of four speakers. Have their speeches be brief and to the point. It is alright, though, to have a group or organization standing with them in support of their message.

5. Strategically place signage or visual pieces for cameras and photographers. If you have a strong visual, such as props, or even children, you greatly increase your chances of a photo of your event making the news or paper. Have small children and families hold signs. Be flamboyant and creative. Dress for the event. Unless there is a particular theme, dress professionally.

6. Prepare a simple press kit to hand to reporters. Include the names and contact information for all of your speakers listed in the order in which they will be speaking. Be sure to include their cell phone numbers in case the press wants to follow up with questions after the event, as well as a name and cell number for the co-coordinator of the event. Also include a list of the talking points from your event as well as the message you are trying to convey to the public. Keep the materials brief and simple. *Reporters have little time to review your information* before they are off to their next assignment.

7. Before the event, send out a press release everyday for two to three days before the event as well as one last notice sent the morning of the event. I would both fax and e-mail your press release to the media. Be sure the newspapers, radio stations, television stations and so on receive your information by 7 A.M. Most assignments and production meetings take place early in the morning or the day before your event.

8. You can assemble a press contact list by finding a citizen advocacy group or nonprofit organization in your area that regularly publicizes events. Ask them if they are willing to share their press contact lists with you. Also, ask them if they are willing to send out releases for you if you are willing to pay them a fee for the use of a press release service they may already subscribe to.

9. Your press release should be modeled after the example that appears on the following page. Follow the simple formula of WHO, WHAT, WHERE, WHEN and WHY. You want your press release to be compelling, unique and newsworthy. Remember, your event has to get past an assignment editor who is trying to cover stories that interest his or her audience. Keep your press release to one page. Always list a knowledgeable contact person on the release who is readily accessible by cell phone and e-mail. Be sure and have your speakers available night and day for interviews several days before and after your event.

10. When the press calls you, be brief, professional, knowledgeable and excited about your event. You must be able to "sell"the event to a reporter. Convince them of the importance and newsworthiness of your event.

11. At your event, go up and introduce yourself to anyone who remotely looks like a reporter, typically the folks carrying a camera and notepad! Thank them for being there. Ask if you can assist them by introducing them to your speakers. Quietly go up without being noticed and send important people to go casually talk to the reporters. It is important that the reporter learns new information to use without being pressured to be able to intelligently cover your event.

12. Stage your event as if it is a movie set. Physically direct people with signs to go stand behind a speaker or the person being

interviewed so the camera catches the signs and the appearance of a huge crowd being present at the event.

13. Ask people to be courteous and respectful at all times. Shouting matches will not get you anywhere.

One time I held a press conference where only 10 or 15 people attended. We only had three members of the press show up to cover the story. One reporter was with the local newspaper and one with a local television news show. The third reporter happened to be with the Associated Press Wire Service. Once I learned for whom that reporter worked, I spent a long time quietly asking every speaker to casually go up and visit with this reporter. Our work paid off. That reporter really took the time to write an article that accurately reflected the message of our 30-minute event. This reporter's story was broadcast on the AP Wire and appeared in over 90 cities around the world! I realized that literally millions of people potentially read this newspaper story and heard our message! It was an amazing accomplishment. To follow your news story to see how it appears in the media and when, you can go to *www.google.com*. Click on the link on the home page for "advanced news search." Here, you can track your event in the news as it hopefully appears throughout the world.

I encourage all of you to become a publicist. It is not as difficult as you think. What a great way to bring attention to actions you are taking as well as to monitor the actions of those who are supposed to be serving our interests in government!

Bring the people back to the government. Monitor election officials' activities. Let them know you are watching them closely. Shine the spotlight on any and all misconduct as well as highlight their accomplishments so we can restore our democracy. We can no longer stay asleep in the times we are living in. Be brave and get involved! It is a great feeling to be of service and getting involved in your community. No less than our country, our world and our childrens' future is at stake!

SAMPLE OF A PRESS RELEASE THAT WENT OUT IN 2004:

September 18, 2004   Contacts: Abbe W. DeLozier (512) 736-5802
For Immediate Release   Vickie Karp, (512) 775-3737
                             Bev Harris, (206) 335-7747
              Andy Stephenson, (206) 778-0524

Attn: Political Assignments Desk

PRESS CONFERENCE
     A Bipartisan Problem:
     Hacking the Presidential Election: Anyone Can Do It!
     Washington, D.C., Wednesday, September 22, 2004.

Two press events: **9:30 A.M. E.S.T. (National Press Club, by invitation only; features a surprise and a three-hour head start for TV news) and 12:30 P.M. E.S.T. (The Ballroom at Heldref Publications, open to all journalists, policymakers and to the public.)**
     Startling demonstrations using real election software proving that any teenager or terrorist with a laptop can create havoc with the election results in November. Or, more onerous—Anyone with an agenda or a profit motive can help themselves to an election with a subtlety that defies detection.

1. **9:30 A.M., The National Press Club**, 529 14th Street NW, Washington, D.C.; Zenger Room (A small gathering by invitation. If you are a member of Congress or a network representative, call (206) 335-7747, (206) 778-0524, (512) 736-5802 or (512) 775-3737 to get on the invite list. Some contact lines are congested, please keep trying.)

2. **12:30 P.M., "The Ballroom"at Heldref Publications,** 1319 Eighteenth St. NW, Washington, D.C. (All press and policymakers welcome; open to the public.)

Bev Harris, Executive Director, Black Box Voting (*www.blackbox voting.org*) will demonstrate a hidden program for vote manipulation which resides on Diebold's election software. This is a secret feature enabled by a two-digit trigger. (Not a "bug" or an accidental oversight; *it's there on purpose*.) The Diebold central tabulator system election software will count 50 million votes, approximately 50 percent of the votes in November's election.

Dr. Herbert H. Thompson, computer security expert and editor/author of 12 books including, *The Mezonic Agenda: Hacking the Presidency,* will demonstrate how easily an election can be rigged by implanting a virus.

Jeremiah Akin, independent computer programmer from Riverside, California, will demonstrate how to manipulate Sequoia Voting Systems software while an election is in progress.

Andy Stephenson, Associate Director, Black Box Voting, will demonstrate how an unscrupulous person with no computer skills whatsoever can sabotage an election with two mouse clicks.

Surprise feature: Highly visual TV demo, features something astonishing. **These 3 minutes will change forever your perspective on voting security.**

Two emergency solutions will be presented by Bev Harris, Black Box Voting, and Sharona Merel and Joan Krawitz, Co-Founders of the National Ballot Integrity Project. These inexpensive and achievable emergency measures to ensure the integrity of the 2004 vote count can be implemented immediately.

Lowell Finley, attorney from Berkeley, California, specializing in election law, will comment about the legal feasibility of the emergency solutions being presented.

❖ ❖ ❖

Conclusion
A Crime Has Been Committed!
Where Do We Go From Here?

Abbe DeLozier and Vickie Karp

GRAND THEFT IS OCCURRING in our country. Elections are being stolen! What are we going to do about it?

Consider the information you have just read:

Victoria Collier has explained the history of vote fraud, which goes back decades, and passed on the warning of her father and uncle regarding the wholesale vote fraud that is possible with electronic voting.

Bev Harris, Harri Hursti, Dr. Herbert Thompson, and Jeremiah Akin and others have proven that the secret software of at least two of these electronic voting machine vendors can be hacked...in fact, that even a chimp can be taught to hack an election! (See *www.blackbox voting.org*, "archives." The Baxter video)

Bev Harris has given proof of over 100 serious election anomalies connected with electronic voting. . . just in one chapter. She has also detailed the almost unbelievable partisan conflicts of interest involved with voting machine vendors and exposed the truth about convicted felons who have been programming our elections.

Kathleen Wynne has detailed evidence she captured on videotape of election officials breaking the law, leading to three criminal indictments from just one lone election incident!

Bob Fitrakis chronicled so much evidence of vote fraud in Ohio, including a rigged recount, that no doubt can remain that Ohio was the focal point of Stolen Election 2004.

We believe that each of our chapters helps build the case: Elections are being hacked on a regular basis! But until now, unlike a typical crime, no one has held anyone accountable! And as Lynn Landes has postulated, "Assume Criminals are in Control!" So if you are waiting for our so-called "elected" officials to fix this one, you've got a long wait coming! Guess what? No one else is going to fix this. . . except *US!*

It is up to We the People to restore integrity, new laws and order to our damaged election systems. We, as editors of this book, were two citizens who became outraged and decided to take action. We urge you to make reclaiming elections YOUR priority! Be creative. Do more reading and research on this subject. We are providing you with a bibliography, a list of Web sites where you can get more information on this topic, and action steps you can take to help save our stolen elections.

A note of warning: We would like to bring to your attention an important point that has currently split the voting rights community in two, and, in our opinion, is moving the entire country in the wrong direction regarding solutions to election problems. Congressman Rush Holt from New Jersey wrote House Bill H.R. 550, The Voter Confidence and Increased Accessibility Act of 2005. You can read his bill at the following link: *http://www.house.gov/sites/members/nj12_holt/ pdf/HR550VCIA.pdf.*

This bill provides an amendment to the Help America Vote Act (HAVA) which would mandate all computerized voting machines to be retrofitted with a printer to produce a ". . . voter verification and mandatory paper record audit capacity; and accessibility and voter verification of results for individuals with disabilities."

Many well-meaning election reform activists are devoting time to support this amendment in hopes of getting it passed. Years ago, many of us believed that a "voter verified paper trail" would be a solution to electronic vote fraud. Because of their dedication to this issue, we admire the motives of the people who still hold this belief.

BUT **NOW THERE IS ABUNDANT EVIDENCE TO INDICATE THAT THIS WILL NOT WORK!** This will only add one more layer of inscrutability to the voting process. Adding a printer does NOT restore our civil right to verify whether our vote is being counted as cast. No one can prove to us that the computer inside the "black box" is actually counting our votes the way the printer indicates! And IF IT'S NOT, with random low 2%, or even higher percentages of audits, this vote fraud could EASILY go undetected.

Therefore, we STRONGLY DISAGREE that adding any other device, even a printer, to an electronic voting machine will solve this problem! We strongly disagree that any change or addition to these machines will bring back the integrity, honesty and transparency needed in our election process.

WE ALSO STRONGLY DISAGREE that relying on a minimum of 2% mandatory audits (or anything less than 100% hand count of paper ballots) will bring integrity and honesty back to our election process.

Why?

As discussed briefly in our book, the proposed H.R. 550 has several provisions that empower the Election Assistance Commission (EAC) with a tremendous amount of authority over elections in our country. This commission, supposedly bipartisan, was created through the Help America Vote Act, with appointees selected by President George W. Bush in the year 2002 to oversee elections in America.

Now that you understand more about the EAC, we can more fully explain our position of opposition to H.R. 550 and why this is important to the future of elections in our country. Important features of this bill include:

A. The Elections Assistance Commission can "randomly" conduct mandatory minimum of 2% audits of the paper receipts of the total precincts in every state within 24 hours of an election. They also must "randomly choose" a minimum of one precinct in every county, and at **the discretion** of the state or county they could conduct further audits. It is important to note that if the EAC detects a problem it is at their *sole discretion* as to whether they continue the audits or recounts any further.

B. Any candidate, person or entity that wants to contest the decisions of the EAC must file complaints with the Attorney General of the United States or seek legal relief.

C. Voters would still be using DREs (touchscreens) equipped with printers. Yes, you would see a printed copy of your vote, verify it is correct and deposit the "receipt" in a secure ballot box. That is the good part of this bill; however, other provisions in the bill render the bill unacceptable.

D. If a candidate requests a recount of the paper receipts, they have to seek legal recourse of suing and bearing the expense of legal fees, court costs and recount fees—which can run into hundreds of thousands of dollars in most counties and states, with limited time to complete the process. Many states only give a few weeks to file such lawsuits and conduct recounts. Meanwhile, the clock is ticking while the public demands to know results and the states, counties and federal government rush to certify the election results. *It sounds great in theory that a recount can be conducted; however, the likelihood of getting a court to agree to a recount, as well as a candidate having the funds to do so, are miniscule.*

E. H.R. 550 places important decisions of audits, recounts and legal recourse in the hands of politically appointed entities: the EAC and the Attorney General of the United States.

HR 550: A Problem Posing as a Solution

Unfortunately, voting activists and citizen advocacy groups from around the country have jumped on the bandwagon in favor of H.R. 550 as the solution to all the problems we are experiencing with computerized voting. *Heed our warning! This is a false salvation.*

Since the year 2000, perhaps earlier, voting activist groups began forming around the country. We believe these people to be true patriots who love this country and cherish the right to vote. Many have been working on this issue for six years, trying to bring public attention to the fact that our elections have been compromised and stolen.

At long last, many of these activists and groups have declared a major victory with H.R. 550 as the solution. A congressman has finally sponsored a bill mandating a paper audit trail that can be verified by the voter. (Several congressional leaders have at this point.) This truly seems to be a step in the right direction.

Unfortunately, that same voter will never know if the computer recorded the vote as indicated by the voter's paper receipt. Unfortunately, millions of votes will be tallied by machines programmed with secret proprietary software, and when the tallies come in, **by law only a 2% (or more) recount is required,** *if deemed necessary by the EAC!* **If you want to demand a further recount, you have to sue the Attorney General of the United States as well as the county, state and federal government!**

After reading Bob Fitrakis' chapter describing the recount in Ohio in 2004, what do you think the chances are of getting a fair recount or audit, especially when the stakes are high?

H.R. 550 is the perfect diversion for these electronic voting machine vendors. The voting activists' complaints fade away and elections go on, business as usual, with compromised electronic voting machines and little or no chance of ever achieving recounts.

WE MUST HAVE A RETURN TO SAFE, PAPER BALLOT ELECTIONS, HAND COUNTED IN PUBLIC VIEW, WITH VOTE TOTALS POSTED AT THE PRECINCT LEVEL!

Many say that it's too late; electronic voting machines have been purchased all across the country, and now we have to use them.

We Say: Citizens get what they settle for. We refuse to settle for electronic voting machines or optical scan counters. Period.

Many say it's the computer age, that's how we have to conduct elections.

We Say: Computers have their place, and they have no place running our elections.

Many say it takes too long to hand count paper ballots.

We Say: In certain cases, it can even be faster to hand count paper ballots than to wait days for uncertain results from highly suspect electronic voting machines. But even if it *did* take longer, WHAT IS MORE IMPORTANT? SPEED? OR ACCURACY?

Many say we will not be able to win the battle of trashing these machines and going back to hand-counted paper ballots without incremental victories. Thus, amendments such as H.R. 550 and the other proposed legislative "solutions" covered in Rep. McKinney's chapter have value.

We Say: How many more years, how many more elections will we allow to be compromised or stolen before we say, conclusively: ENOUGH IS ENOUGH! NO MORE COMPUTERS! NO MORE MACHINES RUNNING OUR ELECTIONS! We will settle for no less than elections held with hand-counted paper ballots!

Appendix
Compendium of problems, continued from Chapter 2

September 1986, Dallas, Texas: The number of voters changed on various report printouts, but votes for individual candidates remained the same. The problem was attributed to a computer programming error. Note the date on this report. Officials have been expressing concerns about computerized vote counting for nearly two decades. "With paper ballots, I can make the numbers add up. . .", said Assistant Texas Attorney General Bob Lemens. "We are running into much tougher problems here." Texas Attorney General Jim Mattox said the computerized vote counting clearly has the potential for fraud. "I can't send a reasonably good programmer to look at this system and determine that it is properly tabulating the ballots," Mattox said.[72]

November 1988, Hillsborough, Broward and Dade counties, Florida: A drop-off was observed in Senate votes from the previous general election, but only in counties that used computerized vote counting machines. Counties without computerized vote counting showed a 1% drop-off, while counties with computerized voting showed a drop-off of 8%. "Something stands out there like a sore thumb," said Michael Hamby, executive director of the Florida Democratic Party.[73]

November 1989, Lima, Ohio: Representatives of Sequoia Pacific, makers of the voting machine software for Lima, failed to appear as requested, and election results were delayed until someone could work out the programming error and recount the votes. Nobody was quite sure how many races were affected, but the mayoral race and the school board races were in question for nearly a week after the election.[74]

November 1990, King County, Washington: Worse than the butterfly ballot, some Democratic candidates watched votes alight, and then flutter away. Democrat Al Williams saw 90 votes wander off his tally between election night and the following day, though no new counting had been done. At the same time, his opponent, Republican Tom Tangen, gained 32 votes. At one point several hundred ballots added to returns didn't result in any increase in the number of votes. But elsewhere, the number of votes added exceeded the number of additional ballots counted. A Republican candidate achieved an amazing surge in his absentee percentage for no apparent reason. The miscounts were sporadic and thus hard to spot, and the errors disproportionately favored just one party.

King County's election manager recommended a countywide recount.[75]

1994, New Orleans, Louisiana: Voting machine tests performed and videotaped by candidate Susan Barnecker demonstrated that votes she cast for herself were electronically recorded for her opponent. This test was repeated several times with the same result. (The video footage of this incident can be seen in Dan Hopsicker's documentary video *The Big Fix 2000*, Mad Cow Productions).[76]

November 1996, Bergen County, New Jersey: Democrats told Bergen County Clerk Kathleen Donovan to come up with a better explanation for mysterious swings in vote totals. Donovan blamed voting computers for conflicting tallies that rose and fell by 8,000 or 9,000 votes. The swings perplexed candidates of both parties. For example, the Republican incumbent, Anthony Cassano, had won by about 7,000 votes as of the day after the election, but his lead evaporated later. One candidate actually lost 1,600 votes during the counting. "How could something like that possibly happen?" asked Michael Guarino, Cassano's Democratic challenger. "Something is screwed up here."[77]

November 1996, Thurston County, Washington: An inexplicably large number of people went to the polls but did not vote in the hot House contest. A whopping 11.5 percent of Thurston County voters ignored the congressional race—nearly twice as many no-votes as other races in Thurston County and twice as many no-votes as other counties recorded. "We have absolute confidence our machine is counting appropriately," said Bob Van Schoorl, Thurston County's chief deputy auditor. J. R. Baker, of Democratic challenger Brian Baird's campaign, was not satisfied. "They have not gone through any special testing to see if their machines are adequately counting the votes. Perhaps they need to do sample hand counts of precincts and compare them with the machine."[78]

November 1996, Guadalupe County, Texas: Officials discovered a voting machine counted more votes in the presidential election than the number of ballots cast. Guadalupe County Elections Administrator J. R. Perez said the problem was with new software for the county's Business Records Corp. Eagle vote counting system. Perez said a problem was identified with the software before the election, and he thought it had been fixed. "I had no reason to believe the system was not tabulating right," Perez said.[79]

1984, Tucson, Arizona: 826 legitimate ballots were discarded in Oro Valley because of a computer error. The error wasn't discovered until after the deadline for counting them.

1996, Tucson, Arizona: A software programming error mixed up the votes cast for two Republican supervisor candidates.

1997, Tucson, Arizona: More than 8,300 votes in the city council race were initially left uncounted because of defective punch-card ballots, which were provided by the voting machine company.

1997, Tucson, Arizona: The city had to hand count 79,000 votes because of a manufacturing defect in the ballots, provided by the voting machine company.

1998: Tucson, Arizona: 9,675 votes were missed in the tabulation. After canvassing, officials realized that no votes had been recorded for 24 precincts even though voter rolls indicated thousands had voted at those polling places. Global Elections Systems (now called Diebold Election Systems) tried to figure out why the computer had failed to record the votes.[80]

November 1998, Franklin County, Ohio: One candidate was incorrectly credited with 14,967 votes; another received 6,889 in error. Deborah Pryce and John R. Kasich gained 13,427 votes and 9,784 votes, respectively, after election officials hand checked vote totals in 371 machines that were affected by a software programming error. A spokesman for Danaher Corp., which supplied electronic voting machines to the county, told the board that such a problem had never before happened in Franklin County. No one caught the error while downloading the data into voting machine memory cartridges.[81]

November 1998, Washoe County, Nevada: A breathtaking number of snafus in the Washoe County registrar's office caused candidates in Reno to liken the election to the movie *Groundhog Day*, in which the lead character relives the same day over and over again. Count votes. Computer failure. Go to court. Recount the votes. Software error. Back to court. Start over counting, and so on.[82]

December 1998, Canada: What was billed as a historic first for the Canadian Wheat Board turned into an embarrassment as a programming error threw the election results into question. The firm hired to count the ballots found a flaw in the computer program that tabulated results for the agency's first ever board of directors.[83]

September 1998, Kansas City, Kansas: Republican John Bacon, a staunch conservative, celebrated a resounding victory for the 3rd District Kansas Board of Education seat, defeating moderate Republican Dan Neuenswander by 3,018 votes. Two weeks later, Neuenswander learned that the race had been dead even with the margin of loss being just 24 votes. No one offered any explanation for the discrepancy.[84]

August 1998, Memphis, Tennessee: In the governor's race, a software programming error in Shelby County began crediting votes to the wrong candidates. Computer cartridges containing 295 individual precinct results were taken to a central location because the scanner couldn't read them. The system that was shut down had posted the incorrect results to newsrooms across the city. At least one television station broadcast the bogus results.[85]

November 1998, Chicago, Illinois: One hundred eight of 403 precincts were not counted. A pin from the cable connecting the ballot reader to the counting computer had gotten bent after three-fourths of the precincts had been counted correctly. No one could explain how a pin inside a cable had become bent during the middle of the count. Democrats requested a full recount; a judge disallowed it.[86]

November 1998, Honolulu, Hawaii: A state senate investigation was conducted into the 1998 malfunction of voting machines in seven precincts at once. ES&S acknowledged the error and paid more than $250,000 for the recount, in which the biggest expense was hand counting, according to Vice President Todd Urosevich. ES&S Financial Officer Richard Jablonski said ES&S would have saved a lot of money if it had been permitted to perform only a machine recount, giving voice to a financial incentive for vendors to get rid of paper ballots.[87]

November 1999, Norfolk, Virginia: Machines showed totals of zero but votes had been cast. Edward O'Neal, Norfolk Electoral Board vice chairman, said, "Somehow, they lost their ability to count the votes."[88]

November 2000, Arapahoe County, Colorado: Officials agreed to reconfigure the vote reading machines for a recount because they had been set wrong and therefore did not read all of the votes. Because Democrats wanted the additional recounts, they had to pay the bill, which came to about $11,000.[89]

November 2000, Denver County, Colorado: Four voting machines malfunctioned. Voting officials mistakenly assumed those machines were not used, but there were 300 votes on them.[90]

Crozet, Virginia (anecdotal report from a voter): "When I pushed the button beside 'No' the machine registered my vote as a 'Yes.' I tried this a couple of more times and got the same result. Finally, I poked my head outside the curtain and asked the 'attendant' what I should do. Whenever I made my choice, the opposite choice lit up. He suggested then that I should intentionally push the wrong button."[91]

November 2000, Volusia County, Florida: A clerk in one precinct could not reach election headquarters to report that the computer had shut down, so the clerk turned the computer off, then turned it back on, accidentally erasing 320 votes. This was discovered only when workers counted all ballots by hand. Election supervisors across Florida say the phone clog happens during most presidential elections, but few people notice.[92]

November 2000, Davidson County, North Carolina: A computer error allowed election software to count about 5,000 early and absentee ballots twice. A reporter brought the discrepancy to light during the county election board's official canvass. The incorrect vote totals appeared only on the official report sent to the State Board of Elections in Raleigh.[93]

November 2000, San Francisco, California: In polling place 2214, machines counted 416 ballots, but there were only 362 signatures in the roster and the secretary of state found only 357 paper ballots.[94]

February 2000, Manatee, Florida: A power surge was reported to be the cause of incorrect computerized vote tallies. A hand count was performed. And because the hand count showed that a candidate lost by just two votes, another hand count was done. All results, including two hand counts, were completed within 48 hours.[95]

November 2000, Albuquerque, New Mexico: A software programming error in New Mexico led officials to withhold about 60,000 ballots from their vote count. According to an AP wire service report: "Their (voting) machines have a problem in the database," Elections Bureau Director Denise Lamb said, "and they can't count any of the straight-party ballots."[96]

November 2001, Buffalo, New York: The poll book showed 96 Republicans signed in to vote at the polling place at Ohio Elementary School, but when the machine was checked, it tallied 121 votes for mayor: 74 for David Burgio and 47 for Mary Kabasakalian.[97]

April 2002, Johnson County, Kansas: Johnson County's new Diebold touchscreen machines, proclaimed a success on election night, did not work as well as originally believed. Incorrect vote totals were discovered in six races, three of them contested, leaving county election officials scrambling to make sure the unofficial results were accurate.

Johnson County Election Commissioner Connie Schmidt said that internal checks revealed that the system had under- and overreported hundreds of votes. Schmidt said the voting machines worked fine, they just tabulated wrong. "The machines performed terrifically," said Robert J. Urosevich, president of Diebold Election Systems. "The anomaly showed up on the reporting part." The problem, however, was so perplexing that Schmidt asked the Board of Canvassers to order a hand recount to make sure the results were accurate. Unfortunately, the touchscreen machines did away with the ballots, so the only way to do a hand recount was to have the machine print simulations of ballots from its internal data. Diebold tried to recreate the error in hopes of correcting it. "I wish I had an answer," Urosevich said. In some cases, vote totals changed dramatically.[98]

November 2002, Palm Beach, Florida: A Florida woman, a former news reporter, discovered that votes were being tabulated in 644 Palm Beach precincts, but only 643 precincts had any eligible voters. An earlier court case in Florida had found the same discrepancy, and the reason for it was never satisfactorily explained.[99]

November 2002, New Jersey: A reporter in New Jersey observed 104 precincts with votes in an area that has only 102 precincts. "Ghost precincts,"no matter what the official explanation, do not provide the transparent accounting needed to protect voting integrity."[99]

March 2002, Palm Beach County, Florida: Touchscreen machines sometimes froze up when voters selected which language to use.

Phil Foster from Sequoia Voting Systems attributed the problem to a software programming error. Elections Supervisor Theresa LePore also said she heard that some people touched one candidate's circle on the screen, only to see an X appear by another candidate's name.[100]

November 2002, Dallas, Texas: When 18 machines were pulled out of action in Dallas because they registered Republican when voters pushed Democrat, Judge Karen Johnson, a Republican, quashed an effort to investigate the accuracy of the tally.[101]

March 2002, Medley, Florida: Voting machines gave the town council election to the wrong candidate. The problem was attributed to a programming error by a voting machine technician. County Elections Supervisor David Leahy said he was concerned because the computer did not raise any red flags; humans had to spot the error.[102]

November 2002, Monterey, California: California machines couldn't add. The problem in Monterey, California, was that the department's mainframe computers refused to add the results of early absentee votes and those cast on touchscreen computers prior to election day. "We didn't have any problems whatsoever during our pre-election tests," said the elections official.[103]

November 2002, South Carolina: A software programming error caused more than 21,000 votes in the close race for South Carolina Commissioner of Agriculture to be uncounted, an error margin of 55 percent. Only a paper ballot hand count was able to sort it out.[104]

November 2002, Taos, New Mexico: Just 25 votes separated the candidates in one race; another race had a 79-vote margin. After noticing that the computer was counting votes under the wrong names, Taos County Clerk Jeannette Rael contacted the programmer of the optical scan voting machine and was told that the problem was a software programming error.[105]

November 2002, Pennsylvania: In Pennsylvania, a voter reported that he had followed his conscience and voted Libertarian. When he reviewed the results for his precinct, though, the Libertarian candidate received zero votes.

There are two ways to look at this: unimportant, just a vote; or a 100 percent error. Either way, this man did not get to vote for whom he wanted.[106]

November 2002, New York: Voting machine tallies were impounded in New York. Software programming errors hampered and confused the vote tally on election night and most of the next day, causing elections officials to pull the plug on the vote reporting Web site. Commissioners ordered that the voting tallies be impounded, and they were guarded overnight by a Monroe County deputy sheriff.[107]

November 2002, North Carolina: Elections officials tried to find 300 voters so they could vote again. In Wake County, North Carolina, one out of four new touchscreen voting machines failed in early voting, losing 294 votes. Election workers looked for the 294 voters to ask them to vote again. (A voter verified paper ballot would have solved this problem.)[108]

November 2002, Florida: Gubernatorial candidate Bill McBride was a tough guy to vote for: One voter said that he tried 10 times, and every time he pressed McBride, the Jeb Bush choice lit up. He could only get his vote to light up the McBride choice when he pressed a dead area of the screen. No paper ballot was available, so no one really knows who got any of the votes, regardless of which candidate lit up. Similar problems were reported in various permutations, for various candidates, by several Florida voters, and an identical problem was noted in Texas.[109]

November 2002, St. Bernard Parish, Louisiana: All the king's horses and all the king's men couldn't put the tally together again: With a 34-vote margin separating the two candidates for justice of the peace in St. Bernard Parish, the machine ate 35 absentee votes and left everyone guessing about the outcome of the race. The ballots became inaccessible when the system locked up; even the technician couldn't get at them.[110]

November 2002, Georgia: In one Georgia county, ballots in at least three precincts listed the wrong county commission races. Officials shut down the polls to fix the problem but didn't know how many wrong ballots were cast or how to correct errant votes. In another, a county commission race was omitted from a ballot. Cards voters needed in order to access machines malfunctioned. Machines froze up, and dozens had been misprogrammed.[111]

November 2002, Nebraska: Charlie Matulka, the Democratic candidate for U.S. Senate in Nebraska, arrived at the polls to vote for himself. When he looked at the optical scan ballot he had been given, he discovered it had already been filled out for his opponent, Chuck Hagel, giving Nebraska the most newfangled voting of all—not just electronic voting, but automatic voting![112]

January 2003, Everett, Washington: If there was any doubt that Republicans were right to ask for a recount of some Snohomish County absentee ballots from November's general election, it was erased by one sobering number: 21.5 percent of the ballots cast in 28 selected precincts were not counted. The Snohomish County Auditor's Office recounted 116,837 absentee ballots after county officials discovered that the optical scan ballot counting machines had miscounted.

The problem was attributed to a faulty "read head" on each of two optical scanners; the heads failed to read ballots with blue ink. The machines had passed the test on blue ink before the election. The Sequoia representative could not recall that the "read head problem" had ever happened before.

When asked by a citizen how many machines of the same make and model number Sequoia has in the United States, she said, "About 1,500." When asked how many years they'd been in use, she said about six years.

"Why, then," asked a citizen, "would this unheard-of problem happen at exactly the same time in exactly the same place on two different machines at once?" The Sequoia rep said she had no idea.[113]

❖ ❖ ❖

This compendium is by no means complete. Worse, these are examples that were noticed and covered in the press. For the 100 examples listed here and in "Can We Trust These Machines?" there are undoubtedly a great many more that were not written up in the newspaper, or were never noticed at all.

72. *The Dallas Morning News*, 24 September 1986; "Dallas Officials Deny Election Fraud Claim."

73. *Atlanta Journal; Atlanta Constitution*, 11 November 1988; "Thin Lead Allows Mack to Proclaim Victory in Senate Race."

74. *The Plain Dealer*, 10 November 1989; "Tally mix-up still under investigation."

75. *Seattle Post-Intelligencer*, 20 November 1990; "Recount of All Election Returns Recommended."

76. *The Las Vegas Review-Journal*, 19 July 1998; "The Clark County vote: How secure is it?" and *The Big Fix, 2000*, Video by Dan Hopsicker, Mad Cow Productions.

77. *The Record*, 16 November 1996; "Bergen County Paper Ballots Finally Counted. . ."

78. *Seattle Post-Intelligencer*, 16 November 1996; "Democrats Seek Recount in 3rd District—Thurston County in Question."

79. *San Antonio Express-News*, 8 November 1996; "Computer glitch skews Guadalupe vote results."

80. *The Arizona Daily Star*, 20 November 2001; "Year-old Votes Discovered in City Precinct Box."

81. *The Columbus Dispatch*, 8 December 1998; "Tallies from November Election Change. . ."

82. *The Las Vegas Review-Journal*, 12 November 1998; "Washoe's nightmare."

83. *Winnipeg Free Press*, 9 December 1998; "Glitch forces recounts in CWB vote."

84. *The Kansas City Star*, 19 August 1998; "Ballot tally change 3,000-vote error. . . ."

85. *The Commercial Appeal*, 7 August 1998; "Computer Glitch Delays Final Vote Total. . . ."

86. *Chicago Daily Herald*, 6 November 1998; "Computer glitch leads to vote error."

87. *Honolulu Star Bulletin*, 10 March 1999; "Vote Recount to Cost $250,000." http://starbulletin.com/1999/03/10/news/story9.html.

88. *The Virginian-Pilot and The Ledger-Star*, 3 November 1999; "Tallying machine malfunction leads to Norfolk recount."

89. *Denver Post*, 29 November 2000; "Recount confirms Polis won seat. . . ."

90. *Denver Post*, 28 November 2000; "Recount adds 300 'lost' votes."

91. *The George Loper Home Page*, letter to the editor, 30 November 2000; "Voting Irregularities in Crozet, Virginia." *http://loper.org/~george/archives/2000/Nov/30.html.*

92. *St. Petersburg Times*, 17 November 2000; "Busy signals taunt clerks at precincts."

93. *Greensboro News & Record*, 15 November 2000; "Davidson Computer Glitch Doubled Votes. . . ."

94. *The San Francisco Chronicle*, 11 February 2002; "2000 election finds work was sloppy."

95. *Sarasota Herald-Tribune*, 10 February 2000; "Election recount makes no change."

96. AP Online, 8 November 2000; "Ballots Withheld in New Mexico."

97. *Buffalo News*, 18 October 2001; "Voting Snafu Won't Change Mayoral Primary."

98. *The Kansas City Star*, 5 April 2002; "Election errors unnerve Johnson County official."

99. Call-in reports; November 2002 election; See also: Dr. Rebecca Mercuri's work on voting machines, where she has similar reports: *www.notablesoftware.com.*

100. *The Palm Beach Post*, 14 March 2002; "Human goofs, not machines, drag vote tally into next day."

101. *The Fort Worth Star-Telegram*, 30 October 2002;"Democrats to appeal voting case ruling."

102. KRTBN Knight-Ridder Tribune Business News: *Miami Herald*, 4 April 2002; "Despite New Voting System, Human Error Mars Medley, Fla., Council Election."

103. *Monterey Herald,* November 2002.

104. *The Herald* (Rock Hill, SC), 7 November 2002; "Machine glitch keeps votes from being counted."

105. *Albuquerque Journal*, 7 November 2002; "Taos To Recount Absentee Ballots."

106. 1 November 2002; Citizen report on the VoteWatch forum: *http://pub103.ezboard.com/fsoldiervoicefrm44.showMessage?topicID=1.topic.*

107. *Democrat & Chronicle* (Rochester, NY), 7 November 2002; "John squeaks out victory."

108. *The News & Observer* (Raleigh, NC), 31 October 2002; "Machines lose 294 early votes."

109. Votewatch citizen reports; *http://www.votewatch.us/election_2002_findings.htm.*

110. *The Times-Picayune*, 7 November 2002; "Machine snag leaves race up in the air; Trapped absentee ballots delays news of JP winner until today."

111. AP Online, 5 November 2002; "Glitches Hit High-Tech Voting Systems."

112. 6 November 2002; interview with Charlie Matulka, Democratic candidate for U.S. Senate in Nebraska.

113. Citizen meeting in Snohomish County, 23 January 2003.

Bibliography and Resources

Here is your opportunity to further educate yourself on the election integrity issue. There is a wealth of knowledge to draw upon, and we encourage you to do your own investigations; then start or join a group in your area and TAKE ACTION! Please dig in and keep learning:

Black Box Voting: Ballot Tampering in the 21st Century, by Bev Harris, January 2004. Order the book from the Web site: *www.blackboxvoting.org;* free downloadable version available.

"The Machinery of Democracy: Protecting Elections in an Electronic World," by Brennan Center Task Force on Voting System Security, Executive Summary, Brennan Center for Justice at NYU School of Law, June 27, 2006. http://*www.brennancenter.org/programs/downloads/ Executive%20 Summary.pdf*

"Nonpartisan GAO Confirms Security Flaws in Voting Machines," by Congressman John Conyers, October 2005. *http://www.dailykos.com/story/ 2005/10/21/115027/30*

"Analysis of an Electronic Voting System," by Aviel D. Rubin, Tadayoshi Kohno, Adam Stubblefield, and Dan S. Wallach, July 23, 2003. An examination of electronic voting software, Diebold, with a conclusion that it is "unsuitable for use in an election." *http://avirubin.com/ vote.pdf*

"Facts about Electronic Voting," by Ellen Theisen. *http://www.voters unite.org/ info/ElectronicVotingInBrief.pdf*

Sleuthing Stolen Election 2004: John Brakey and the "Hack and Stack," by David L. Griscom, Ph.D.

"Paper Trails: Ballots vs. Receipts," by Roy Lipscomb, Technology Director, The Illinois Ballot Integrity Project. *http://e-grapevine.org/papertrail.htm*

"Residual Votes Attributable to Technology—An Assessment of the Reliability of Existing Voting Equipment, The CalTech/MIT Voting Technology Report, Version 2: March 2001. The report states that manually counted paper ballots have the lowest average incidence of spoiled, uncounted and unmarked ballots. *http://www.hss.caltech.edu/~voting/CalTech_MIT_Report_Version2.pdf*

"We're Counting the Votes: An Election Preparedness Kit for New Hampshire Citizens, Candidates, and Campaigns and for All the Good and Honest Election Officials, Election Workers, and Poll Workers of New Hampshire," by Nancy Tobi, Democracy for New Hampshire Fair Elections Committee, July 2006. *http://www.democracyfornewhampshire.com/files/were_counting_the_votes_formatted_2006_07_12.pdf*

"Myth Breakers: Facts about Electronic Elections. Essential Information for Those Entrusted with Making Decisions about Election Systems in the United States," 2nd edition, by Ellen Theisen, January 2005. *http://www.votersunite.org/MB2.pdf*

"The Silent Scream of Numbers," by Robert Koehler, Tribune Media Services, April 14, 2006. *http://www.commonwonders.com/archives/col290.htm*

"How They Could Steal the Election This Time," by Ronnie Dugger, August 16, 2004, *The Nation,* cover story. *http://www.thenation.com/doc.mhtml?i=20040816&s=dugger*

"Statement Against the Use of Money Allocated under the Help America Vote Act for the Purchase of Electronic Voting Systems for New York," by Teresa Hommel, October 18, 2004. *http://www.wheresthepaper.org/NYCChearing10_18.htm*

"Where's the Paper Trail for Each Ballot Cast?," by Teresa Hommel. An electronic voting simulation. *http://wheresthepaper.org/index.html*

"Was the 2004 Election Stolen? Republicans prevented more than 350,000 voters in Ohio from casting ballots or having their votes counted—enough to have put John Kerry in the White House," by Robert F. Kennedy, Jr., *Rolling Stone,* Issue 1002, June 15, 2006. **Article:** *http://www.rollingstone.com/news/story/10432334/was_the_2004_election_stolen.* **Exclusive documents, sources, charts & commentary:** *http://rollingstone. com/news/story/10463875*

"Some Might Call It Treason: An Open Letter to Salon," by Mark Crispin Miller, Huffington Post, June 16, 2006, A defense of Robert F. Kennedy's piece in Rolling Stone. *http://www.huffingtonpost.com/mark-crispin-miller/some-might-call-it-treaso_b_23187.html*

Fooled Again: How the Right Stole the 2004 Election, by Mark Crispin Miller, October 2005. Miller's meticulous and thorough account of how the numbers just don't add up to a Bush re-election. Miller's sharp analysis points in one direction: George W. Bush did not rightfully win the 2004 election and Bush's "victory" was borne out of vote suppression, manipulating the electoral process, fraud and theft.

"Paper Ballots Now!," by Chuck Herrin, December 2004.
A computer "geek" expounds on why paper ballots, hand counted, are much safer than electronic voting. *www.chuckherrin.com/paperballots.htm*

U.S. map of some of the 2004 election anomalies. *http://www.voters unite.org/info/mapflyer2004.pdf*

Ohio map of some of the 2004 election anomalies. *http://www.voters unite.org/info/mapflyerohio2004.pdf*

"What's Wrong with the Holt Bill? Part 1," by Nancy Tobi, Democracy for New Hampshire, February 2006. Analysis of H.R. 550, Rep. Rush Holt's proposed amendment to HAVA providing for paper trails on electronic voting machines. *www.democracyfornewhampshire.com/node/view/2040*

"What's Wrong with the Holt Bill? Part 2," by Nancy Tobi, Democracy for New Hampshire, February 2006. Part 2 provides further analysis of Rush Holt's H.R. 550. *www.democracyfornewhampshire.com/node/view/2103*

How the GOP Stole America's 2004 Election and Is Rigging 2008, by Bob Fitrakis and Harvey Wasserman, 2006. A special investigative report revealing massive voter theft, fraud and illegalities in Ohio's presidential balloting. The theft of the 2004 election has been catalogued, footnoted and thoroughly documented in this special digest, more than 180 bullet points, compiled by these Ohio based investigative reporters. *http://freepress.org/store.php#donate*

Did George W. Bush Steal America's 2004 Election?, by Bob Fitrakis, Harvey Wasserman, and Steve Rosenfeld, May 2005. This collection of news analysis, legal documents and sworn statements from suppressed and disenfranchised voters may very well tilt the balance in revealing the election fraud in Ohio during the 2004 election. Foreword by Rev. Jesse Jackson. *www.freepress.org/dispatches/2005/display/193*

"Ten preliminary reasons why the Bush vote does not compute, and why Congress must investigate rather than certify the Electoral College," by Bob Fitrakis, Steve Rosenfeld, and Harvey Wasserman, *Free Press,* Columbus, Ohio, January 3, 2005. *http://www.freepress.org/departments/display/19/2005/1065*

"Even a Remote Chance," by Pokey Anderson, July 2006. *http://www.votersunite.org/info/EvenARemoteChance.asp*

"Election Incident Reports," Over 40,000 reports for November 2004, including a map of frequency Election Incident Reporting System. *https://voteprotect.org/index.php?display=EIRMapNation&tab=ED04*

"Ohio's Odd Numbers," by Christopher Hitchens, *Vanity Fair. http://www.vanityfair.com/commentary/content/printables/050214roco05?print=true*

Voting by Paper Ballots and Hand Counts, on Lynn Landes' Web site, under "How to Use Paper Ballots." *www.ecotalk.org*

"Malfunctions and Miscounts, Sorted by Vendor," by VotersUnite.org. *http://www.votersunite.org/info/messupsbyvendor.asp*

"What Went Wrong in Ohio: The Conyers Report on the 2004 Presidential Election," by Congressman John Conyers. This fascinating and disturbing book is the official record of testimony taken by the Democratic Members and Staff of the House Judiciary Committee,

presided over by Rep. John Conyers of Michigan, the Ranking Member. Originally released in January, 2005 by the Committee. **Report**: *http://www.house.gov/judiciary_democrats/ohiostatusrept1505.pdf.* **Executive Summary**: *http://www.truthout.org/docs_05/010605Y.shtml*

"The Black Box Report, Security Alert: Critical Security Issues with Diebold Optical Scan Design," by Harri Hursti, July 2005. Details Hursti's findings in the Leon County, Florida, investigation of Diebold optical scan equipment used to count paper ballots. *http://www.blackboxvoting.org/BBVreport.pdf*

"Security Analysis of the Diebold AccuBasic Interpreter," by David Wagner, David Jefferson, and Matt Bishop. Voting Systems Technology Assessment Advisory Board for the State of California, February 2006. Evaluation of Hursti's findings on the Diebold optical scanners validating the severity of the security flaws he found. *http://www.ss.ca.gov/elections/voting_systems/security_analysis_of_the_diebold_accubasic_ interpreter.pdf*

"Fourth of July Fireworks: Unredacted Hursti Reports, Photos Released," by Bev Harris and Harri Hursti, Black Box Voting.org, July 2006. Hursti's analysis of Diebold DREs (touchscreens), in Emery County, Utah. His discovery of a fundamental security flaw stuns the nation's computer scientists. "Hursti II" (unredacted). *http://www.bbvforums.org/cgi-bin/forums/board-auth.cgi?file=/1954/32863.html*

"Scientists Call Diebold Security Flaw 'Worst Ever,'" by Ian Hoffman, May 11, 2006, *Inside Bay Area.* Commentary on Hursti report. *http://www.truthout.org/docs_2006/051206F.shtml*

"Backdoor Found in Diebold Voting Machines," by Robert McMillan, May 15, 2006, *PC World.* More commentary and validation regarding the Hursti report. *http://www.pcworld.com/news/article/0,aid,125700,tk,dn051506X,00.asp*

"Why Do Diebold's Touchscreen Voting Machines Have Built-In Wireless Infrared Data Transfer Ports?," by Brad Friedman, February 22, 2006. *http://www.bradblog.com/archives/00002458.htm*

"Hand Counted Paper Ballots in 2008," by Sheila Parks, April 2006, *Tikkun. www.truthout.org/docs_2006/041106L.shtml*

"Key Component of Voting System Undergoes No Review." VotersUnite.org, June 18, 2006. h*ttp://www.votersunite.org/info/Ballot Programming.pdf*

*"Vote-Switching Software Provided by Vendors: A Partial List—51 Ballot Programming Flaws Reported in the News."*VotersUnite.org, June 2006. *http://www.votersunite.org/info/mapVoteSwitch.pdf*

"Evidence of Election Irregularities in Snohomish County, Washington General Election, 2004," by Paul R. Lehto, J.D. and Jeffrey Hoffman, Ph.D. *http://www.votersunite.org/info/SnohomishElectionFraud Investigation.pdf*

"The 2004 Presidential Election: Who Won The Popular Vote? An Examination of the Comparative Validity of Exit Poll and Vote Count Data," by Jonathan Simon, J.D. and Ron P. Baiman, Ph.D., December 29, 2004. *http://www.freepress.org/departments/display/19/2004/1054*

"Response to Edison/Mitofsky Election System 2004 Report," by Josh Mitteldorf, Ph.D., Kathy Dopp, M.S. in mathematics, Steven F. Freeman, Ph.D., Brian Joiner, Ph.D., Frank Stenger, Ph.D., Richard G. Sheehan, Ph.D., Elizabeth Liddle, M.A. (UK), Ph.D. candidate, Paul F. Velleman, Ph.D., Victoria Lovegren, Ph.D., Campbell B. Read, Ph.D., U.S. Count Votes. *http://www.uscountvotes.org/ucvAnalysis/US/USCountVotes_Re_Mitofsky-Edison.pdf*

Was the 2004 Presidential Election Stolen? Exit Polls, Election Fraud, and the Official Count by Steve Freeman and Joel Bleifuss, June 2006.

Votescam: The Stealing of America, by James M. Collier and Kenneth F. Collier, 1992, Victoria House Press.

The Best Democracy Money Can Buy, by Greg Palast, 2003. Describes how the Florida election was stolen for Bush in 2000.

Armed Madhouse, by Greg Palast, 2006. How the election will be stolen in 2008, and other explosive political exposes.

"Computerized Election Fraud in America: A Brief History," by Victoria Collier, October 25, 2003. *http://www.votescam.com/abriefhistory.php*

"All the President's Votes?," by Andrew Gumbel, October, 2003, *Independent*/UK. Re: the 2002 Mid-term U.S. Election. *http:// www.common dreams.org/headlines03/1013-01.htm*

VIDEOs, DVDs, CDs

"Help America Vote on Paper," A documentary on the dangers to democracy posed by privately owned voting machines, and what citizens, officials and activists are doing about it. Features attorney Lowell Finley (of "VoterAction"); Representatives Stephanie Tubbs-Jones and Cynthia McKinney. 2006 DVD $15. *http:// www.eon3.net/pages/main.html (415) 868-1900*

"Vote Rigging 101"and "Got Democracy," (a shorter version of "Vote Rigging 101"). National teach-in in Oakland, on February 26, 2005, with presentations by Bob Fitrakis, Lynn Landes, Emily Levy, Dr. Jonathan Simon, Warren Stewart, Medea Benjamin, John Gideon, Larry Bensky, Jim March, and Paul Lehto. Ecological Options Network (415) 868-1900. http://www.eon3.net/pages/navigation/ projects/electionreform/voterig101.html

"Votergate: The Presidential Election Special Edition," Video exposes new computer voting systems. Free shorter version online; a theatrical-length version is anticipated in fall 2006. http://www.votergate.tv

"The Truth About the 2004 Election: Why We Must Not Get Over It," Multimedia CD about the 2004 election. SolarBus Election Justice Center. http://www.solarbus.org/election/cd

"Invisible Ballots: A Temptation for Electronic Vote Fraud," A feature-length 90-minute documentary and a shorter 50-minute version. Includes Dr. David Dill, Professor of Computer Science at Stanford University; Dr. Rebecca Mercuri, Research Fellow at Harvard University's Kennedy School of Government; Bev Harris, author of *Black Box Voting;* Dr. Avi Rubin, Technical Director of the Information Security Institute at Johns Hopkins University. Also Kim Alexander, Lynn Landes, Kim Zetter, and Congressman Rush Holt. Several years old; proposes the voter verified paper trail as the solution. DVD or VHS. http://www.invisibleballots.com

WEB SITES

banvotingmachines.org
BlackBoxVoting.org

BradBlog.com

Coalition for Visible Ballots: *http://coalition4visibleballots.homestead.com*

www.ecotalk.org

fairnessbybeckerman.blogspot.com

www.freepress.org

www.infowars.com

National Ballot Integrity Project: *http://www.NBIP.org*

OnlineJournal.com (Elections and Voting section): *http://onlinejournal. com/ artman/publish/cat_index_26.shtml*

Opednews.com

Scoop (New Zealand) (USA Coup, Voting Machines):

http://www.scoop.co.nz/features/usacoup.html

www.solarbus.org/election

VoterAction.org (covers litigation)

VoteRescue.org

VotersUnite.org (to receive a daily e-mail news digest, send an e-mail to: DVN@votersunite.org)

www.votescam.com

www.wheresthepaper.org

For booking and speaking information:

ABBE WALDMAN DELOZIER
adelozier@hackedelections.com

VICKIE KARP
vkarp@hackedelections.com

Books may be purchased at our Web site
www.hackedelections.org

or

www.barnesandnoble.com and *www.Amazon.com*

Books may be available to nonprofit organizations
in quantity at a discount.

Abbe Waldman DeLozier was born in Dallas, Texas. Her parents were very involved in The Jewish Welfare Federation as well as volunteering in community activities and charitable organizations. Their work and dedication greatly influenced and developed her own keen interest in citizen community involvement. She attended college in Mexico for 6 months at the University of the Americas and lived with a local family while studying Mexican language, culture, and history. She then spent a year studying overseas in Israel, living, studying and working on a kibbutz for 9 months and then continued her travels in Europe. She received an associate's degree in General Education at Palomar College. She has owned and managed her own businesses in landscaping and real estate. She has also created and co-produced sizeable charitable events as well as volunteered extensively helping political organizations with strategy and publicity. Ms. DeLozier also created and produced two charitable fundraising events that benefited the Susan G. Komen Breast Cancer Foundation. In addition she has co-produced press conferences in Washington, D.C., and Austin, Texas, on the issue of vote fraud, one being on September 22nd, 2004, at the National Press Club titled, "Hacking the Presidential Election: A Bipartisan Problem, Anyone Can Do It." There, Bev Harris, computer security expert Dr. Herbert

Thompson, and Jeremiah Akin demonstrated six ways election software could be easily hacked. The other was co-produced in conjunction with True Majority.org and took place at the State Capitol in Austin, Texas, coinciding with national activities supporting "The Computer Ate My Vote Day!" Contact: adelozier@hackedelections.com

Vickie Karp is a *Realtor in Austin, Texas. She grew up in Houston and holds a B.A. in Sociology from the University of Houston; she did graduate work in journalism at The University of Texas. An activist in the '60s, Karp learned about electronic vote fraud in 2003 and called Bev Harris to investigate further. As a Toastmaster for 15 years, she began following the story and giving speeches on it to political groups of all persuasions. She has written accounts of national election reform conferences for online journals and has been a guest on numerous radio shows exposing the vote fraud issue; she has appeared on local Austin TV news as a spokesperson, has testified at both the Texas Secretary of State's office and the House Committee on Elections in Austin regarding the dangers of Diebold software, and was a guest on MSNBC prior to the 2004 presidential election, discussing two press conferences in Washington, D.C. during which Harris and computer experts showed six ways to hack an election. She is currently the president of the Board of Directors of Black Box Voting; the National Chair of the Coalition for Visible Ballots (G. Edward Griffin, founder); and works on the issue locally in Austin, Texas with activist Karen Renick's VoteRescue group. You can contact Vickie at vkarp@hackedelections.com*